SUBSTANTIVE LAW FOR THE LEGAL PROFESSIONAL

DELMAR CENGAGE Learning

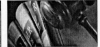

Options.

Over 300 products in every area of the law: textbooks, online courses, CD-ROMs, reference books, companion websites, and more – helping you succeed in the classroom and on the job.

Support.

We offer unparalleled, practical support: robust instructor and student supplements to ensure the best learning experience, custom publishing to meet your unique needs, and other benefits such as Delmar Cengage Learning's Student Achievement Award. And our sales representatives are always ready to provide you with dependable service.

Feedback.

As always, we want to hear from you! Your feedback is our best resource for improving the quality of our products. Contact your sales representative or write us at the address below if you have any comments about our materials or if you have a product proposal.

Accounting and Financials for the Law Office • Administrative Law • Alternative Dispute Resolution • Bankruptcy Business Organizations/Corporations • Careers and Employment • Civil Litigation and Procedure • CLA Exam Preparation • Computer Applications in the Law Office • Constitutional Law • Contract Law • Court Reporting Criminal Law and Procedure • Document Preparation • Elder Law • Employment Law • Environmental Law • Ethics Evidence Law • Family Law • Health Care Law • Immigration Law • Intellectual Property • Internships Interviewing and Investigation • Introduction to Law • Introduction to Paralegalism • Juvenile Law • Law Office Management • Law Office Procedures • Legal Nurse Consulting • Legal Research, Writing, and Analysis • Legal Terminology • Legal Transcription • Media and Entertainment Law • Medical Malpractice Law Product Liability • Real Estate Law • Reference Materials • Social Security • Sports Law • Torts and Personal Injury Law • Wills, Trusts, and Estate Administration • Workers' Compensation Law

DELMAR, CENGAGE Learning
Executive Woods
5 Maxwell Drive
Clifton Park, New York 12065

For additional information, find us online at:
www.cengage.com/delmar

SUBSTANTIVE LAW FOR THE LEGAL PROFESSIONAL

By Judy A. Long, J.D.

Australia • Brazil • Japan • Korea • Mexico • Singapore • Spain • United Kingdom • United States

Substantive Law for the Legal Professional
Judy A. Long

Vice President, Career Education Strategic
  Business Unit: Dawn Gerrain

Director of Learning Solutions: John Fedor

Managing Editor: Robert Serenka, Jr.

Acquisitions Editor: Shelley Esposito

Editorial Assistant: Melissa Zaza

Director of Content and Media Production:
  Wendy Troeger

Senior Content Project Manager: Glenn Castle

Art Director: Joy Kocsis

Technology Project Manager: Sandy Charette

Director of Marketing: Wendy E. Mapstone

Channel Manager: Gerard McAvey

Marketing Coordinator: Jonathan Sheehan

Cover Design: Elizabeth Wood

For product information and technology assistance, contact us at
Cengage Learning Customer & Sales Support, 1-800-354-9706

For permission to use material from this text or product,
submit all requests online **www.cengage.com/permissions**
Further permissions questions can be emailed to
permissionrequest@cengage.com

Library of Congress Control Number: 2007001725

ISBN-13: 978-1-4180-1837-5

ISBN-10: 1-4180-1837-6

Delmar
Executive Woods
5 Maxwell Drive
Clifton Park, NY 12065
USA

Cengage Learning is a leading provider of customized learning solutions with office
locations around the globe, including Singapore, the United Kingdom,
Australia, Mexico, Brazil, and Japan. Locate your local office at
www.cengage.com/global

Cengage Learning products are represented in Canada by Nelson Education, Ltd.

To learn more about Delmar, visit **www.cengage.com/delmar**

Purchase any of our products at your local college store or at our preferred online
store **www.cengagebrain.com**

Printed in the United States of America
2 3 4 5 6   19 18 17 16 15

DEDICATION

To my grandson

Nicholas

Brief Contents

CONTENTS

The legal assistant or legal administrative assistant is a very important member of the law office team. In the past, the legal administrative assistant was often called a *legal secretary,* and in some areas still retains that title. The goal of this textbook is to provide an overview of the various areas of substantive law that law offices practice. In general, the paralegal is more highly specialized in one or more substantive law areas and requires a substantially more in-depth study of the law. However, the legal assistant may not be required to perform the same tasks as the paralegal, and will likely be required to have a more generalized knowledge of the substantive law.

Oran's *Dictionary of the Law*[1] defines *substantive law* as:

> The basic law of rights and duties (contract law, criminal law, accident law, law of wills, etc.) as opposed to procedural law (law of pleading, law of evidence, law of jurisdiction, etc.)

The primary focus of this text will be the rights and duties of individuals and entities in the different legal areas, as well as the responsibilities of the legal assistant in each of these areas.

The larger the law office, the more specialized the members of the law office team. For example, a large law firm of several hundred attorneys would be divided into departments for litigation, estate planning, corporate law, family law, and criminal law. Within each of those departments would be paralegals and legal assistants working on cases in only that particular specialty.

However, an attorney in a very small law office would probably handle cases in two or more of the preceding specialty areas. Therefore, although the paralegal and legal assistant must be highly specialized when working for the large law firm, they would provide more generalized assistance in the smaller firm. Smaller firms may employ one individual who performs the function of the paralegal and legal assistant, while larger firms would have several individuals fulfilling these responsibilities.

ORGANIZATION OF THE TEXT

The text begins with a very general background of substantive law. It defines substantive law and describes where it is found. Statutes and cases, the two main sources of substantive law, are discussed. The reader will also learn the difference between state and federal law, and when each is used in a case in a law office.

[1]Daniel Oran, *Oran's Dictionary of the Law,* 3rd ed. (Albany, NY: West Legal Studies, 2000).

Each chapter describes the law, as well as the duties and responsibilities of the legal assistant in each of the areas of law. The law presented is merely an overview of each substantive area. Bear in mind that separate textbooks are written on each of these areas. After taking a course using this text, the student is encouraged to take classes in the substantive law fields that are of special interest.

LEGAL ASSISTANT SERIES

The author has written a series of textbooks to train the legal assistant. These books include the following:

1. *Office Procedures for the Legal Professional*, 2005.
2. *Administrative Procedures for the Legal Professional*, 2008.
3. *Substantive Law for the Legal Professional* (this text)

Students who have already taken one of the courses and/or used one of these books will be familiar with the format. The chapter layout will be similar in each of these texts, as will the questions and projects. Notebooks will be used for special projects in all of the series. Those students who are not familiar with the Project Notebooks should read the next section carefully.

PROJECT NOTEBOOKS

Students should be required to prepare a reference notebook that will be useful not only during this course but later as well. A logo beside documents and projects in the text indicates that they should be placed in the notebook. To prepare the notebook, the student will need a three-ring binder with dividers and tabs. Each section in the notebook should coincide with a chapter in the text. The student should be required to prepare the "skeleton" notebook before beginning the textbook assignments.

As each chapter is studied, documents or forms with the notebook logo should be added to the notebook along with instructions in the text for preparing the document. Whenever the instructor gives the student specific instructions on the manner in which a document is prepared, served, or filed, the directions should be added to the notebook along with a sample of the document. All checklists in the text should be included in the notebook under the appropriate subject heading. Each chapter concludes with projects that require the student to work with documents and forms in the chapter. After the projects are graded, they should be put in the notebook. At the end of the course, the instructor should again check the notebook to be sure all required items are included.

The student should be encouraged to add to the notebook as he takes more courses in the program. Some of the material encountered in subsequent courses will fit under the headings established for this course. In some cases, new headings will be added as the student progresses through the course of study.

The notebook will prove valuable after graduation from the program. Most employers require a writing sample to be submitted with the employment application. The assignments in the notebook can be used for this purpose. The notebook will also assist in teaching organizational skills and will provide models to use when similar documents are prepared on the job. Since documents prepared in law offices tend to be repetitive in nature, the student may follow the format of a document in the notebook and simply fill in the names and other new information.

Each time the student prepares something new on the job or in another class, it should be included in the notebook. The student should add to the notebook throughout his legal career. Former students have agreed with the benefits of keeping a notebook after several years in the legal profession. Instructors are encouraged to use this "notebook" approach throughout the course of study in the paralegal or legal assistant programs.

SPECIAL FEATURES

State-Specific Information boxes are included in each chapter. These boxes provide space for students to write down information on the laws in that particular state.

Key terms are printed in bold font and defined in the margin where they first appear within the chapter.

Self Tests in short-answer format appear at the end of each chapter to provoke additional review of chapter concepts.

Notebook Projects at the end of each chapter provide students with practical experience in performing the tasks of legal assistants using the substantive law studied in each chapter.

Notebook logos precede projects that students should place in their notebooks.

Notebooks must be prepared by all students and are explained in the introduction to the text. Pages from the text should be placed in the notebooks if the notebook logo appears therein.

SUPPLEMENTARY MATERIALS

This text is accompanied by support material that will aid instructors in teaching and students in learning. The following supplements accompany the text.

Instructor's Manual—This supplement is designed for instructors to assist in presenting text material in an organized and comprehensive manner. The manual includes a detailed overview of each chapter, lesson plans (including suggestions for speakers and field trips), answers to the Self Tests, and suggestions for additional projects. A comprehensive test bank contains more than 200 objective test questions and answers. The *Instructor's Manual* is also available online at

http://www.paralegal.delmar.cengage.com

in the Instructor's Lounge under Resource.

Online Companion™—The Online Companion Web site can be found at

http://www.paralegal.delmar.cengage.com

in the resource section of the Web site. The Online Companion contains study notes and outside activities for the students. Links are also provided to different state and federal sites where substantive law information is found.

Web page—Come visit our Web site at

http://www.paralegal.delmar.cengage.com

where you will find valuable information such as hot links and sample materials to download, as well as other Paralegal Studies products.

WESTLAW®—Delmar's online computerized legal research system offers students "hands-on" experience with a system commonly used in law offices. Qualified adopters can receive 10 free hours of WESTLAW®. WESTLAW® can be accessed with Macintosh and IBM-compatible computers. A modem is required.

ABOUT THE AUTHOR

Judy Long is a retired attorney and college professor. She taught at a community college for 25 years and developed a paralegal program that was approved by the American Bar Association. Prior to teaching, she spent 12 years working as a legal assistant in private law offices and corporate law departments. Her first legal position was as a part-time legal assistant in a small private law firm while she was in high school. She has written several legal textbooks, including the following:

Basic Business Law (co-author 2nd edition), Prentice-Hall, 1994

California Supplement to Civil Litigation, West, 1995

Law Office Procedures, West, 1997

California Legal Directory, West, 2000

Legal Research Using the Internet, West, 2000

Legal Research Using Westlaw, West, 2001

Computer Aided Legal Research, West, 2002

Office Procedures for the Legal Professional, West, 2005

Administrative Procedures for the Legal Professional, West, 2008

ACKNOWLEDGMENTS

Many individuals provided valuable assistance in the preparation of this textbook.

First and foremost, I would like to thank my editor, Shelley Esposito, and assistant editor Brian Banks for their numerous suggestions and considerable assistance, and developmental editor Robin Reed for her assistance in preparing the manuscript.

The following individuals provided very valuable suggestions and recommendations in their reviews of the text:

Julie Abernathy
NALS

Dee Beardsley
Latham & Watkins LLP

Michele Bradford
Gadsden State Community College

Joni Montez
Lewis-Clark State College

Sharolyn Sayers
Milwaukee Area Technical College

Caryn Wolchuck
Thomas Whitelaw & Tyler LLP

I sincerely appreciate the considerable support I received from the following individuals, who provided suggestions and materials to use in this text:

John Callinan for his material and charts on the California court structure.

Rachel Sotelo for her landlord/tenant materials.

Finally, I would like to thank all the other people whose names have inadvertently been omitted.

FEEDBACK

The user may contact the author at Jaler@aol.com with questions, suggestions, or comments about the text or supplements.

Judy A. Long, J.D.

GENERAL BACKGROUND OF SUBSTANTIVE LAW

CHAPTER OUTCOMES

After studying this chapter, the student will understand

1. the definitions of substantive and procedural law.
2. the difference between substantive and procedural law.
3. the difference between legal and equitable issues.
4. the classification and description of statutory and case law.

INTRODUCTION

Substantive law may be created by the legislature or by appellate and supreme courts. Laws created by the legislature are known as *statutory law,* and laws created by the courts are called *case law.* State legislatures and courts create state law, and the United States Congress and the federal appellate courts and Supreme Court create federal law. When there is a controversy over federal or state case law, the United States Supreme Court or that state's highest state court prevails. In controversies over case and statutory law, the statutory law prevails.

Some classifications of **procedural law** include administrative regulations issued by state and federal administrative agencies. Each agency maintains its own set of laws and regulations that govern that particular organization. For instance, the Internal Revenue Code establishes the laws that govern the Internal Revenue Service. The procedural rules that govern court cases are generally found in the Code of Civil Procedure (for civil cases) and the Code of Criminal Procedure (for criminal cases). Procedural rules for state courts are found in that state's codes, and procedural rules for federal courts are found in the federal codes. Other classification systems refer to the laws that are promulgated by administrative arms of the federal and state governments as administrative laws.

The federal and most state systems of case law are based on English common law, which maintains that earlier cases establish precedents for later cases. The exception is the state of Louisiana, which bases its laws on the Napoleonic Code. Case law is handed down by appellate and supreme court justices based on their interpretation of standards established in earlier cases or statutes. The system of relying on a prior case to establish precedent in deciding a later case is known as *stare*

procedural law the rules for enforcing one's rights in court; the procedures that must be followed

decisis. State and federal legislatures create statutory law to maintain order and protect the public's safety.

STATUTORY LAW

State laws are enacted by the legislature of that particular state. All people or organizations within that state, and those who interact with them, are required to adhere to the state statutes or **statutory law.** For instance, if a resident of Arizona violates a California law while in California, even though the law is not valid in Arizona, the individual may still be prosecuted for violating the law in California.

When the United States Congress establishes a federal law, all people and entities within the country must adhere to that law. Laws enacted by the legislature remain valid until they are repealed by the legislature or deemed unconstitutional in a judicial proceeding before the United States Supreme Court.

State laws may not contradict the state or federal Constitution. Federal laws must be consistent with the United States Constitution.

CASE LAW

New laws based on precedent-setting cases may be established in the appellate and supreme courts. All reported judicial decisions create **case** law. If a state court decides that a state statute is unconstitutional, that case may be appealed to the United States Supreme Court. If a party to a case at the trial court level determines that the court interpreted the law incorrectly or that the court did not apply the legal principles appropriately, the party may appeal the case. The appellate and/or supreme court then decides the issues involved in the appeal and makes a ruling, which may establish a precedent for future cases.

FINDING THE LAW

Most state appellate cases are reported in that state's reporter series. State supreme court cases are also reported. Some states report their appellate and supreme court cases in the same series of volumes, while others report their cases in two separate series of volumes. The appropriate state series references for your state may be found at

http://www.paralegal.delmar.cengage.com.

statutory law laws established by the state legislature or United States Congress

case law judicial opinions of appellate and supreme courts that establish precedents for future cases

Federal appellate cases and United States Supreme Court cases are published in separate series of volumes. Federal cases are published in the *Federal Reporter* series. United States Supreme Court cases are published in the *United States Reports* and the *Supreme Court Reporter.* The official version for the Supreme Court is the *United States Reports* and must be used when quoting portions thereof in court documents. Some federal trial court cases are published in the *Federal Supplement.*

Exhibits 1-1 and 1-2 show sample cases from appellate and supreme courts.

EXHIBIT 1-1 Court Opinion

Rael v. Cadena, 604 Pacific Reporter 2d 822 (1979); reprinted with permission from West, a Thomson business.

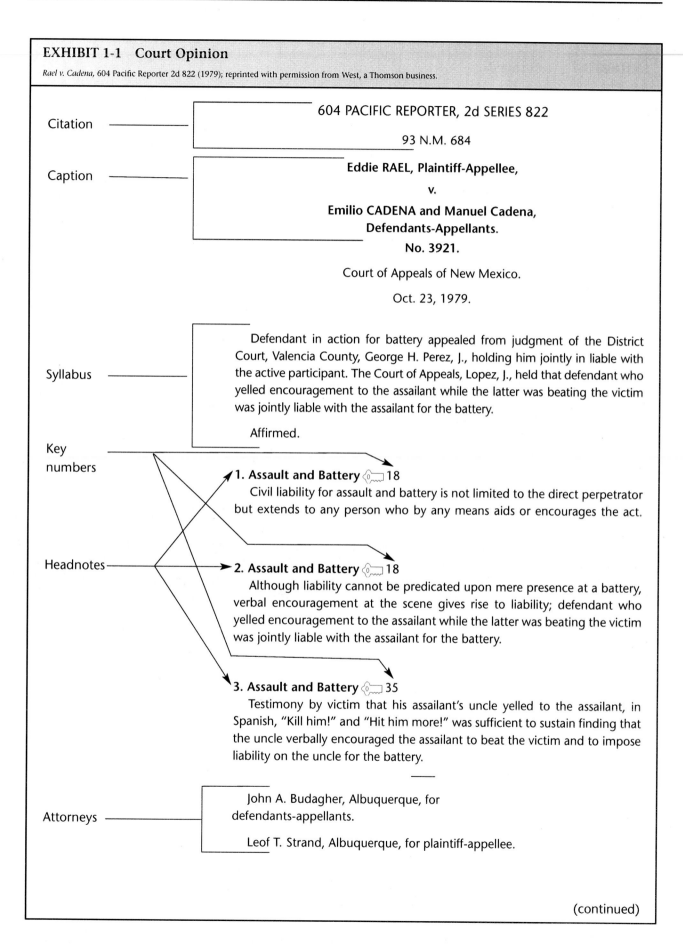

Citation

604 PACIFIC REPORTER, 2d SERIES 822

93 N.M. 684

Caption

Eddie RAEL, Plaintiff-Appellee,

v.

Emilio CADENA and Manuel Cadena,
Defendants-Appellants.

No. 3921.

Court of Appeals of New Mexico.

Oct. 23, 1979.

Syllabus

Defendant in action for battery appealed from judgment of the District Court, Valencia County, George H. Perez, J., holding him jointly in liable with the active participant. The Court of Appeals, Lopez, J., held that defendant who yelled encouragement to the assailant while the latter was beating the victim was jointly liable with the assailant for the battery.

Affirmed.

Key numbers

Headnotes

1. Assault and Battery ⚷ 18

Civil liability for assault and battery is not limited to the direct perpetrator but extends to any person who by any means aids or encourages the act.

2. Assault and Battery ⚷ 18

Although liability cannot be predicated upon mere presence at a battery, verbal encouragement at the scene gives rise to liability; defendant who yelled encouragement to the assailant while the latter was beating the victim was jointly liable with the assailant for the battery.

3. Assault and Battery ⚷ 35

Testimony by victim that his assailant's uncle yelled to the assailant, in Spanish, "Kill him!" and "Hit him more!" was sufficient to sustain finding that the uncle verbally encouraged the assailant to beat the victim and to impose liability on the uncle for the battery.

Attorneys

John A. Budagher, Albuquerque, for defendants-appellants.

Leof T. Strand, Albuquerque, for plaintiff-appellee.

(continued)

EXHIBIT 1-1 (continued)

OPINION

Judge ———— LOPEZ, Judge.

Body of the opinion — Defendant Emilio Cadena, a non-active participant in the battery of plaintiff Eddie Rael, appeals the judgment of the trial court finding him, along with the active participant, jointly and severally liable for the battery. We affirm.

The issue on appeal is whether a person present at a battery who verbally encourages the assailant, but does not physically assist him, is civilly liable for the battery.

On a visit in Emilio Cadena's home, Eddie Rael was severely beaten on the head and torso by Emilio's nephew, Manuel Cadena. As a result of the beating, he suffered a fractured rib and was hospitalized. Eddie Rael testified that once the attack had started, Emilio yelled to Manuel in Spanish, "Kill him!" and "Hit him more!" The trial court sitting without a jury found that Emilio encouraged Manuel while Manuel was beating Eddie. Based on this finding, the court held the Cadenas jointly and severally liable for the battery.

Emilio urges that in order for the trial court to have held him jointly liable for the battery, it had to find either that he and Manuel acted in concert, or that Manuel beat and injured Eddie as a result of Emilio's encouragement. This is a misstatement of the law.

[1] This is an issue of first impression in New Mexico. It is clear, however, that in the United States, civil liability for assault and battery is not limited to the direct perpetrator, but extends to any person who by any means aids or encourages the act. *Hargis v. Herrine*, 230 Ark. 502, 323 S.W.2d 917 (1959); *Ayer v. Robinson*, 163 Cal. App.2d 424, 329 P.2d 546 (1958); *Guilbeau v. Guilbeau*, 326 So.2d 654 (La.App.1976); *Duke v. Feldman*, 245 Md. 454 226 A.2d 345 (1967); *Brink v. Purnell*, 162 Mich. 147, 127 N.W. 322 (1910); 6 Am.Jur.2d *Assault and Battery* § 128 (1963); 6A C.J.S. *Assault and Battery* § 11 (1975); Annot., 72 A.L.R.2d 1229 (1960). According to the Restatement:

[f]or harm resulting to a third person from the tortious conduct of another, one is subject to liability if he

(b) knows that the other's conduct constitutes a breach of duty and gives substantial assistance or encouragement to the other so to conduct himself.* * *

Restatement (Second) of Torts § 876 (1979).

[2] Although liability cannot be predicated upon mere presence at a battery, *Duke, supra*; 6 Am.Jur., *supra*, verbal encouragement at the scene gives rise to liability. *Hargis, supra; Ayer, supra; Brink, supra*.

[A] person may be held liable for the tort of assault and battery if he *encouraged* or incited *by words* the act of the direct perpetrator.* * * (Emphasis added.)

6 Am.Jur., *supra* at 108. Because he yelled encouragement to his nephew while the latter was beating Eddie Rael, Emilio Cadena is jointly liable with his nephew for the battery.

[3] Contradictory evidence was offered as to whether Emilio Cadena did yell anything during the beating. Eddie Rael claimed that Emilio urged Manuel to beat him; Emilio denied that he said anything; and Manuel testified that he never heard Emilio. However, the trial court found that Emilio did verbally encourage Manuel to beat Eddie. Although the evidence was in conflict, the court could conclude from the testimony of Eddie Rael that Emilio Cadena verbally encouraged his nephew to attack. This testimony, if believed, is substantial evidence to support the trial court's finding. It is not the function of the appellate court to weigh the evidence or its credibility, or to substitute its judgment for that of the trial court. So long as the findings are supported by substantial evidence, they will stand. *Getz v. Equitable Life Assur. Soc. of U.S.*, 90 N.M. 195, 561 P.2d 468, *cert. denied*, 434 U.S. 834, 98 S.Ct. 121, 54 L.Ed.2d 95 (1977).

The judgment of the trial court is affirmed.
IT IS SO ORDERED.
SUTIN and ANDREWS, JJ., concur.

* * * * * *

EXHIBIT 1-2   Supreme Court Case from WESTLAW (p. 1)

United States v. American Library Association, Inc., et al., 59 U.S. 194, 123 S. Ct. 2297. Reprinted from WESTLAW with permission of Thomson/West.

123 S.Ct. 2297   page 1

539 U.S. 194, 123 S.Ct. 2297, 2003 Daily Journal D.A.R. 6824, 156 L.Ed.2d 221, 16 Fla. L. Weekly Fed. S415,
71 USLW 4465, 03 Cal. Daily Op. Serv. 5397, 29 Communications Reg. (P&F) 438
(Cite as: 539 U.S. 194, 123 S.Ct. 2297)

Briefs and Other Related Documents

Supreme Court of the United States
UNITED STATES, et al., Appellants,
v.
AMERICAN LIBRARY ASSOCIATION, INC., et al.
No. 02-361.

Argued March 5, 2003.
Decided June 23, 2003.

Group of public libraries, library associations, library patrons, and Web site publishers challenged constitutionality of Children's Internet Protection Act (CIPA), which required public libraries to use Internet filters as condition for receipt of federal subsidies. Upon convening of a three-judge court pursuant to CIPA, the United States District Court for the Eastern District of Pennsylvania, 201 F.Supp.2d 401, held CIPA facially invalid under the First Amendment. The United States appealed. The Supreme Court, Chief Justice Rehnquist, held that: (1) CIPA did not violate First Amendment free speech clause, and (2) CIPA did not impose unconstitutional condition on public libraries.

Reversed.

Justice Kennedy concurred in judgment and filed opinion.

Justice Breyer concurred in judgment and filed opinion.

Justice Stevens filed dissenting opinion.

Justice Souter filed dissenting opinion in which Justice Ginsburg joined.

West Headnotes

[1] **Constitutional Law 92** 🔑 **90.4(3)**

92 Constitutional Law
  92V Personal, Civil and political Rights
    92k90 Freedom of Speech and of the Press
      92k90.4 Obscenity and Pornography
        92k90.4(3) k. Entertainment in General;

Telecommunications. Most Cited Cases

United States 393 🔑 **82(2)**

393 United States
  393VI Fiscal Matters
    393k82 Disbursements in General
      393k82(2) k. Aid to State and Local Agencies in General. Most Cited Cases
First Amendment public forum principles, which require strict scrutiny of an alleged restriction on speech, did not apply to analysis of First Amendment validity of Children's Internet Protection Act (CIPA), under which a public library could not receive federal assistance to provide Internet access unless it installed software both to block images that constituted obscenity or child pornography and to prevent minors from obtaining access to material that was harmful to them; Internet access in public libraries was neither a traditional nor a designated public forum. U.S.C.A. Const.Amend. I; Children's Internet protection Act, § 1701, 114 Stat. 2763A-335.

[2] **Constitutional Law 92** 🔑 **90.4(3)**

92 Constitutional Law
  92V Personal, Civil and Political Rights
    92k90 Freedom of Speech and of the Press
      92k90.4 Obscenity and Pornography
        92k90.4(3) k. Entertainment in General;
Telecommunications. Most Cited Cases

United States 393 🔑 **82(2)**

393 United States
  393VI Fiscal Matters
    393k82 Disbursements in General
      393k82(2) k. Aid to State and Local Agencies in General. Most Cited Cases
Children's Internet Protection Act (CIPA), under which public library could not receive federal assistance to provide Internet access unless it installed software to block obscene or pornographic images and to prevent minors from obtaining access to harmful material, did not violate the First Amendment free speech clause; it was reasonable, given quantity of material on Internet and library's traditional role in identifying material suitable for inclusion, for library to exclude certain categories of

CATEGORIES OF LAW

Laws are categorized by whether they are civil or criminal, and by whether they are procedural or **substantive.** All laws fall into one of each of these two categories. For example, a law may be civil and procedural, civil and substantive, criminal and procedural, or criminal and substantive. Criminal laws are enacted to protect the public, whereas **civil laws** are created to protect private rights and deal with the rights and responsibilities of individuals.

Criminal law deals with wrongful acts against society. In a criminal action, the plaintiff is the state or society as a whole, not the individual victim of the crime. Criminal offenders are prosecuted by attorneys who represent the government. Criminal law defines the crime and determines what acts are prohibited and what the punishment is for committing those acts. It also establishes the degree of intent required for criminal liability. Criminal law will be discussed more extensively in Chapter 6.

Cases involving civil law are instituted by individuals or entities against other individuals or entities. Civil lawsuits are brought by plaintiffs who seek to enforce a right or to redress a wrong. Civil suits involve money damages or equity issues.

EQUITABLE ISSUES

In earlier times, two different types of civil courts existed: law and **equity.** In modern times, these courts have been merged under the civil court system. However, different remedies exist for legal and equitable issues.

In a legal action, the plaintiff sues the defendant for money damages or something of value. In an equitable action, the plaintiff seeks to stop the defendant from committing an act or to make the plaintiff perform an act that he is legally obligated to perform. Typical equitable actions involve injunctions or temporary restraining orders. A court issues an injunction to prevent a person or entity from infringing on another's property or to prevent a company from dumping toxic wastes. A restraining order may be issued to stop an individual from injuring another. They are typically used in domestic violence situations to keep the abuser away from the abused.

SUBSTANTIVE AND PROCEDURAL LAW

Substantive law, typically called *black letter law,* involves law related to basic rights and duties of the individuals and the general public. Procedural law deals with the methods of enforcing the rights and responsibilities given in substantive law. For example, contract and civil law are both substantive. The laws of evidence and civil procedure are procedural. They tell how to file a lawsuit, what evidence will be allowed, what time lines are required to file documents, and what other procedures are required in a case.

substantive law the law that describes one's rights and duties; also known as *black letter law*

civil law laws protecting individuals and entities; used to redress wrongs and enforce rights

criminal law law that protects society from wrongful conduct

equity a court's power to act when no law governs the situation; a court order to stop an individual or entity from doing an act or to require that an act be done

EXHIBIT 1-3   Geographic Boundaries of United States Courts of Appeal and United States District Courts

Source: http://www.uscourts.gov/courtlinks/

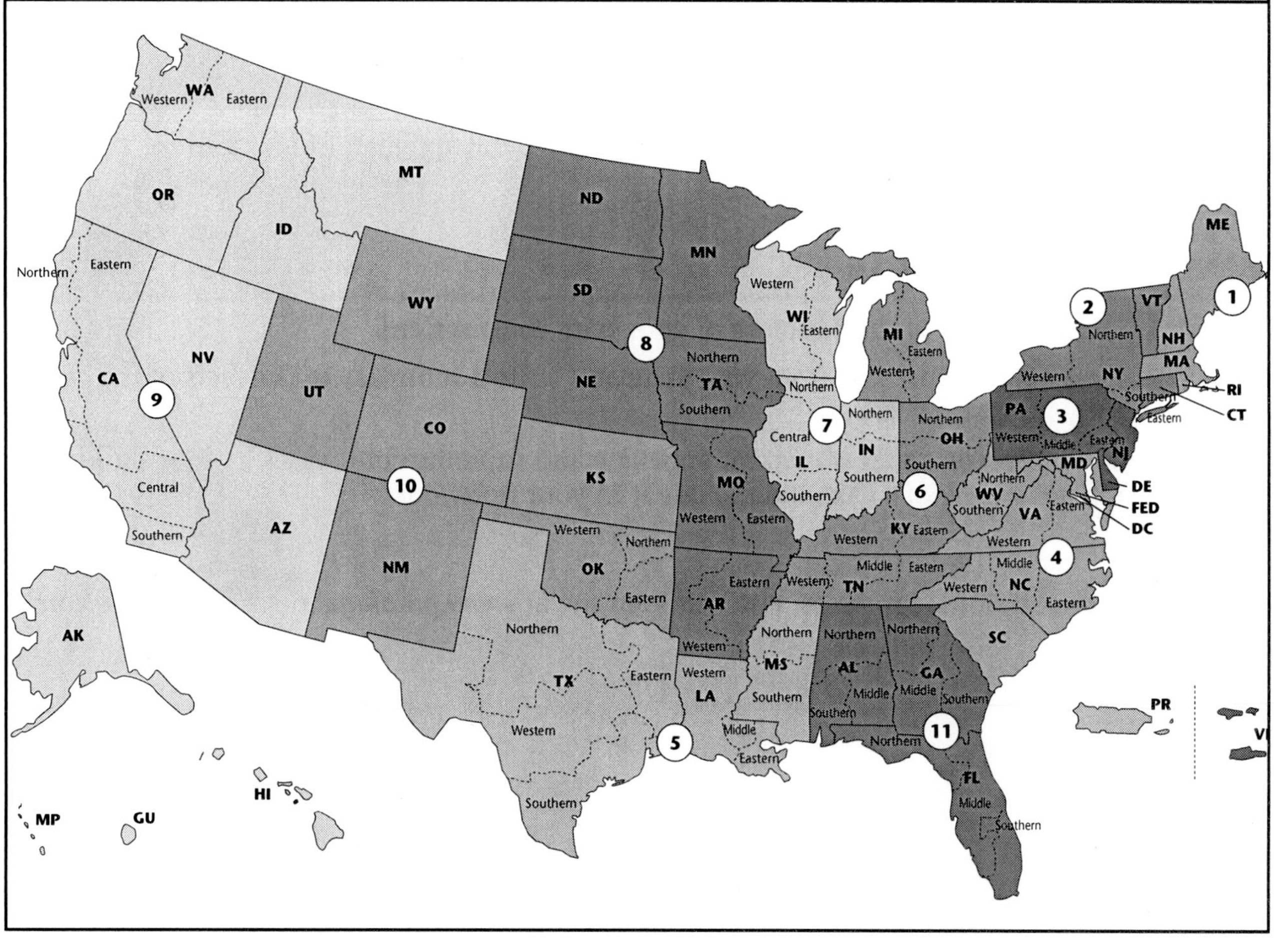

FEDERAL COURT SYSTEM

The federal courts of appeals and district courts are divided into *circuits* based on areas of the country. The district courts are the trial courts on the federal level. Exhibit 1-3 shows a map of the geographic boundaries for these courts. For instance, if your office is in Texas, you would be in the Fifth Circuit.

● KEY TERMS

case law	procedural law
civil law	statutory law
criminal law	substantive law
equity	

● SELF TEST

1. Describe the difference between substantive and procedural law.

2. Give two examples of substantive law.

3. Give two examples of procedural law.

4. Describe the difference between statutory and case law.

5. Which law takes precedence, a federal statute or a federal appellate court case?

● NOTEBOOK PROJECTS

1. Obtain a copy of the structure of your state court system.

2. Find a state court case from your state and write a summary of the facts of the case for your instructor.

3. What reporter series is used for appellate and supreme court cases in your state? Obtain a copy of a case and include it in your notebook.

For additional resources, visit our Web site at **www.paralegal.delmar.cengage.com.**

CONTRACT LAW

CHAPTER 2

CHAPTER OUTCOMES

After studying this chapter, the student will understand

1. the elements of a contract.
2. the specific requirements for making a contract.
3. the requirements of written contracts under the Statute of Frauds.
4. the different types of contracts.
5. the legal elements of a breach-of-contract action.

INTRODUCTION

Contracts are legally binding agreements among two or more parties that create a legal obligation on the part of the parties. They may involve mutual promises between the parties to perform a lawful act or not to perform a lawful act. The law requires that certain criteria be met before a legally binding contract is formed. The basic elements of a contract are offer, acceptance, and consideration. If the contract involves a legitimate business relationship, the courts generally intervene to establish the validity of the contract.

One of the parties (the **offeror**) makes an *offer* to enter into a contract with the other party (the **offeree**). The offeree must *accept* the offer and both parties must make a bargained-for exchange, called *consideration*. In other words, each party must give up something of value and receive something of value in return.

Suppose I offer to sell you this book for $75 and you accept my offer. The consideration is as follows:

Benefit to me—I receive $75.

Detriment to me—I lose my book.

Benefit to you—You receive my book.

Detriment to you—You lose $75.

Making contracts is a day-to-day activity of all businesses. The parties to the contract set the terms and requirements of the contract. Contracts are used as basic planning tools in the business world.

contract a legally binding agreement among two or more parties; requires an offer, acceptance, and consideration

offeror the person or entity who makes an offer to enter into a contract

offeree the person or entity who accepts an offer to enter into a contract

9

TYPES OF CONTRACTS

Written Contracts

Certain contracts must be in writing to satisfy the *Statute of Frauds,* which derives from the old English law on which our laws are based. The individual states determine which contracts must be in writing, but the following are generally included:

1. contracts for the sale of goods over $500 (or other amounts in some states)
2. contracts for the sale of real estate
3. leases for a year or more
4. contracts to guarantee another's debt
5. certain long-term contracts

Research contract law for your state and complete the requirements for written contracts in the following box.

> **STATE-SPECIFIC INFORMATION**
>
> The state of _____ requires that the following types of contracts be in written form:
>
> _____
>
> _____
>
> _____

Most businesses make all of their contracts in writing. Good business practice dictates that every contract be in writing so that the contract can be proven in a court of law if a problem arises. The courts, however, will not honor an agreement made for an unlawful purpose or one that violates public policy. The courts generally prohibit contracts made in restraint of trade or those that limit competition in business.

The courts will not read into the contract any terms that were not agreed on by the parties. Therefore, all business contracts should be in writing and should include within the writing all of the terms required by the business. Under the *Parol Evidence Rule,* courts interpret the contract terms by looking at the "four corners of the contract" and do not make any assumptions as to the intent of the parties outside the contract itself.

CONTRACT CLASSIFICATION

Contracts are classified into the following categories:

Formal Contract or Simple Contract

A *formal contract* is made under seal. It is required in certain states for leases for property for more than a year, for giving a bond, for deeds to property, or for contracts for the sale of real estate. Most states, however, do not require this type of formal contracts. Formal contracts also include those incorporated into a court record when the loser in court agrees to pay the court's judgment amount. The latter are also called *contracts of record.*

Simple contracts comprise all other contracts and may be oral or written.

Oral Contract or Written Contract

Oral contracts are based on words spoken between the parties and require all of the terms of a written contract, including offer, acceptance, and consideration. *Written contracts* are in writing and are signed by both parties. Business contracts should all be in writing so that they can be proven in a court of law.

Express Contract or Implied Contract

An *express contract* is set forth in oral or written words. All of the terms of the contract are stated explicitly. *Implied contracts* are based on the conduct of the parties (*implied in fact*). For example, if you hire a housekeeper to clean your house, you are expected to pay her for performing that service. A *quasi contract* (*implied in law*) is based on actions of one party that benefit the other party. If the benefiting party receives unjust enrichment because of the actions of the other party, the courts generally require that the enriched party pay the other party the reasonable value of her services. Suppose you go to the ATM to withdraw $100 from your account, and the machine pays you $10,000 instead. The courts would hold that you had been unjustly enriched and require that you pay back the excess $9,900. (See the section on quasi contracts later in the chapter.)

Bilateral Contract or Unilateral Contract

A **bilateral contract** consists of mutual promises by both parties. However, a **unilateral contract** is based on a promise by one party and the action of the second party.

Void Contracts and Voidable Contracts

Void contracts are illegal contracts that the courts will not enforce. *Voidable contracts* are based on fraud and may be set aside by the courts. For instance, suppose you bought a painting for $1,000, but when it was delivered it turned out to be a $5 print of the same painting. You could have the contract set aside in a court of law because you purchased not a $5 print but the $1,000 painting.

In *Oubre v. Entergy Operations, Inc.,* 522 U.S. 422, 118 S. Ct. 838 (1998), the Court made this distinction between void and voidable contracts:

> To determine whether a contract is voidable or void, courts typically ask whether the contract has been made under conditions that would justify giving one of the parties a choice as to validity, making it voidable, e.g.,

bilateral contract a contract formed by mutual promises

unilateral contract a contract formed by the promise of one party and an act by the other party

a contract with an infant; or whether enforcement of the contract would violate the law or public policy irrespective of the conditions in which the contract was formed, making it void, e.g., a contract to commit murder.

REQUIREMENTS FOR MAKING A CONTRACT

Legal Capacity

States have laws that restrict certain individuals from making valid contracts. The parties must be legally competent to enter into a contract.

Contracts by Minors. Contracts made by minors can be legally voided by the minor up to the time the minor reaches the age of majority and for a reasonable amount of time thereafter. The age of majority varies among the states from 18 to 21. However, if the minor purchases the necessities of life, she will be liable for the reasonable value of these items furnished to her at the minor's request. Included under necessities are food, shelter, medical care, and education. Some states also consider any property or services necessary for the minor to make a living to be necessities. Most states consider a minor who has been legally emancipated to be an adult.

Intoxicated Persons. Most states consider an intoxicated person or one under the influence of drugs to be incompetent to enter into a contract if the person cannot comprehend the nature of her actions in entering into the contract.

Mental Incapacity. If a person is under mental incapacity such that she does not know she is entering into a contract, the contract is voidable.

Licensing

Individuals in certain professions and occupations are required to be licensed by the states in which they practice. *Regulatory licenses* require them to meet certain standards of education, experience, and expertise. Contracts made by individuals without licenses in a profession that requires one are not enforceable, provided the license is not merely a fee to be paid to obtain the license but a regulatory license that requires certain qualifications of the individual. The states provide various exceptions to this rule, however, particularly when the individual has performed the work but has not been paid.

Agreement Not to Compete

Most states provide that contracts are void if they require that an individual is restrained from engaging in a lawful occupation. An exception would be if one sells a business and goodwill, the seller may be restricted from opening the same type business for a reasonable period of time, such as one year. For instance, if a lawyer leaves one law firm, she cannot be required to change occupations and not practice law.

Exculpatory Clauses

One may not be relieved of responsibilities required by law by the addition of an *exculpatory clause* in a contract. For instance, if a clause in a contract relieves the party from ordinary negligence should the other party become injured, the courts will favor the injured party and not the contract clause. Many states have statutes prohibiting such clauses where a party owes a duty to protect the public. The clause may be considered valid if a private agreement does not involve the public interest and the state does not have a statute prohibiting the clause.

OFFER

In most business contracts, a considerable amount of preliminary negotiation takes place prior to the actual **offer.** Depending on the complexities of the contract, the negotiation phase could take hours, days, or, in the case of some international contracts, months before an offer is made. When all preliminary negotiations are completed, the offeror makes an offer sufficient to justify the offeree's understanding that her acceptance will conclude the negotiations and a contract will be formed if consideration is made a part of the bargain. Once both parties agree to enter into a contract, the contract is finalized. Both parties must agree to all terms when the contract is created. Although not all contracts are required to be in writing, it is good business practice to reduce all negotiated terms to a writing signed by both parties.

The following conditions must be present in order to have a valid offer:

1. The offeror must show intent to enter into a contract at this point in time.
2. The offeror must communicate her intentions to the offeree.
3. The terms must be unambiguous and specific.

The offer must be made at the present time and must be made with appropriate intent. All terms of the contract must be specified, including the parties, price, subject matter, and time for performance. For example, the following may be considered valid offers:

1. I offer to give you $100 if you clean my home located at 122 Sunset Drive in Anytown by Monday, January 24, 2008.
2. I will sell you my 1995 Lexus SC400 for $5,000 cash, but you must accept or decline the offer by April 1, 2008.
3. ABC Company will sell to XYZ Company 100 widgets at $1 each, for cash. Acceptance is required by June 5, 2008, and delivery will be made on July 30, 2008.

offer   a proposal to enter into a contract

However, the following are not considered valid offers:

1. My car is a lemon and I will get rid of it for a nickel.
2. I do not like farming, so I will sell you the family farm for a dollar.

Offers that are made in jest or frustration are not considered valid offers, and if an individual overhearing such a statement accepts the offer, a valid contract is not created.

In *Mastrobuono v. Shearson Lehman Hutton, Inc.*, 514 U.S. 52, 115 S. Ct. 1212 (1995), the Court held that a court should construe ambiguous language against the interest of the party that drafted it. Therefore, a contract clause that is proven to be ambiguous would be construed in favor of the party who did not draft the contract.

Newspaper advertisements to sell merchandise are considered genuine offers if they are specific as to their terms. A private ad in the newspaper to sell a specific car for a specific price would likely be considered a valid offer. However, a newspaper advertisement offering 10 percent off the list price of all automobiles in stock may not be considered sufficiently specific to constitute a valid offer.

Exhibit 2-1 shows several valid offers.

EXHIBIT 2-1   Examples of Valid Offers

Date: January 24, 2008

GEEK Computer Company offers to sell to JOHN DOE a WHIZ 1.8-gigahertz computer, including the following items: 19-inch WHIZBANG flat-screen monitor, 250-gigabyte hard drive, 1 gigabyte RAM, and a WHIZTOUCH 500 keyboard, for the price of $1,500 cash. The computer and all of its components will be delivered to JOHN DOE by the end of next month. Acceptance of this offer must be in writing, signed by JOHN DOE, sent via Express Mail by February 18, 2008.

_____
(Signature)
M. GEEK, President

Advertisement placed in local newspaper:

2004 Lexus GS300 for sale; low mileage; good condition; price not negotiable; $25,000. Car may be viewed at 12345 Sixth Street, Your Town, from 10 A.M. to 1 P.M. For more information, call Jane Doe at 555-1255.

John states to his friend Jim, "I will sell you my 1999 Chevrolet Impala for $3,000 if you accept by tomorrow at 5:00 P.M."

In an offer, the offeror's promise must consist of an explicit declaration that she wishes to enter into a contract. It must include a firm commitment to perform or not to perform an act. For instance, if you tell your friend that you may sell her your car if you feel like it tomorrow, this promise is not explicit and may be considered illusory. However, if you tell him that you will sell him your car if he pays you $500, this offer tells him unequivocally that you want to sell your car and the price. If you are a car collector and do not specifically state which car you would like to sell, then the promise is not definite and does not constitute a valid offer.

The *Uniform Commercial Code* governs business contracts for the sale of goods. Article 2, Section 2–204 states that if one or more terms of the contract for sale are left open, the contract will not fail for indefiniteness "if the parties have intended to make a contract and there is a reasonably certain basis for giving an appropriate remedy." The issue in this case is whether both parties intended to make a contract. The Uniform Commercial Code provides, in Article 2, terms that supplement the terms provided in the contract itself if these particular terms are missing. The following provisions appear in Article 2, Section 3:

1. price
2. time of shipment or delivery
3. place for delivery
4. terms for payment or credit
5. warranties—title, merchantability, fitness

ACCEPTANCE

The offeree must accept the contract in the same manner in which the offer was presented. That is, if the offer was oral, then the acceptance must be oral. If the offer was written, the acceptance must also be written. It is considered good business practice to have all offers and acceptances in writing.

The acceptance must be clear and unequivocal. If the offeree states, "I will accept your offer if I get up before 9:00 A.M. tomorrow and if it rains," the acceptance is not considered valid and no contract is created.

CONSIDERATION

Consideration for a contract must be a bargained-for exchange. Each party must give up something of value and receive something of value. In Exhibit 2-1, the items sold constitute something of value that the offeror is giving up; the price paid for those items constitutes something of value being given up by the offeree. However, the offeror receives the money and the offeree receives the items, which constitutes the value received by each party. See Exhibit 2-2 for the steps within a contract.

consideration something of value given in a contract

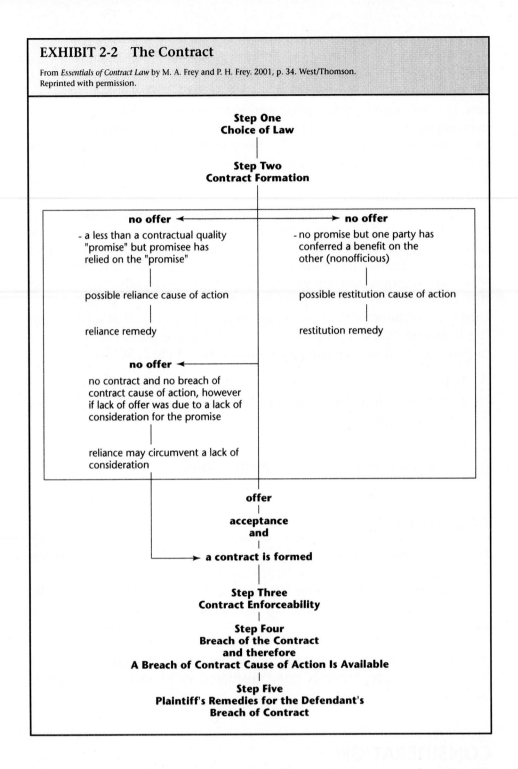

EXHIBIT 2-2   The Contract

From *Essentials of Contract Law* by M. A. Frey and P. H. Frey. 2001, p. 34. West/Thomson.
Reprinted with permission.

Step One
Choice of Law

Step Two
Contract Formation

no offer
- a less than a contractual quality "promise" but promisee has relied on the "promise"

possible reliance cause of action

reliance remedy

no offer
- no promise but one party has conferred a benefit on the other (nonofficious)

possible restitution cause of action

restitution remedy

no offer
no contract and no breach of contract cause of action, however if lack of offer was due to a lack of consideration for the promise

reliance may circumvent a lack of consideration

offer
acceptance
and
a contract is formed

Step Three
Contract Enforceability

Step Four
Breach of the Contract
and therefore
A Breach of Contract Cause of Action Is Available

Step Five
Plaintiff's Remedies for the Defendant's
Breach of Contract

QUASI CONTRACTS (Implied in Law)

In order to prevent unjust enrichment on the part of one party, the courts generally apply the principles of contract law when a benefit has been conferred on one party by the other and the benefited party has not paid the other party for her services. However, if that individual performs the service without the knowledge or consent of the benefited party, the courts generally find that the performing party committed an intrusive act and interfered in the other's affairs. Consider the difference between the following examples.

1. John moves to another state to care for his aging uncle, with the understanding that he will be compensated for his services. His uncle refuses to pay.
2. John mows his next-door neighbor's lawn and asks the neighbor to pay him for his services.

In the first case, John's uncle would be unjustly enriched if he did not pay John for his services. However, in the second case, John's neighbor did not expect to have his lawn mowed by John, who meddled in his neighbor's affairs.

WRITING A CONTRACT

Legal assistants are often asked to draft simple contracts for the attorney. Although the only contracts that are required to be in writing were outlined previously, it is good and sound business practice to require that all contracts be in writing.

Good writing skills are essential for the successful legal assistant. Some attorneys develop an outline for certain types of contracts, and the legal assistant must complete the terms in their proper order. If an outline is not provided, the legal assistant should develop her own outlines for the different types of contracts drafted most frequently. For instance, a legal assistant in a family law firm may draft marital settlement agreements, prenuptial agreements, and contracts of sale for marital assets. In a corporate law firm, the legal assistant may draft business contracts, merger agreements, and acquisitions contracts. Several computer programs are available for drafting different types of contracts. However, the legal assistant may need to complete the required information.

The legal assistant should use a checklist to be sure that all the terms of the contract are included in their proper order. Exhibit 2-3 shows a checklist for drafting a contract and includes the items that the contract should address.

BREACH OF CONTRACT

Contract lawsuits involve one party claiming that the other party has not fulfilled her part of the contract because the second party has not performed her obligations as required in the contract. A person may also breach the contract by announcing that she will not perform at the promised time. Because this performance requirement has not yet occurred, the breach is often called **anticipatory breach** or **anticipatory repudiation.**

For example, suppose you order personalized Christmas cards to send out for the holiday to be delivered to you on December 20, and the printer does not have the cards ready until December 29. If he notifies

anticipatory breach (anticipatory repudiation) breaching a contract by refusing to fulfill one's obligations once the contract has been entered into but before the time for performance

---

EXHIBIT 2-3 Contracts Checklist

From *Essentials of Contract Law* by M. A. Frey and P. H. Frey. 2001, p. 127. West/Thomson. Reprinted with permission.

1. Choice of law

    The applicable state law if the parties decide to select the applicable state law (that is, choice-of-law provision)

2. Contract formation

    a. The offeror's duties

    b. The offeree's duties

    c. The timing and dependence of the performance of the duties to one another

    d. Events or conditions necessary to create the duty

    e. Events or conditions necessary to terminate the duty

    f. Whether all the terms of this contract will be set forth in this writing and, if so, whether the writing should so state (that is merger clause)

3. Enforcement

    a. If the contract must be in writing to be enforceable, the terms the writing should contain and who must sign

    b. If a clause in the contract could be held unenforceable, what remains of the contract

4. Breach

    a. Definition of breach

    b. Significance of breach

5. Remedies for the aggrieved party

    a. The aggrieved party's remedies

    b. Alternative methods of dispute resolution in lieu of litigation (e.g., negotiation, mediation or arbitration)

    c. A statement relating to costs and attorneys' fees

    d. The forum in which litigation would take place

---

you on December 18 that the cards will not be ready on December 20, he has breached the contract as of December 18 based on anticipatory repudiation. If instead he does not notify you and does not deliver the cards on December 20, he has breached the contract as of December 20.

Most states require the preparation of a Complaint for Breach of Contract, a sample of which is shown in Exhibit 2-4.

Remedies for Breach of Contract

Various remedies are available to the plaintiff in a breach-of-contract action. They are designed to protect the plaintiff's expectations that the defendant will perform her portion of the bargain. The plaintiff is also

EXHIBIT 2-4   Complaint for Breach of Contract

From *Essentials of Contract Law* by M. A. Frey and P. H. Frey. 2001, p. 202. West/Thomson. Reprinted with permission.

IN THE DISTRICT COURT OF [NAME] COUNTY
STATE OF [NAME]

[NAME], dba [Name]	)	
Plaintiff,	)	
v.	)	Case No. _____
[NAME], a [Name of State]	)	
corporation	)	
Defendant.	)	

COMPLAINT FOR BREACH OF CONTRACT

1. Plaintiff is an individual residing in [Name] County, [Name of State], doing business as [Name].

2. Defendant is a corporation incorporated under the laws of the State of [Name of State].

3. On or about [date], Plaintiff and Defendant entered into a written contract whereby Plaintiff promised to design a marketing plan for Defendant and Defendant promised to pay [$ dollars] and 1% of Defendant's net profits earned during the first year after the marketing plan was implemented. The contract also provided that in the event of litigation, reasonable attorney fees could be awarded to the prevailing party. A copy of the contract is attached as Exhibit A.

4. On or about [date], Plaintiff presented the completed marketing plan to the Defendant.

5. All conditions precedent have been performed by Plaintiff or have occurred and Defendant has not been excused from performance.

6. Defendant has breached the contract by failing to pay the Plaintiff for the services rendered.

7. As a result of Defendant's breach of contract, Plaintiff has sustained damages in the sum of $ [dollars].

Accordingly, Plaintiff demands judgment against Defendant for the sum of $ [dollars], interest, and costs, including reasonable attorney fees.

[Attorney's name signed]

[Attorney's name typed]

Attorney for plaintiff

[Bar membership number]

[Address]

[Telephone number]

protected based on her reliance on the defendant's promise and is entitled to **restitution** damages—that is, being restored to as good a position as if both parties had performed their sides of the contract. Damages are based on the reasonable value of the benefit that the plaintiff would have received if the defendant had performed on the contract. Alternatively, the court may require the defendant to perform her part of the contract and thereby confer the benefit required to the plaintiff. This remedy is known as **specific performance.** In some cases, the court may issue an **injunction** that directs the defendant to stop performing certain acts specified in the order.

For example, suppose Jane and Sally enter into a contract under which Jane will pay Sally $15,000 for the purchase of Sally's car. Sally delivers the car to Jane, but Jane does not pay Sally. Sally could sue Jane for $15,000 damages (the amount agreed on for the sale of the car). In reverse, suppose Jane pays Sally $15,000 for the car, but Sally does not deliver the car. Jane could sue Sally for specific performance on the contract; that is, Sally could be required to deliver the car to Jane.

In another example, Mr. Hope contracts with the Bad Painting Company to paint his house for $5,000. After entering into the contract, the painting company refuses to paint the house, and Mr. Hope must hire the Good Painting Company to do the job. Good charges Mr. Hope $6,000. Mr. Smith could then sue Bad for $1,000, the additional amount it cost Mr. Hope to have his house painted. Mr. Hope had an *expectation interest* in having his house painted for $5,000. When Bad breached the contract and Mr. Hope was required to pay $1,000 more, he became entitled to recovery from Bad because of this expectation interest.

Whether the defendant breaches the contract intentionally or unintentionally, the damages to which the plaintiff is entitled are the same. In most cases, **punitive damages** are not awarded for breach of contract unless the defendant has committed fraud or an egregious willful act against the plaintiff.

In most monetary damage awards, the courts grant **compensatory damages** for the actual loss the plaintiff suffers because of the defendant's breach of the contract. However, the courts require that the plaintiff mitigate the damages by acting reasonably to avoid or limit her losses. For instance, if the plaintiff orders merchandise and the defendant does not deliver it, the plaintiff cannot recover damages for doing without the merchandise when it is readily available from another individual or company.

Defenses to Breach of Contract

Performance. The defendant may respond to the complaint by alleging performance of her obligations under the contract. For instance, a defendant who was required to pay the plaintiff for an item may prove payment by producing a copy of the canceled check.

Substantial Performance. A defendant who has performed the majority of her obligations under the contract may allege **substantial performance;** the courts will allow money damages for the part that is

---

restitution restoring the plaintiff to the position she would have held had the defendant performed according to the contract

specific performance requirement to perform on a contract to the precise agreed-upon terms

injunction a court order requiring an individual to perform an act or to refrain from performing an act

punitive damages a monetary award to punish the defendant for her actions; also called *exemplary damages;* used when the wrong was as a result of gross negligence or intentional, willful, or wanton conduct of the defendant; used most often in civil actions

compensatory damages damages awarded for the actual loss of the plaintiff

substantial performance the condition in which one party has performed most of the obligations required under the contract; may be used as a defense in a breach-of-contract action

not completed. Whether the extent of the performance was substantial would be an arguable issue for the courts to decide.

Impossibility.   If the parties did not know at the time the contract was made that it would have been impossible for the defendant to perform, she may be excused from performance. For instance, suppose the plaintiff rents a house from the defendant and the house has been destroyed by fire. If neither of the parties knew about the destruction when the contract was made, the defendant may claim impossibility of performance.

Prior Breach by Plaintiff.   If the plaintiff was required to perform her part of the contract before the defendant's performance, the defendant may claim that the plaintiff breached the contract and therefore the defendant was not required to perform. For instance, if Michael had made a contract with Nicholas to deliver a certain automobile to him on a specified date and Michael did not deliver the car, then Nicholas would not be obligated to pay for it. If Michael sued Nicholas for breach of contract, Nicholas could claim this defense.

Destruction.   If the subject of the contract is destroyed, then the defendant cannot be required to perform. For instance, if Dan promises to paint a specific house owned by Jeff and the house burns down, Dan is not obligated to perform.

Death or Disability.   If the contract can be performed by only one individual and that person dies or is disabled and is unable to perform, she is not obligated to perform. But if the work can be done by others, then the defendant must hire others to perform the contract. If an artist contracts to paint a picture or an author contracts to write a book, those acts require personal skill and must be performed only by the defendant. However, if the contract requires the defendant to paint the plaintiff's house, then others may perform her obligation under the contract.

Bankruptcy.   If the defendant has filed for bankruptcy in federal court, some of her debts will be discharged in the bankruptcy. While ordinary business contracts may generally be discharged, some other specific contracts must be performed.

● KEY TERMS

anticipatory breach (anticipatory repudiation)

bilateral contract

compensatory damages

consideration

contract

injunction

offer

offeree

offeror

punitive damages

restitution

specific performance

substantial performance

unilateral contract

● SELF TEST

1. Describe the difference between a bilateral and a unilateral contract.

2. Which types of contracts must be in writing to satisfy the Statute of Frauds?

3. Under what circumstances is an individual excused from performance under the contract?

4. What is a breach-of-contract action?

● NOTEBOOK PROJECTS

1. Prepare a contract for the sale of your automobile to John Smith.

2. Suppose John does not pay you for the automobile. Prepare a Complaint for Breach of Contract. You may use the format shown in Exhibit 2-4 or find the proper format for your state.

For additional resources, visit our Web site at **www.paralegal.delmar.cengage.com**.

SALES AND COMMERCIAL PAPER

CHAPTER OUTCOMES

After studying this chapter, the student will understand

1. the sales concepts governed by the Uniform Commercial Code.
2. the difference between sales and bailments.
3. the methods to transfer title.
4. the types of commercial paper.
5. the defenses to transfer of negotiable instruments.

INTRODUCTION

Simply stated, business law involves the laws that regulate businesses. Major components include contract law (see Chapter 2), sales, commercial paper, forms of business organization and their functions, the law of agency, and the growing field of international business.

SALES

The law of sales was established to provide a standardized system for sales contracts. The sale and distribution of **goods** may be conducted more proficiently and promptly with a uniform code for making sales contracts. Thus, the **Uniform Commercial Code (UCC)** was established to provide a uniform system of laws related to sales contracts among the states.

Uniform Commercial Code

The Statute of Frauds requires all contracts for the sale of goods for $500 or more to be in writing. The UCC creates uniformity among these contracts. *Oran's Dictionary of the Law* defines the Uniform Commercial Code as follows:

> A comprehensive set of laws on every major type of business law, including contract law as it applies to the sale of goods, banking law, and negotiable instruments law. It has been adopted by every state, in whole or in part. . . .[1]

[1]Daniel Oran, *Oran's Dictionary of the Law,* 3rd ed. (Clifton Park, NY: West Legal Studies, an imprint of Thomson Delmar Learning, 2000), 502.

goods tangible and movable merchandise

Uniform Commercial Code (UCC) a comprehensive set of laws governing sales contracts with merchants

Contracts covered by the UCC must be for the sale of "goods" (or merchandise) that are tangible and movable. Real estate contracts are not covered by the UCC. Contracts for the sale of stocks and bonds and other intangibles are not covered.

Goods may be either specific items or bulk amounts of *fungible* goods, such as rice, oil, wheat, or flour. A unit of goods that is identical to every other unit of that type of goods is considered fungible. These goods may be readily substituted for each other.

Article 2 of the UCC requires a higher standard for merchants, or those who hold themselves out as having knowledge and skill of that particular product, or those who are engaged in the sale of the type of goods being sold.

Sales Forms

Many businesses use preprinted **sales forms** for their sales transactions. These forms may go back and forth between the seller and the buyer on a regular basis. In most cases, the language of the seller's form favors the seller, and the buyer's forms use language that favors the buyer. Unless the seller specifically states that the exact terms specified on his forms are required to form a valid sales contract, the UCC allows the exchange of forms with slightly different language. In that case, the contract is binding only as to the terms agreed on by both parties. Any new terms suggested by the buyer on the seller's forms must be specifically agreed to by the seller. Likewise, if the seller requests terms that differ from those on his original forms, then those terms will be made a part of the contract only if the buyer subsequently agrees to them. However, no sales contract will be formed if the buyer's terms are inconsistent with the seller's terms. When absolute inconsistencies occur on both sides, the courts generally hold that no contract has been formed. If the final sales agreement leaves out a term that later might come into dispute, the courts insert the missing terms based on the prior business dealings of the parties, established customs, or the provisions of the UCC.

Bailment

sales forms preprinted forms used by businesses for their sales transactions

bailment a temporary delivery of property by the owner into another person's custody (keeping)

bailor the person who possesses the personal property and turns it over to the other party

bailee the person who gets custody of the property in a bailment

A **bailment** is defined in *Oran's Dictionary of Law* as "a temporary delivery of property by the owner into another person's custody (keeping)."[2] Examples of bailments include the loan of a book to a friend, the storage of property in a commercial warehouse, and the repair of an automobile in a repair shop. A *bailment for term* is a delivery of property for a set length of time. Bailment has been defined by the courts as a transfer of possession but not a change or transfer of ownership.

The person who possesses the personal property and turns it over to the other party is known as the **bailor;** the party who gets custody of the property is called the **bailee.** The owner of the property is not necessarily the bailor, because the property may have been stolen

[2]Oran, *Oran's Dictionary of the Law,* 502.

by or lent to the individual who is then transferring it temporarily to another for repair. Suppose your friend borrows your tennis racket, breaks a string, and takes it to a repair shop to be restrung. Your friend becomes the bailor, and the repair shop is the bailee. However, if you take the racket to the repair shop, you would be the bailor.

The courts require that when a bailment occurs, the bailee must return the identical item to the bailor in its original condition. An exception to this requirement is in the case of fungible goods, as they are not readily distinguishable. Thus, if you temporarily deliver ten gallons of gasoline, the recipient is not required to return the same ten gallons to you but must return gasoline of the same quality.

Valet Parking

When you have your car parked by a valet at a restaurant, store, or other facility, the valet retains the keys to your automobile. You receive a small ticket with identification for your car. In many cases, the ticket contains, in small print, an exculpatory clause to avoid legal responsibility for your automobile. Most courts have held that these clauses are not a defense against negligence. However, when the exculpatory clause does not avoid liability completely but limits it, the courts may be more willing to accept the validity of the clause.

Special Bailments

Hotel operators are required to maintain full responsibility for protecting the baggage and property of their guests. In most cases, the hotel is liable for damages for stolen or damaged property. Most state statutes limit liability for stolen valuables unless the articles are placed in a safe in the hotel office or, in some cases, in a safe in the guest's hotel room.

A *common carrier* (an entity that transports goods or people) has a special duty to deliver the goods or people safely to their destination. Various exceptions occur in the cases of natural disaster, acts of war, or other uncontrollable events.

Options

An **option** is a separate contract under which one party pays money for the right to buy something from or sell something to the other party at a set price within a specified time period. An example would be a *commodity option,* in which the buyer may buy a commodity (such as wheat, rice, or cotton) at a certain price by the end of the month (or some other agreed-on time period). One may also have a commodity option to sell a commodity for a certain price by the end of the specified time period.

For instance, suppose you are not sure whether you wish to buy a piece of property and need some time to decide. You may request an option to purchase the property by an agreed-on date. The seller will charge you a set fee for the option. If you do not exercise the option to purchase the property by the agreed-on date, then the seller is free to sell the property to someone else. The seller may also keep the fee you paid to keep the option open.

option a separate contract under which one party pays money for the right to buy something from or sell something to the other party at a set price within a specified time period

Conditional Sales

If the seller of an item of real or personal property retains the title to the property until the buyer has paid the total price, a *conditional sale* has occurred. Under the UCC, the conditional sale is known as a *security agreement.*

A seller of real property who enters into a conditional sales agreement retains title to the property until the buyer has paid the full price for it. If you sell your car under a conditional sale, then you keep the title to the car until the buyer has paid you the full price for the car.

Although the buyer obtains possession of the property, the seller may retake possession of the property if the buyer defaults on his payments. If the property is destroyed while in the possession of the buyer and before full payment has been made to the seller, the buyer is still required to pay the balance due on the contract to the seller.

Fungible Goods

Products or items that have elements that are not distinguishable are known as **fungible** goods. In this case, all parts are the same as the other parts. For example, in a ton of rice, each grain is indistinguishable and thus the rice is considered fungible.

In this case, a person who buys a portion of the fungible goods owns them in common with the seller until they are separated from the seller's portion. For instance, if the seller has 1,000 tons of rice and the buyer buys 500 tons, they own the 1,000 tons in common until the seller separates out the buyer's 500 tons.

Transfer of Title

In most cases, title to property transfers when the seller delivers the item to the buyer and the buyer pays for it. For instance, if you deliver your golf clubs to the buyer and the buyer pays your price, the title to the golf clubs transfers to the buyer. However, sales transactions are usually more complicated and other contingencies come into play. For instance, the following questions may have to be answered in cases of controversy:

1. Which party has an insurable interest in the property?
2. Do any creditors have claims against the property, and whose are valid?
3. Where were the goods transferred, for tax purposes?
4. When does the risk of loss pass from the seller to the buyer?
5. May the seller require the return of the property if the buyer does not pay?

fungible describes a unit of goods that is identical to every other unit of that type of goods

All of these matters may be settled by the parties in advance and made a part of the contract itself. Otherwise, the UCC governs the transfer of title and risk of loss in a sales contract with a business. It is recommended, however, that the parties register all of the terms for transfer of title and risk of loss in the contract itself so that there will be no problems interpreting the contract at a later date.

COMMERCIAL PAPER

Negotiable instruments relating to business are known as **commercial paper.** A signed document in which a party promises to pay a specific sum of money to a specific person or entity, on demand or at a specified future date, is a negotiable instrument. Examples of negotiable instruments are checks, bills of exchange, and promissory notes. Therefore, a check from a business that represents payment to another business on a contract is known as commercial paper. Commercial paper may also include stock certificates or bonds concerning business debts. Instruments used in business that require payment in money may be considered commercial paper.

Article 3 of the UCC requires that an item must include the following elements in order to be considered commercial paper:

1. a sum certain of money
2. the signature of the maker
3. an unconditional promise or order
4. payable on demand or at a specific time
5. payable to the bearer

Types of Commercial Paper

Various types of checks constitute commercial paper, including customer checks, cashier's checks, certified checks, and traveler's checks. Also included in the category of commercial paper are bills of exchange, certificates of deposit, and promissory notes. Note that each of these items must be negotiable in order to constitute commercial paper.

A person who writes a check from his checking account promising to pay a stipulated amount of money to an identified third-party business has prepared commercial paper (or a negotiable instrument). A *cashier's check* may be required for some purchases. In that case, the check is drawn by the bank on itself and signed by the bank's cashier. The check may be written for a third party, who has paid the money to the bank for this purpose.

A *certified check* is guaranteed by the bank on which it is drawn. The bank is verifying that the amount and the maker's signature are valid. A *traveler's check* is useful for those who are traveling and must carry large sums of money. It is executed by the addition of the holder's signature, which must match the original signature on the check. The second signing must occur in front of the individual or business to whom the check is being made.

A *bill of exchange* (or *bank draft*) is written by one party directing a second party to pay a definite sum to a third party. A typical bank draft comes into play when a debtor owes money to a creditor who wishes the debtor to pay a third party to whom he owes money instead of

commercial paper
negotiable instruments relating to business

paying him directly. To simplify this type of payment, remember the following formula:

A pays B for the benefit of C = bill of exchange

A *promissory note* is a written promise to pay a specific amount of money on a date specified in the note to an authorized person. The individual signing the note is known as the *payor;* the person or entity to which the money is to be paid is called the *payee.* This type of note becomes a negotiable instrument when it is made payable to the bearer of the note or to a specific named individual. The amount or rate of interest must be specified on the promissory note.

Time for Payment

The time for payment is generally specified within the particular negotiable instrument. However, if the time in which payment must be made is left out, the instrument is payable on demand of the other party.

Holder in Due Course

One who has legal possession of commercial paper is called a *holder.* The holder is entitled to payment on the paper. A *holder in due course* purchases commercial paper thinking it is valid and has no knowledge that there are some problems with validity. Perhaps the paper is overdue or fraudulent. The holder in due course has greater rights than a holder and cannot be charged for defective merchandise by a buyer of the merchandise involved in the negotiable instrument.

Article 3 of the UCC establishes the following requirements for a holder in due course:

1. The holder takes the paper for value, with good faith, and without notice that there is a deficiency or problem with the instrument.
2. The payee may be the holder in due course.
3. The holder may not purchase the instrument at a judicial sale or under legal process.
4. The holder may not acquire the paper as a result of an estate or as part of a bulk transaction not in the ordinary course of business.
5. The purchaser of a limited interest may be a holder in due course only of the amount of the interest he purchased.

Consumer Sales

While the holder-in-due-course principles still hold true in sales among merchants, many states have enacted legislation limiting or eliminating the principles in consumer buying and financing. Many states require that the consumer be advised if the obligation (such as a promissory note) is sold to a third party and allow the consumer a certain period of time to advise of claims against the seller. State laws vary on the rights of consumers under these principles; research your state's laws and identify them in the following box.

STATE-SPECIFIC INFORMATION

Laws in the state of _____ related to consumers in the application of holder-in-due-course principles include the following:

_____

_____

_____

_____

_____

_____

The Federal Trade Commission (FTC) governs the prohibition of unfair or deceptive practices that affect interstate commerce. The courts have held this to include transactions using the telephone or mail. The FTC requires all consumer credit contracts to include printed notices that any holder of the consumer's obligation has all of the same rights the original consumer may have against the seller. The FTC Web site (http://www.ftc.gov) is shown in Exhibit 3-1.

Transfer of Commercial Paper

Commercial paper may be transferred by way of an **endorsement** (sometimes spelled *indorsement*) on the back of the paper. A person who signs the back of a check made out to him is making an endorsement that transfers the check to a third party. A *restrictive endorsement* limits either the recipient or the purpose of the transfer. For instance, a check made that has been endorsed on the back as follows:

Pay to the order of William Smith
(Your signature)

restricts the person who may cash the check to William Smith. A check signed on the back with

For Deposit Only
(Your signature)

restricts the payment of the check to your bank account. Further restrictions might include your bank account number and bank name. A *blank endorsement* is merely the signature on the back of the check, which enables anyone who possesses the check to cash it.

Defenses for Nonpayment

In order to refuse payment on a negotiable instrument, the maker may assert a defense against the individual or entity that holds the commercial paper.

endorsement/indorsement transferring a negotiable instrument to a third party by signing it in such a manner as to transfer the rights to another

EXHIBIT 3-1   FTC Web Site

Source: Federal Trade Commission Web site, http://www.ftc.gov.

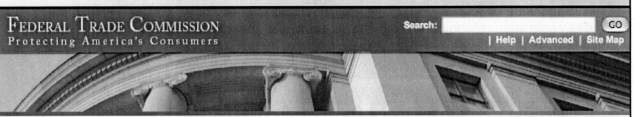

FEDERAL TRADE COMMISSION
Protecting America's Consumers

Search: [_____] GO

| Help | Advanced | Site Map

Privacy Policy | About FTC | Commissioners | File a Complaint | HSR | FOIA | IG Office | En Español

Contents

FOR CONSUMERS

FOR BUSINESS

NEWSROOM

FORMAL ACTIONS

ANTITRUST & COMPETITION

CONGRESSIONAL RESOURCES

ECONOMIC RESOURCES

LEGAL RESOURCES

Hot Topics

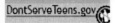

FTC Headlines

For Release: November 13, 2006

Court Shuts Down Media Motor Spyware Operation

Trojan Program Downloaded Spyware, Adware, Porno Pop-Ups to Consumers' Computers

A U.S. district court has shut down an operation that secretly downloaded multiple malevolent software programs, including spyware, onto millions of computers without consumers' consent, degrading their computers' performance, spying on them, and exposing them to a barrage of disruptive advertisements. More...

For Release: November 7, 2006

Federal Trade Commission/Department of Justice Hearings On Single-Firm Conduct to Continue On November 15

Session To Be Held in Washington, DC to Focus on Exclusive Dealing

The Federal Trade Commission and the Department of Justice's (DOJ) Antitrust Division today announced that the latest in a series of joint public hearings designed to examine the implications of single-firm conduct under the antitrust laws will take place on November 15, 2006, in Washington, DC. More...

Last Updated: Monday, November 13, 2006 10:57 AM

Of Interest

View the FTC's
PRIVACY POLICY

PRIVACY INITIATIVES

HISTORY OF THE FTC

JOBS AT THE FTC

EARLY TERMINATIONS

CONFERENCES & WORKSHOPS

HEARINGS

REPORTS

INTERNATIONAL ACTIVITIES

RN DATABASE

Fair Credit Reporting Act (including FACT Act)

FTC Merger Best Practices

FTC/DOJ Hearings and Report on Section 2 of the Sherman Act: Single-Firm Conduct As Related to Competition

E-CONSUMER.GOV

NO FEAR ACT DATA

WEBSITE POLICIES

RELATED SITES

XML RSS News & Info Feeds

HOME | CONSUMERS | BUSINESSES | NEWSROOM | FORMAL | ANTITRUST | CONGRESSIONAL | ECONOMIC | LEGAL
Privacy Policy | About FTC | Commissioners | File a Complaint | HSR | FOIA | IG Office | En Español | Contact Us

Federal Trade Commission, 600 Pennsylvania Avenue, N.W., Washington, D.C. 20580

Fraud. A person who is induced to sign a document believing that the document is something other than what it purports to be may not be forced to pay. However, fraud cannot be used as a defense merely because the individual signed the document without reading it. If the document is in a language that the signer does not understand and he is told the document is something that it is not, then the signer can use fraud as a defense.

Illegality. The courts will not intervene in an illegal agreement. If the contract on which the commercial paper is based is illegal, then the instrument is void.

Duress. The UCC requires that the degree of duress must render "the obligation of the party a nullity." A person who signed a check while someone was pointing a loaded gun at him could assert the defense of duress.

Other defenses may also be available in different states. Research the laws in your state and list the results in the following box.

STATE-SPECIFIC INFORMATION

Defenses against payment on a negotiable instrument in the state of
_____ are as follows:

_____

_____

_____

● KEY TERMS

bailee	fungible
bailment	goods
bailor	option
commercial paper	sales forms
endorsement/indorsement	Uniform Commercial Code (UCC)

● SELF TEST

1. Describe the difference between a sale and a bailment.
2. What is the difference between an option and a contract?
3. Describe how title is transferred in a typical sales contract.
4. List the types of negotiable instruments and how they are transferred.

● NOTEBOOK PROJECTS

1. Find any laws in your state that govern sales contracts under the UCC and write a memorandum to your instructor describing these laws.

2. Prepare a contract for the sale of fungible goods under the UCC.

3. Describe the laws in your state that relate to holder-in-due-course requirements.

4. Complete the State-Specific Information boxes in this chapter and include the information in your notebook.

For additional resources, visit our Web site at **www.paralegal.delmar.cengage.com.**

ORGANIZATION OF BUSINESSES

CHAPTER OUTCOMES

After studying this chapter, the student will understand

1. the different types of business organizations and how they are structured.
2. how mergers, consolidations, and dissolutions are accomplished.
3. how agency relations are created and terminated.
4. government regulations that control businesses.
5. the treaties that affect international business.

TYPES OF BUSINESS ORGANIZATIONS

The most common types of business organizations are the following:

1. sole proprietorship—an unincorporated business usually owned by one individual
2. partnership—an organization composed of two or more individuals who have jointly agreed to operate a business for profit
3. corporation—a business entity existing separate and apart from its owners, who are called shareholders

Sole Proprietorship

The **sole proprietorship** is the mainstay of the United States economy and is generally a small business owned by one individual. It is usually smaller than a partnership or a corporation and possesses limited resources. Although a sole proprietorship is easy to establish, the owner faces unlimited personal liability if a problem arises. For example, a customer who is injured in a store owned by a sole proprietor may be awarded damages from the owner's business and personal assets in order to settle the claim.

If the owner hires a manager to run the business, the owner is vicariously liable for the acts of the manager that are made in the scope of her employment. Both the owner's business and personal assets may be used.

The owner usually must obtain a loan from a bank or other financial institution in order to provide capital to open and run the business.

sole proprietorship an unincorporated business usually owned by one individual

Both the assets of the business and the owner's personal assets will be reviewed. The owner's business and personal debts will also be evaluated to determine her potential for repayment of the loan.

If the state imposes a sales tax and the business sells items to the public, the owner must obtain a sales tax permit. If the business operates under a name other than the owner's, a **Fictitious Business Name Statement** must be filed in the county in which the business is located. A business license must be obtained in the city where the business is located. A sample Fictitious Business Name Statement is shown in Exhibit 4-1.

STATE-SPECIFIC INFORMATION

Fill in the following blanks with the requirements in your state:

The state of _____ imposes a sales tax of _____%. The owner (is / is not) required to obtain a sales tax permit.

A business license (is / is not) required in the city where the business is located.

A Fictitious Business Name Statement (is / is not) required.

Special requirements:

_____

_____

_____

Partnership

Partners share expenses and have increased capital to run the business. They generally pool their resources. Partners must declare their share of the **partnership** profits on their individual personal income tax returns. Partners have unlimited liability for the acts of the other partners in dealings on behalf of the partnership. For instance, if one partner purchases a limousine in the partnership's name, each of the partners is also liable for payment of the purchase price. The assets of the partnership are used to pay for the limousine. However, if insufficient funds exist to pay for any item purchased for the partnership, each partner's individual funds may be used for that purpose.

If one partner enters into a contract for the partnership, all other partners are liable for the terms of the contract. If a partner enters into illegal activities on behalf of the partnership, the other partners may also be held liable.

A large partnership may include general partners and limited partners. General partners take part in the day-to-day operations of the business and invest money in the company. Limited partners invest capital in the business but have no management responsibility and are not personally

Fictitious Business Name Statement a certificate required to be filed in the county in which a business operates if the business functions under a name other than the owner's

partnership an organization composed of two or more individuals who have jointly agreed to operate a business for profit

EXHIBIT 4-1   Fictitious Business Name Statement

FICTITIOUS BUSINESS NAME STATEMENT

File No. AB-45903

The following persons are doing business as:

GOLFF FOR LESS, 433 East Main Street, Phoenix, AZ 85012

Danielle M. Gallo, 455 Sunset Boulevard, Prescott, AZ 85011

Jeffrey W. Flogg, 908 Desert Dunes Drive, Scottsdale, AZ 85911

_____   _____

DANIELLE M. GALLO   JEFFREY W. FLOGG

This statement was filed with the County Clerk of Maricopa County on December 22, 2004. The registrants commenced to transact business under the fictitious name listed above on December 21, 2004.

NOTICE: This Fictitious Business Name Statement expires five years from the date it was filed with the office of the County Clerk. A new Fictitious Business Name Statement must be filed before that time. The filing of this statement does not of itself authorize the use in this state of a Fictitious Business Name in violation of the rights of another under Federal, State, or common law (See Section 9222 et seq., Business Code.)

liable for the partnership's activities. Most states require that each partnership have at least one general partner who is responsible and liable for the partnership. Some states have more stringent regulations on limited partners. List your state's requirements in the following box.

STATE-SPECIFIC INFORMATION

Requirements in the state of _____ for limited partnerships are as follows:

_____

_____

_____

The General Partnership Agreement. When the partnership involves only general partners, they must negotiate an agreement for the operation of the business. Because of the complexity, responsibilities, and liabilities involved in this type of business arrangement, it is advisable to have a written partnership agreement that enumerates the following elements:

1. title—name and address of partners
2. name—name, purpose, and location of the partnership
3. duration of the partnership
4. each partner's contribution in money and time
5. division of profits and allocation of expenses and losses
6. how a partner may transfer her interests
7. how a partner's interest may be "bought out" or purchased by the other partners (this issue is particularly critical if your client is the partner whose interest is purchased)
8. the procedure for voting on issues
9. duties and responsibilities of each partner
10. procedures for dissolving the partnership
11. procedures for removing a partner or obtaining new partners
12. how policy disagreements will be settled
13. accounting procedures used in the business
14. each partner's liability to the other partners
15. how partners will be compensated
16. what effect the death or resignation of a partner will have
17. signatures of the partners

A sample general partnership agreement is shown in Exhibit 4-2.

Format for General Partnership Agreement

Title. The title of the partnership agreement should identify the parties and the nature of the agreement. For instance, in Exhibit 4-2, Adams and Harmon are identified as the parties to the agreement. The nature of the agreement is that it is a general partnership agreement.

Name, Nature, and Location. Exhibit 4-2 shows that the partnership is being formed to manufacture candles and that the partnership name is Adams & Harmon. Its principal place of business is given under item 4.

Capital Contribution. Under the section titled "Initial Capital," the agreement indicates the initial capital that each partner must contribute as well as how the partners share in profits and losses. It also indicates accounting procedures, management rights, compensation, and allocation of profits.

The partnership agreement shown in Exhibit 4-2 also indicates the procedures for dissolution of the partnership or dealing with the death of one of the partners, as well as procedures for the purchase and sale by the partners. It is signed by both partners.

EXHIBIT 4-2   General Partnership Agreement

Reprinted with permission from *Office Procedures for the Legal Professional*, Judy Long, 2005: Thomson/Delmar Learning.

ADAMS AND HARMON
GENERAL PARTNERSHIP AGREEMENT

This Agreement is made on May 6, 2009 by Gregory Adams and Lisa Harmon, referred to as "Partners" under the following provisions.

1. The Partners shall associate to form a General Partnership for the purpose of manufacturing candles and any other businesses agreed upon by the Partners.

2. The Partnership name shall be Adams & Harmon.

3. The Partnership shall commence on the execution of this Agreement and shall continue until dissolved by agreement of the Partners or terminated under the Agreement.

4. The Partnership's principal place of business shall be 24 Colonial Road, Salem, Massachusetts.

Initial Capital

5. The Partnership's initial capital shall be $100,000. Each Partner shall contribute toward the initial capital by depositing the following amounts in the Partnership checking account at the Main Office of the Community Bank in Salem, Massachusetts, May 20, 2009:
Each party shall contribute $50,000.

6. No Partner shall withdraw any portion of the Partnership capital without the other Partner's express written consent.

7. The Partners shall share equally in Partnership net profits and shall bear Partnership losses equally.

8. Partnership books of account shall be accurately kept and shall include records of all Partnership income, expenses, assets, and liabilities. The Partnership books of account shall be maintained on a cash basis. Each Partner shall have the right to inspect the Partnership books at any time.

9. The Partnership's fiscal year shall end on December 31 each year.

10. Complete accountings of the Partnership affairs at the close of business on the last days of March, September, and December of each year shall be rendered to each Partner within 10 days after the close of each such month. At the time of such accounting, the net profits of the Partnership shall be distributed to the Partners as provided in this Agreement. Except as to errors brought to the Partners' attention within 10 days after it is rendered, each accounting shall be final and conclusive.

11. Each Partner shall devote undivided time to and use utmost skill in the Partnership business.

12. Each Partner shall have an equal right in the management of the Partnership. Each Partner shall have authority to bind the Partnership in making contracts and incurring obligations in the Partnership name or on its credit. No Partner, however, shall incur obligations in the Partnership name or on its credit exceeding $10,000 without the other Partner's express written consent. Any obligation incurred in violation of this provision shall be charged to and collected from the Partner who incurred the obligation.

13. In compensation for services in the Partnership business, each Partner shall be entitled to a salary of $3,000 per month. The Partnership shall deduct the Partners' salaries as ordinary business expenses prior to computing net profits. A Partner's salary may be increased or reduced at any time by mutual agreement of the Partners.

14. The term "net profits," as used in this Agreement, shall mean the Partnership net profits as determined by generally accepted accounting principles for each accounting period specified in this Agreement.

15. Upon 30-days written notice of intent to the other Partner, either Partner may withdraw from the Partnership at the end of any accounting period specified in this Agreement.

continued

Exhibit 4-2 *continued*

16. On dissolution of the Partnership by the death, withdrawal, or other act of either Partner, the remaining Partner may continue the Partnership business by purchasing the outgoing Partner's interest in the Partnership assets and goodwill. The remaining Partner shall have the option to purchase the outgoing Partner's interest by paying to the outgoing Partner or the appropriate personal representative the value of the outgoing Partner's interest as determined under Paragraph 17 of this Agreement.

17. On exercise of the option described in Paragraph 16 of this Agreement, the remaining Partner shall pay to the outgoing Partner or appropriate personal representative the value of the outgoing Partner's Partnership interest as determined by the last regular accounting preceding dissolution plus the full unwithdrawn portion of the outgoing Partner's share in net profits earned between the date of that accounting and the date of dissolution.

18. If the Partnership is dissolved by the death of either Partner, the remaining Partner shall have 30 days from the date of death in which to purchase the deceased Partner's Partnership interest. The purchase price for the deceased Partner's interest shall be determined under Paragraph 17 of this Agreement. During the 30-day period following either Partner's death, the remaining Partner may continue the Partnership business. The liability of the deceased Partner's estate for Partnership obligations incurred during the period of continuation shall be limited to the amount that the deceased Partner had invested or involved with the Partnership at the time of death and that is includable in the deceased Partner's estate. The deceased Partner's estate shall be entitled, at the election of the personal representative, to either one-half of the Partnership profits earned during the period of continuation or to interest at 10 percent (10%) per annum for the Partnership's use of the deceased Partner's interest as determined under Paragraph 17 of this Agreement during the period of continuation.

19. On any purchase and sale made pursuant to Paragraphs 16, 17, or 18 of this Agreement, the remaining Partner shall assume all Partnership obligations. The remaining Partner shall hold the withdrawing Partner or the deceased Partner's estate and personal representative, as well as any property belonging to either a withdrawing or deceased Partner, free and harmless from all liability for Partnership obligations. Immediately upon purchase of a withdrawing or deceased Partner's interest, the remaining Partner shall prepare, file, serve, and publish all notices required by law to protect the withdrawing Partner or the deceased Partner's estate and personal representative from liability for future Partnership obligations. All costs incident to the requirements of this Paragraph shall be borne by the remaining Partner.

20. On dissolution of the Partnership, except as provided in Paragraphs 16, 17, and 18 of this Agreement, the Partnership affairs shall be wound up, the Partnership assets liquidated, its debts paid, and the surplus divided among the Partners according to their then net worths in the Partnership business.

21. All notices between the Partners shall be in writing and shall be deemed served when personally delivered to a Partner, or when deposited in the United States mail, certified, first-class postage prepaid, addressed to a Partner at the Partnership's principal place of business or to such other place as may be specified in a notice given pursuant to this Paragraph as the address for service of notice on such Partner.

22. All consents and agreements provided for or permitted by this Agreement shall be in writing. Signed copies of all consents and agreements pertaining to the Partnership shall be kept with the Partnership books.

23. On all accountings provided for in this Agreement, the goodwill of the Partnership business shall be valued at one dollar ($1) and no more.

24. This instrument contains the Partner's sole agreement pertaining to their Partnership. It correctly sets out the Partners' rights and obligations. Any prior agreements, promises, negotiations, or representations not expressly set forth in this instrument have no force or effect.

Executed at Salem, Massachusetts, This _____ day of May, 2009.

_____
GREGORY ADAMS

_____
LISA HARMON

Limited Liability Partnership (LLP).   Each state has its own statutes that govern limited liability partnerships (LLPs) in that state. An LLP is similar to a general partnership but limits the liability of the partners for certain commitments and responsibilities. The organization is recorded with the state secretary of state's office; this can generally be done on the individual state's Web page.

STATE-SPECIFIC INFORMATION

The Web site for the state of _____ may be found at
_____.

The state secretary of state's office is located at _____.

The state requirements for a limited liability partnership are as follows:

_____

_____

_____

State requirements may include periodic filing of reports and renewals with the state; restrictions on the degree of limited liability; and special requirements for negligence in torts, contracts, or wrongful acts by a partner.

Corporations

A **corporation** is a business entity that exists separate and apart from its owners, who are called shareholders. Some corporations have just a few shareholders; others have thousands. A corporation is said to have *perpetual life* because it is not dissolved on the death of any of the shareholders. A shareholder's ownership interest is represented by shares of stock and can easily be transferred to another by selling the stock.

The primary advantages of the corporate structure are the ability to raise considerably larger sums of capital, the limited liability of the shareholders, and the corporation's perpetual life. Because many individuals pool their capital to form a corporation, potentially large sums of money can be raised. Unlike sole proprietors and general partners, owners of shares of a corporation's stock are not liable for damages if a lawsuit is brought against the corporation. If the corporation must pay damages, only the corporate assets may be used to satisfy the claim. Having perpetual life means that when a shareholder dies, her shares of stock pass to the heirs, but the corporation itself continues. As we have seen, in other forms of business organization the death of an owner may mean the dissolution of the business.

In some cases, a corporation enjoys lower tax rates than other forms of business organization. In a small, closely held corporation, business income may be divided between the owner and the corporation. When

corporation   a business entity that exists separate and apart from its owners, who are called shareholders

the income is divided, the owner is in a lower tax bracket and is assessed lower taxes than a sole proprietor who reports all the business income on her personal tax return. For instance, an owner who works in the business and collects a salary must report the salary on her personal income tax return, but that salary is deducted from the income of the corporation, which pays no tax on it. If the corporation's income amounts to $150,000 a year or less after deducting all expenses including salaries, this method of dividing the corporate income between the owner and the business will probably result in lower taxes than if the business were run as a partnership or a sole proprietorship. Obviously this system is advantageous only in a small corporation with a few owners who collect a salary from the corporation.

One disadvantage of corporations is that they are regulated more stringently than other types of organizations. Creating and maintaining the corporate structure can involve a considerable amount of paperwork. The government may require various documents including articles of incorporation, bylaws, minutes of meetings, and proxy statements. The next sections will discuss pre-incorporation concerns to discuss with the client as well as how the corporation is formed.

Preliminary Considerations. The attorney and client must discuss some preliminary matters before the corporate documents are prepared. The following items must be addressed:

1. the type of corporate structure
2. the form of stock ownership
3. the corporation's purpose
4. the financial foundation
5. the state of incorporation (usually the state where the attorney and client are located)

State of Incorporation. Although most corporations are incorporated in the state where the attorney and client are located, some clients choose a state where the statutes and taxes are more favorable to the corporate structure. The legal assistant may be asked to research the laws of different states to determine the feasibility of incorporating in the client's state or in another state with greater advantages for the client. In an office specializing in corporate law, the statutes of different states for corporations will be readily available for such research. The state that is chosen for the incorporation is known as the *domicile state* of the corporation.

Exhibit 4-3 shows a checklist for the formation of a corporation.

close corporation a corporation owned by a few individuals who run the corporation and control business operations

Special Types of Corporations

Close Corporation. A **close corporation** is formed by a few individuals who run the corporation and may control the business. The close corporation may choose not to offer its stock to the public. The number of shareholders is restricted.

EXHIBIT 4-3   Checklist for Corporate Formation

Reprinted with permission from *Basics of Legal Document Preparation*, Robert Cummins, 1997: Thomson/Delmar Learning.

TICKLER/CHECKLIST FOR INCORPORATION OF

1. Name:
    Call secretary of state re: name availability   _____
    Reserve corporate name   _____

2. Draft incorporation documents:
    Articles   _____
    Designation of registered agent   _____
    Bylaws   _____
    Minutes and waiver or consent   _____
    Subscriptions   _____
    Stock certificates   _____

3. Prepare miscellaneous forms:
    Application for federal employer identification number   _____
    Application for sales tax   _____
    Application for business license   _____

4. Prepare miscellaneous letters:
    Secretary of state/articles   _____
    City/business licenses   _____
    IRS filing, subchapter S, election and power of attorney.   _____

5. Prepare minute books   _____

6. Send articles to secretary of state   _____
    Rec'd _____

7. Send city/business licenses   _____
    Rec'd _____

8. Send application for federal employer identification number   _____
    Rec'd _____

9. Send application for sales tax   _____
    Rec'd _____

10. Order corporate seal/corporate kit   _____
    Rec'd _____

11. Schedule organizational meeting of board of directors   _____

12. Hold organizational meeting of board   _____

13. Prepare corporate bank account resolution   _____

14. Prepare the waiver of notice of the annual shareholders'
    and directors' meeting   _____

15. Prepare the annual shareholders' and directors' resolution   _____

Professional Corporation. State statutes enable professionals to incorporate. These **professional corporations** may be formed by doctors, lawyers, psychologists, optometrists, or other professionals. The name of the corporation will have *PC* after the professional's name, or in some states *PS* or *PSC*. Many professional licensing boards have stringent rules for professional corporations for that profession. States also have specific requirements. Professionals who incorporate may be held personally liable for their own malpractice and that of those whom they supervise. Most professionals are required to carry malpractice insurance.

Since state statutes vary as to the rules for professional corporations, find the rules for your state and complete the following box.

STATE-SPECIFIC INFORMATION

Rules or statutes governing professional corporations in the state of
_____ are as follows:

_____

_____

_____

---

professional corporation
a special corporation owned by professionals, such as doctors, lawyers, psychologists, or optometrists

subchapter S corporation
a corporation with no more than 25 shareholders whose tax status enables it to be taxed similarly to a partnership. The corporation does not pay corporate income tax, but the shareholders declare income and losses on their personal tax returns.

franchise a business arrangement whereby the owner obtains the right to market a company's goods or services in a particular territory

nonprofit corporation
a corporation operated for charitable, religious, scientific, educational, or literary purposes, and not for profit

Subchapter S Corporation. A **subchapter S corporation** is similar to a close corporation. It may have no more than 25 shareholders and is limited to domestic operations. Corporate income and losses are reported on the owners' personal tax returns. Owners may deduct losses from their personal income tax returns only up to the amount they have invested in the corporation.

Franchises. A **franchise** owner obtains the right to market a company's goods or services in a particular territory. The term also refers to the right itself. The individual owns the business itself but leases the facilities from the franchise organization (the parent company that grants the franchise and allows the business to use its name.) The owner usually must purchase certain supplies from the franchise organization. Some fast-food establishments also require the owner to buy ingredients from certain suppliers to maintain uniform quality.

Nonprofit Corporations. An organization operated entirely for charitable, religious, scientific, educational, or literary purposes may qualify as a **nonprofit corporation** for tax purposes under the Internal Revenue Code. The corporation may not engage in other unrelated activities or benefit the owners economically, although the owners may collect a reasonable salary if they work in the business. All corporate profits must be used to benefit the purpose for which the corporation was formed. The corporation may not engage in political activities. States may impose additional restrictions. Find the rules for your state and complete the following box.

STATE-SPECIFIC INFORMATION

Rules for nonprofit corporations in the state of _____ are as follows:

_____

_____

_____

_____

Limited Liability Corporation.   The rules for limited liability corporations (LLCs) vary by state. Their owners are known as *members* and are not personally liable for the debts and liabilities of the corporation. Each member has an ownership interest. In many states, each member is required to sign the operating agreement (or articles of organization), which are filed with the secretary of state for the state in which the corporation operates. These companies may be managed by the members, who make management decisions, or by managers appointed by the members. In the latter case the managers will make most decisions, with major resolutions being decided by the members. Since the organization is not technically a corporation, it can usually be taxed as a general partnership. These rules vary by state.

STATE-SPECIFIC INFORMATION

The rules for the organization of limited liability corporations in the state of _____ are as follows:

_____

_____

_____

_____

_____

_____

Pre-Incorporation Agreement.   If more than one individual is establishing the corporation, it is advisable to prepare a **pre-incorporation agreement** that lists the preliminary agreements of the parties, known as the *promoters* of the corporation. These individuals are responsible for the organization of the corporation, including obtaining funds for the corporation and complying with all necessary statutes of the state of incorporation.

pre-incorporation agreement   an agreement setting forth the preliminary arrangements of the parties who are forming the corporation

The pre-incorporation agreement should contain all preliminary agreements of the promoters and should be signed by all parties. Included therein should be the name and address of the corporation, its purpose, information about stock subscriptions and corporate capital, and the choice of corporate officers. A sample pre-incorporation agreement is shown in Exhibit 4-4.

Agent for Process.   Once the client decides on a state of domicile and the type of corporation, an **agent for process** must be chosen. In some states this individual is called a *registered agent.* The agent is authorized to act for the corporation and receives service of process and other communications from the office of the state's secretary of state for the benefit of the corporation. An agent must be chosen for each state in which the corporation operates.

The agent should be a trusted employee of the corporation and should be chosen with the utmost care. The legal professional or paralegal should keep a record of the agent's name and address; the address will generally be the office of the corporation.

Choosing a Name.   Before choosing a name for the corporation, permission must be obtained from the state's secretary of state. Various methods are used in different states. Some states have forms on their Web sites for this purpose. Other states allow a telephone inquiry if a prepaid account has been established with the secretary of state's office. Most states require that the name contain the word *Corporation, Company, Incorporated,* or some other word that indicates the corporate structure.

In addition, other laws should be checked to determine the rights to the reservation of a name, including the following:

1. Federal Trademark act (15 U.S.C. § 1051)
2. the state's Trademark act
3. the state's Fictitious Business Name act
4. common-law rights, including rights to a trade name

Complete the rules for your state in the following box.

STATE-SPECIFIC INFORMATION

A name for a corporation may be reserved in the state of _____ by the following procedure:

_____

_____

_____

_____

_____

_____

agent for process   an individual chosen by the corporation to act on its behalf; an agent must be chosen for each state in which the corporation operates

STATE LAWS RELATED TO NAME RESERVATION

1. Fictitious Business Name Statement—Section _____ of the
   _____ Code

2. State Trademark Act, found at

   _____

3. Other pertinent state statutes:

   _____

   _____

EXHIBIT 4-4   Sample Pre-Incorporation Agreement
Reprinted with permission from *Office Procedures for the Legal Professional*, Judy Long, 2005: Thomson/Delmar Learning.

AGREEMENT TO INCORPORATE

Agreement made this 30th day of February, 2008, between WALTER GATES, of City of Boulder, County of Citrus, State of Fremont, and HUGH PACK, City of Boulder, County of Citrus, State of Fremont, hereinafter sometimes called the "incorporators."

In consideration of the mutual promises herein contained, the incorporators agree to form a corporation under the laws of the State of Fremont, and particularly the General Corporation Law of the state, for the purpose of undertaking and carrying on a business or businesses, as follows:

SECTION ONE
NAME OF CORPORATION

Subject to availability, the name of the corporation shall be CYBERSPACE, INCORPORATED.

SECTION TWO
PURPOSE AND POWERS

The corporation shall be formed for the purpose of engaging in and maintaining a computer software business and such other lawful businesses as may from time to time be determined by the board of directors. The authorized corporate purposes shall include any lawful business purpose or purposes which a corporation organized under the General Corporation Law may be permitted to undertake.

SECTION THREE
PRINCIPAL OFFICE

The principal office for the transaction of the business of the corporation shall be located in the County of Citrus, State of Fremont.

SECTION FOUR
CAPITALIZATION

The authorized capital of the corporation shall be Ten Thousand Dollars ($10,000.00). The authorized capital stock of the corporation shall be all common stock with a par value of One Dollar ($1.00) per share.

continued

Exhibit 4-4   *continued*

SECTION FIVE
STOCK SUBSCRIPTION

Each of the incorporators subscribes as capital of the corporation the sum set out opposite his name below and agrees to accept in exchange for the amounts so specified the shares of stock following his name:

Name of Subscriber	Subscription	Stock
WALTER GATES	$5000.00	5000 shares
HUGH PACK	$5000.00	5000 shares

SECTION SIX
INCORPORATION; PERMIT TO ISSUE SHARES;
PAYMENT OF SUBSCRIPTION

The incorporators shall cause the corporation to be formed under the provisions of section 1010 of the Fremont Business Corporation Act, formed within ninety (90) days from the date of this agreement, and thereupon with all reasonable diligence shall cause the corporation to apply for and secure a permit authorizing issuance of stock as hereinabove subscribed.

SECTION SEVEN
SIGNING ARTICLES; FIRST DIRECTORS

The parties to this agreement, or so many of them as may be necessary for the purpose, shall sign the articles of incorporation as incorporators. The persons named below shall be designated in the articles of incorporation as the first directors of the corporation and shall serve as such until their respective successors are duly elected and qualified:

Office	Name of officer
President	WALTER GATES
Vice president	HUGH PACK
Secretary-treasurer	I. B. HEMMINGWAY

IN WITNESS WHEREOF the undersigned incorporators have executed this agreement at Boulder, Fremont, the day and year first above written.

_____
WALTER GATES

_____
HUGH PACK

articles of incorporation
the first document prepared for corporate formation; it includes corporate name, purpose, agent, stock structure, duration, and names of incorporators and members of the board of directors. The articles must be filed with the secretary of state's office in the state of formation. A name is reserved with that same office.

Articles of Incorporation.   The first document prepared for corporate formation is the **Articles of Incorporation,** which include the following:

1. name of the corporation
2. purpose of the corporation
3. name and address of the agent for process
4. stock structure (number of shares issued and value)
5. duration of corporation and names of initial incorporators and members of the board of directors (not required in all states)

Exhibit 4-5 shows an example of Articles of Incorporation. A corporation may not use the name of another corporation, nor may it use a

EXHIBIT 4-5   Sample Articles of Incorporation

Reprinted with permission from *Office Procedures for the Legal Professional*, Judy Long, 2005: Thomson/Delmar Learning.

ARTICLES OF INCORPORATION
OF
ABC CORPORATION

I.

The name of this corporation is: ABC CORPORATION.

II.

The purpose of this corporation is to engage in any lawful act or activity for which a corporation may be organized under the General Corporation Law of California other than the banking business, the trust company business, or the practice of a profession permitted to be incorporated by the California Corporations Code.

III.

The name and address in the State of California of this corporation's initial agent for service of process is:

> Dana M. Morrison
> 45 Sunset Boulevard
> Memphis, CA 90555

IV.

This corporation is authorized to issue only one class of shares of common stock; and the total number of shares which this corporation is authorized to issue is two hundred (200).

V.

The liability of the directors of the corporation for monetary damages shall be eliminated to the fullest extent permissible under California law.

VI.

The corporation is authorized to provide indemnification of agents, as that term is defined in Section 317 of the California Corporations Code, for breach of duty to the corporation and its shareholders in excess of that expressly permitted by said Section 317 under any bylaw, agreement, vote of shareholders or disinterested directors or otherwise, to the fullest extent such indemnification may be authorized hereby, subject to the limits on such excess indemnification set forth in Section 204 of the California Corporations Code. The corporation is further authorized to provide insurance for agents as set forth in Section 317 of the California Corporations Code, provided that, in cases where the corporation owns all or a portion of the shares of the company issuing the insurance policy, one of the two sets of conditions set forth in Section 317, as amended, is met.

VII.

Any repeal or modification of the foregoing provisions of Articles V and VI, by the shareholders of this corporation, shall not adversely affect any right or protection of a director or agent of this corporation existing at the time of such repeal or modification.

DATED: June 27, 2009

_____

WILLIAM M. LANGLEY
Sole Incorporator

name so similar that they could be confused. Software packages are available to determine via modem or fax whether a particular name is available.

Once the name is obtained, the articles are prepared for mailing to the secretary of state's office. A certificate of incorporation is returned if the articles have been prepared properly. At that point, the legal assistant orders the corporate seal and minute book from a legal stationery store.

At this time an organizational meeting is held to elect directors and to draft **bylaws**, which are the rules governing the operations of the corporation. Bylaws include the location of the corporation, the date and place of annual shareholders' meetings, powers of the board of directors, types of officers and their terms and responsibilities, and information about corporate stock. Exhibit 4-6 shows an example of corporate bylaws.

Annual Meetings. All corporations are required to have meetings each year and must file an annual report for the shareholders and the state's secretary of state. The report describes the actions and business in which the corporation was engaged during the previous year. It lists the corporation's income and expenses for the year, along with assets and liabilities.

Corporate Board of Directors. The board of directors is responsible for the running of the corporation. The directors have a fiduciary duty to use ethical and sound judgment in managing the corporation's affairs. They owe a duty of loyalty that includes placing the organization's needs before their own personal business interests. They may not be involved in conflicts of interest, nor may they commit acts beyond the scope of their enumerated responsibilities. They may not be held personally liable for their mistakes unless it can be proven that they engaged in fraudulent, illegal, or unethical practices.

Corporate Minute Book. The legal professional or paralegal may keep the minute book, which contains a record of the business of the corporation, including the articles of incorporation, bylaws, meeting minutes, and stock transfer ledgers. It may be purchased from a legal stationery store.

Corporate seals are also available from the same supplier. They are embossed and make imprints on the paper. Other seals may be stamped on the paper. They are used for various legal documents.

Derivative Suits. Shareholders may file a lawsuit called a **derivative suit** against the corporation to prevent a wrong to the corporation or to provide a remedy for that wrong. The shareholders sue as representatives of the corporation If the shareholders are injured, then the director or officer who caused the injury may be sued directly. The shareholders must have held their stock when the act occurred and must first have demanded that the board of directors act to protect the corporation's rights in this instance. If the board fails to act, then the shareholders may file a derivative suit. To win the suit, the shareholders must prove that the director or officer deliberately mismanaged or committed fraud against the corporation.

bylaws rules and regulations adopted by a corporation

derivative suit a lawsuit filed by shareholders against the corporation if a director or officer of the corporation commits an *ultra vires* act, which includes actions outside the scope of the powers or activities permitted by the Articles of Incorporation

---

EXHIBIT 4-6   Example of Corporate Bylaws

Reprinted with permission from *Office Procedures for the Legal Professional*, Judy Long, 2005: Thomson/Delmar Learning.

**Bylaws
of
ABC Corporation
Article One: Shareholders**

Section 1. MEETINGS.

(A) TIME. An annual meeting of the shareholders shall be held each year on the first day of April at 2:00 p.m., unless such day should fall on a legal holiday. In such event, the meeting shall be held at the same hour on the next succeeding business day that is not a legal holiday.

(B) PLACE. Annual meetings shall be held at the principal executive office of the corporation or at such other place within the state of California as may be determined by the board of directors and designated in the notice of such meeting.

(C) CALL. Annual meetings may be called by the directors, by the Chairman of the Board, if any, Vice-Chairman of the Board, if any, the President, if any, the Secretary, or by any other officer instructed by the Directors to call the meeting.

(D) SPECIAL MEETINGS. If in any year, the election of directors is not held at the annual meeting of the shareholders or an adjournment of the meeting, the board of directors shall call a special meeting of the 104 shareholders as soon as possible thereafter as is reasonably possible for the purpose of holding the election and transacting such other business as may properly be brought before the meeting.

In the event the board of directors fails to call a special meeting within three months after the date set for the annual meeting, any shareholders may call such a meeting; at such a meeting, the shareholders may elect directors and transact all other business as may be properly brought before the meeting.

(E) NOTICE. Written notice stating the place, day, and hour of each meeting, and, in the case of a special meeting, the general nature of the business to be transacted or, in the case of an Annual Meeting, those matters which the Board of Directors, at the time of mailing of the notice, intends to present for action by the shareholders, shall be given not less than ten (10) days (or not less than any such other minimum period of days as may be prescribed by the General Corporation Law) or more than sixty (60) days (or more than any maximum period of days as may be prescribed by the General Corporation Law).

(F) ACTION BY WRITTEN CONSENT. Any action required by law to be taken at a meeting of the shareholders, except for the election of the directors, and any other action that may be taken at a meeting of shareholders may be taken without a meeting if written consent, setting forth the action so taken, is signed by the holders of outstanding shares having not less than the minimum number of votes that would be necessary to authorize or take such an action at a meeting at which all shares entitled to vote thereon were present and voted, if the consents of all shareholders entitled to vote were solicited in writing. Directors may not be elected by written consent except by unanimous written consent of all shares entitled to vote for the election of directors.

continued

Exhibit 4-6 *continued*

(G) WAIVER OF NOTICE. A shareholder may waive notice of any annual or special meeting by signing a petition notice of waiver either before or after the date of such meeting.

(H) RECORD DATE. For the purpose of determining those shareholders entitled to notice of or to vote at any meeting of shareholders, or to receive payment of any dividend, or in order to make a determination of shareholders for any other proper purpose, the board of directors may fix, in advance, a date as the record date for the determination of shareholders. Such date shall not be more than sixty (60) days, and for a meeting of shareholders, not less than ten (10) days, or in the case of a meeting where a merger or consolidation will be considered, not less than twenty (20) days, immediately preceding such meeting.

If a record date is not fixed for the determination of shareholders entitled to notice of or to vote at a meeting of shareholders, the record date shall be at the close of business on the business day next preceding the day on which notice is given, or, if notice is waived, at the close of business on the business day next preceding the day on which the meeting is held.

If no record date is fixed, the record date for determining shareholders entitled to give consent to corporate action in writing without a meeting shall be the day on which the first written consent is given, when no prior action by the board of directors is necessary.

If no record date is fixed, the record date for determining shareholders for any other purpose shall be at the close of business on the day on which the board of directors adopts the resolution relating thereto or the 60th day prior to the date of such other action, whichever is later.

When a determination of shareholders entitled to vote at any meeting of shareholders has been made as provided in this section, such determination shall apply to adjournment of such meeting, unless the board of directors fixes a new record date for the adjourned meeting.

(I) QUORUM. The presence, at the shareholders' meeting, in person or by proxy, of persons entitled to vote a majority of the shares of the corporation then outstanding shall constitute a quorum for the transaction of business. In determining whether quorum requirements for a meeting have been met, any share that has been enjoined from voting or that cannot be lawfully voted for any reason shall not be counted.

(J) PROXIES. Every person entitled to vote at a shareholders' meeting of the corporation, or entitled to execute written consent authorizing action in lieu of a meeting, may do so either in person or by proxy executed in writing by the shareholder or by his duly authorized attorney in fact. No proxy shall be valid after 11 months from the date of its execution unless otherwise provided in the proxy.

(K) VOTING. Except in elections of directors, in which each shareholder shall have the right to cumulate his votes, each outstanding share, regardless of class, shall be entitled to one vote on each matter submitted to a vote at a meeting of shareholders. The affirmative vote of the majority of shares represented at a meeting at which a quorum is present shall be the act of the shareholders unless the vote of a greater number or a vote by classes is required by the articles, these bylaws, or the laws of the State of California.

(L) ORDER OF BUSINESS. The order of business at the annual meeting of the shareholders and, insofar as possible, at all other meetings of shareholders, shall be as follows:

continued

Exhibit 4-6   *continued*

1. Call to order.
2. Proof of notice of meeting.
3. Reading and disposing of any unapproved minutes.
4. Reports of officers.
5. Reports of committees.
6. Election of directors.
7. Disposition of unfinished business.
8. Disposition of new business.
9. Adjournment.

Article Two: Board of Directors

Section 1. GENERAL POWERS.

(A) AUTHORITY. Subject to the limitations of the articles of incorporation, these bylaws, and the Corporations Code of the State of California, and the provisions of the Corporations Code concerning corporate action that must be authorized or approved by the shareholders of the corporation, all corporate power shall be exercised by or under the authority of the board of directors, and the business and affairs of the corporation shall be controlled by the board.

(B) NUMBER, TENURE, QUALIFICATIONS, AND ELECTION. The board of directors shall consist of ten persons who shall be shareholders of the corporation. The number of directors may be increased or decreased by approval of the outstanding shares. Directors of the corporation shall be elected at the annual meeting of the shareholders, or at a meeting held in lieu thereof as provided in Article One above, and shall serve until the next succeeding annual meeting and until their successors have been elected and qualified.

Section 2. MEETINGS.

(A) ORGANIZATIONAL MEETING. The board of directors shall hold an organizational meeting immediately following each annual meeting of the shareholders. Additionally, regular meetings of the board of directors shall be held at such times as shall be fixed by resolution of the board. Special meetings of the board may be called at any time by the president or, if the president is absent or refuses to act, any vice-president or any two members of the board.

(B) NOTICE. Notice need not be given of regular meetings of the board of directors, nor is it necessary to give notice of adjourned meetings. Notice of special meetings shall be in writing by mail at least four days prior to the date of the meeting or 48 hours' notice delivered personally or by telephone or telegraph. Neither the business to be transacted at nor the purpose of any such meeting need be specified in the notice. Attendance of a director at a meeting shall constitute a waiver of notice of that meeting except when the director attends for the express purpose of objecting to the transaction of any business in that the meeting is not lawfully called or convened.

(C) QUORUM AND VOTING. A majority of the authorized number of directors shall constitute a quorum for the transaction of business, and the acts of a majority of directors present at a meeting at which a quorum is present shall constitute the acts of the board of directors. At any meeting of the board of directors, if less than a quorum is present, a majority of those present may adjourn the meeting until a

continued

Exhibit 4-6 *continued*

quorum is present. If the meeting is adjourned for more than 24 hours, notice of any adjournment to another time or place shall be given prior to the time of the adjourned meeting to the directors who were not present at the time of adjournment.

(D) COMPENSATION. Directors who are not employed as officers of the corporation shall be entitled to receive from the corporation as compensation for their services as directors such reasonable compensation as the board may determine, and shall also be entitled to reimbursement for any reasonable expenses incurred in attending meetings of directors.

(E) INDEMNIFICATION. The corporation shall indemnify all persons who have served or may serve at any time as officers or directors of the corporation, and their heirs, executors, administrators, successors, and assigns, from and against any and all loss and expense, including amounts paid in settlement before or after suit is commenced, and reasonable attorneys' fees, actually and necessarily sustained as a result of any claim, demand, action, proceeding, or judgment that may be asserted against any such persons, or in which any such persons are made parties by reason of their being or having been officers or directors of the corporation. However, this right of indemnification shall not exist in relation to matters where it is adjudged in any action, suit, or proceeding that any such persons are liable for negligence or misconduct in the performance of duty.

(F) COMMITTEES. The board of directors may, by resolution adopted by a majority of the whole board, designate two or more directors to constitute an executive committee. The executive committee, to the extent provided in the resolution, shall have and may exercise all of the authority of the board of directors in the management of the corporation, except that the committee shall have no authority in reference to amending the articles of incorporation, adopting a plan of merger or consolidation, suggesting to shareholders the sale, lease, exchange, mortgage, or other disposition of all or substantially all the property and assets of the corporation other than in the usual course of business, recommending to the shareholders a voluntary dissolution or a revocation thereof, amending, altering, or repealing any provision of these bylaws, electing or removing directors or officers of the corporation, or members of the executive committee, fixing the compensation of any member of the executive committee, declaring dividends, or amending, altering, or repealing any resolution of the board of directors which, by its terms, provides that it not be amended, altered, or repealed by the executive committee. The board of directors shall have power at any time to fill vacancies in, to change the size or membership of, and to discharge any such committee.

Any such executive committee shall keep a written record of its proceedings and shall submit such record to the whole board at each regular meeting, and at such other times as may be requested by the board. However, failure to submit such record, or failure of the board to approve any action indicated therein shall not invalidate such action to the extent it has been carried out by the corporation prior to the time the record thereof was or should have been submitted to the board as provided herein.

Article Three: Officers

(A) ENUMERATION OF OFFICERS. The corporation shall have as officers a president, vice-president, secretary, and chief financial officer. The board of directors, at its discretion, may appoint such officers as the business of the corporation may require.

(B) ELECTION AND TERM OF OFFICE. The principal officers of the corporation shall be elected by the board of directors at its organizational meeting immediately following the annual meeting of

continued

Exhibit 4-6   *continued*

shareholders or as soon thereafter as is reasonably possible. Subordinate officers may be elected as the board may see fit. Each officer shall hold office until his successor is elected and qualified, or until his resignation, death, or removal.

(C) REMOVAL. Any officer may be removed from office at any time, with or without cause, on the affirmative vote of a majority of the board of directors. Removal shall be without prejudice to any contract rights of the officer removed.

(D) VACANCIES. Vacancies in office, however caused, may be filled by election of the board of directors at any time for unexpired terms of such offices.

(E) OFFICERS—POWERS AND DUTIES. The president, vice-president, secretary, chief financial officer, and other officers appointed by the board of directors shall have such powers and duties as prescribed by the board of directors.

(F) ABSENCE OR DISABILITY OF OFFICERS. In the case of the absence or disability of any officer of the corporation and of any person hereby authorized to act in his place during his absence or disability, the board of directors may, by resolution, delegate the powers and duties of such officer, or to any director, or to any other person whom it may select.

(G) SALARIES. The salaries of all officers of the corporation shall be fixed by the board of directors.

Article Four: Stock Certificates

(A) FORM. The shares of the corporation shall be represented by certificates signed by the chairman or a vice-chairman of the board of directors, if any, or the president or a vice-president, and by the chief financial officer or an assistant financial officer, or the secretary or an assistant secretary. Any or all of such signatures may be facsimile. Each such certificate shall also state:

1. The name of the record holder of the shares represented by such certificate;

2. The number of shares represented thereby;

3. A designation of any class or series of which such shares are a part;

4. That the shares are without par value;

5. Any rights of redemption and the redemption price;

6. Any rights of conversion, and the essential terms and periods for conversion;

7. Any liens or restrictions on transfer or on the voting power of such shares;

8. That the shares are assessable, if that is the fact;

9. That assessments to which the shares are subject are collectible by personal action, if that is the fact;

10. When the shares of the corporation are classified or any class has two or more series, the rights, preferences, privileges, and restrictions granted to or imposed on the respective classes or series of

continued

Exhibit 4-6 *continued*

shares and the holders thereof, as established by the articles or by any certificate of determination of preferences, as well as the number of shares constituting each series and the designation thereof; or a summary of such preferences, privileges and restrictions with reference to the provisions of the articles or certificate or certificates of determination of preferences establishing same; or the office or agency of the corporation from which stockholders may obtain a copy of a statement of such right, preferences, privileges, and restrictions or of such summary.

11. Any right of the board of directors to fix the dividend rights, dividend rate, conversion rights, voting rights, rights in terms of redemption, including sinking fund provisions, the redemption price or prices, or the liquidation preferences of any wholly unissued class or of any wholly unissued series of any class of shares, or the number of shares constituting any unissued series of any class of shares, or designation of such series, or all or any of them; and

12. For any certificates issued for shares prior to the full payment therefor, the amount remaining unpaid, the terms of payment to become due, and any restrictions on the transfer of such partly paid shares on the books of the corporation.

13. All certificates for shares of the corporation shall bear the following legend: "These securities have not been registered under the Securities Act of 1933, and may not be offered, offered for sale, or sold in the absence of an effective registration statement under that Act or an opinion of counsel satisfactory to the corporation that registration is not required."

(B) LOST, DESTROYED, AND STOLEN CERTIFICATES. No certificate for shares of stock in the corporation shall be issued in place of any certificate alleged to have been lost, destroyed, stolen, or mutilated except on production of such evidence and provision of such indemnity to the corporation as the board of directors may prescribe.

Article Five: Corporate Actions

(A) CONTRACTS. The board of directors may authorize any officer or officers, and any agent or agents of the corporation, to enter into any contract or to execute and deliver any instrument in the name of and on behalf of the corporation, and such authority may be general or confined to specific instances.

(B) LOANS. No loans shall be made by the corporation to its officers or directors, and no loans shall be made by the corporation secured by its shares. No loans shall be made or contracted on behalf of the corporation and no evidence of indebtedness shall be issued in its name unless authorized by resolution of the board of directors. Such authority may be general or confined to specific instances.

(C) CHECKS, DRAFTS, OR ORDERS. All checks, drafts, or other orders for the payment of money by or to the corporation and all notes and other evidence of indebtedness issued in the name of the corporation shall be signed by such officer or officers, agent or agents of the corporation, and in such manner as shall be determined by resolution by the board of directors.

(D) BANK DEPOSITS. All funds of the corporation not otherwise employed shall be deposited to the credit of the corporation in such banks, trust companies, or other depositories as the board of directors may select.

continued

Exhibit 4-6 *continued*

Article Six: Miscellaneous

(A) INSPECTION OF CORPORATE RECORDS. The corporation shall keep correct and complete books and records of account and shall also keep minutes of all meetings of shareholders and directors. Additionally, a record shall be kept at the principal executive office of the corporation, giving the names and addresses of all shareholders, and the number and class or classes of shares held by each. Any person who is the holder of a voting trust certificate or who is the holder of record of at least ten percent of the outstanding voting shares of the corporation shall have the right to examine and copy, in person or by agent or attorney, at any reasonable time or times, for any proper purpose, the books and records of account of the corporation, the minutes, and the record of shareholders.

(B) INSPECTION OF ARTICLES OF INCORPORATION AND BYLAWS. The original or a copy of the articles of incorporation and bylaws of the corporation, as amended or otherwise altered to date, and certified by the secretary of the corporation, shall at all times be kept at the principal executive office of the corporation. Such articles and bylaws shall be open to inspection to all shareholders of record or holders of voting trust certificates at all reasonable times during the business hours of the corporation.

(C) FISCAL YEAR. The fiscal year of the corporation shall begin on the first day of April of each year and end at 11:59 p.m. on the 31st day of March of the following year.

(D) CORPORATE SEAL. The board of directors shall adopt an official seal for the corporation, which shall be inscribed with the name of the corporation, the state of incorporation, and the words "Corporate Seal."

(E) CONSTRUCTION AND DEFINITION. Unless the context requires otherwise, the general provisions, rules of construction, and definitions in the Corporations Code of the State of California shall govern the construction of these bylaws.

Without limiting the foregoing, the masculine gender includes the feminine and neuter; the singular number includes the plural, and the plural number includes the singular; "shall" is mandatory and "may" is permissive, and "person" includes a corporation as well as a natural person.

Article Seven: Amendments

These bylaws may be altered, amended, or repealed by approval of the outstanding voting shares or by a majority vote of the board of directors of the corporation.

Corporate Dissolution. At least 50 percent of the voting power of shareholders must vote for voluntary **dissolution.** The board of directors may also dissolve the corporation without shareholder approval if all of the following have occurred:

1. No shares have been issued by the corporation.
2. The corporation has filed a chapter 7 bankruptcy.
3. All corporate assets have been disposed of.
4. No business has been conducted for the past five years.

Creditors and shareholders must be notified, and a notice indicating that the corporation is being dissolved must be filed with the state's secretary of state. After the creditors are notified and paid and the assets are liquidated, the corporation is dissolved. Any funds left are distributed to shareholders. The dissolution is then reported to the state.

An involuntary dissolution may be instituted by the state. Some states allow shareholders to petition the courts for involuntary dissolution if they can prove that the directors are not managing the corporation prudently or that management problems are affecting the operation of the corporation. Creditors may apply for an involuntary dissolution if they are owed substantial sums and are not being paid in some cases.

Determine the rules for involuntary dissolution in your state and fill in the following box.

STATE-SPECIFIC INFORMATION

In the state of _____, involuntary dissolution may be obtained by the following methods:

_____

_____

_____

_____

_____

_____

Acquisitions. The purchase or acquiring of assets of one corporation by another is known as an *acquisition.* This may be accomplished in the following ways:

1. One corporation may purchase another corporation's assets.
2. One corporation may purchase the stock of another corporation.
3. One corporation may purchase the assets of another corporation by issuing shares of its own stock to the seller.
4. One corporation may trade its stock for the stock of the other corporation.

dissolution the dissolving of a corporation; may be voluntary or involuntary (by the state)

Shareholder approval is not required unless the purchased corporation can no longer carry on its business. In that case, both the shareholders and the board of directors must approve the sale. State laws vary on this type of transaction.

STATE-SPECIFIC INFORMATION

The rules for acquisition in the state of _____ are as follows:

_____

_____

_____

_____

_____

_____

Consolidations.   A **consolidation** occurs when two or more corporations dissolve and form a new corporation. Shareholders of both original corporations must approve the dissolution of their own corporation and the formation of the new one. In this case, the following occurs:

$$A + B = C$$

Mergers.   A **merger** occurs when one corporation takes over another corporation, which disappears from the structure. In this case, the following occurs:

$$A \text{ absorbs } B = C$$

Mergers must be approved by the shareholders of the corporation that will no longer exist. Either corporation's shareholders who do not want to have stock in the new corporation can sell their shares back to the corporation. Articles providing notification of the merger must be filed with the state's secretary of state.

THE LAWS OF AGENCY

An **agency** relationship exists when one party, the agent, acts for or represents another party, the principal, by the latter party's authority. In this situation, the principal may be held liable for the acts of the agent in business transactions. The association exists based on an express or an implied contract.

The courts have held that an employer controls the activities of an employee and therefore will be held responsible for the employee's

consolidation   the formation of a new corporation from two or more dissolved corporations

merger   the taking over of a corporation by another corporation

agency   a relationship in which one party acts for another by the latter party's authority

actions when the employee is acting within the scope of her employ-ment. The employer may be held liable for torts committed by the employee under these circumstances. An agent may be distinguished from an employee in that she acts in place of and for the benefit of the principal in creating or changing a legal relationship with a third party. Employees generally lack the authority to act in this manner.

In the case of an independent contractor, the principal has no right to control the work of the contractor or the manner in which it is performed. The independent contractor is hired to achieve a certain result, rendering her services based on a contract that specifies the result to be achieved. The principal is generally not responsible for the actions of the independent contractor. The principal does not hire and fire employees of the independent contractor, nor can the principal have independent control over the project itself.

Businesses use both general and special agents. *General agents* have authority to act for the principal in transacting any type of business. *Special agents* have authority to act for the principal in a specific matter. Personal-services contracts, such as the painting of a picture, may not be delegated to agents. The agent may not perform any act that the principal may not do for herself.

The principal may appoint an agent by either an express or an implied contract. Although the contract may not have to be written, most business contracts establishing an agency relationship are in writ-ing. Consideration is not required in an agency contract. In order to prove in court that an agency relationship exists, the individual who claims the benefit from the agency must initiate the action and estab-lish the proof.

Responsibilities

The principal and agent are required to perform their duties in a responsible manner in their relationship with each other. The agent is held to a standard of reasonable care and expertise. The agent owes a fiduciary duty to the principal and may not divulge confidential information about the business that is obtained during the course of her agency, even after the agency relationship terminates. The agent may not take any position that diverges from the interests of the prin-cipal unless without obtaining consent from the principal. The princi-pal may invalidate the agency relationship if the agent violates her fiduciary duties.

The principal must cooperate with the agent and may not obstruct the agent's performance. The principal must pay any sums due to the agent by way of salary or other compensation. However, the agent is not due compensation for acts that were prohibited by the principal. Illegal acts of the agent also may not be compensated.

Contracts

If the agent makes a contract for the principal, then the principal becomes liable for any breach of contract if the agent is acting within the scope of her responsibilities. In that case, the only recourse the third party to the contract would have would be against the principal.

However, if the agent acts outside the scope of her responsibilities and the contract is breached, then the third party may sue the agent directly. An agent who is negligent is always liable for any injuries caused to third parties. Likewise, an agent who commits a malicious or fraudulent act is also liable.

Health Plans

In recent years, a number of different health plans have been developed in which subscribers receive a list of doctors who practice within their organization. The subscriber usually must go to one of the doctors on the health plan's list.

In order for the health plan to be responsible for the doctor's actions, the plan must control the doctor's work. Under the theory of respondeat superior, the health plan is responsible for most harm caused by doctors who are acting within the scope of their employment. In that case, the health plan has *vicarious liability,* or legal responsibility for the doctor's acts. The courts look at several items to determine whether the health plan is responsible for the doctor's actions:

1. everyday interaction between the health plan and the doctor
2. the doctor's contract with the health plan
3. the amount of control the health plan exercises over the doctor

Lawsuits arise under this theory when the health plan refuses to allow the patient to seek certain treatment or when the doctor is negligent and the patient is injured as a result. These cases are decided differently depending on the state law that applies. For instance, California law states that both the health plan and the doctor may be responsible in the case of the negligent actions of the doctor. Cases under this theory are relatively new. The legal theories will become clearer as additional cases are heard in the courts.

Independent Contractors

In most cases, independent contractors are liable for their own negligence. Third parties may not seek recourse against the principal who hires the independent contractor unless the contract was specifically created to evade liability for a dangerous project. For instance, the courts may impose absolute liability on the principal for the use, storage, or transportation of hazardous materials.

Travel

Several cases relate to employees who travel for business. If the employee has an automobile accident in which someone else is injured, the employer may be held liable if the employee is acting within the scope of her employment. If the employee is traveling to a business meeting from her office, the employer may be held liable. However, if the employee is traveling from home to work on a regular business day, the courts have generally held that the employee, and not the employer, is liable for any negligence that occurs.

Agency Termination

When the principal terminates an agency relationship, the withdrawal does not come into effect until the agency receives notice. Likewise, the principal must notify all third parties who deal with the agent in order to escape liability. Third parties who are not notified may bind the principal to a contract made by the agent prior to notification of the third party.

The agency relationship may be ended by the following means:

1. specific agreement between the agent and principal
2. expiration of a period of time specified in the agency agreement
3. revocation by the principal
4. death or legal incapacity of one of the parties
5. agent withdrawal
6. loss or destruction of the subject matter of the agency
7. physical impossibility

Employer Liability for Negligence

The courts use two basic requirements to determine whether the employer will be liable for the employee's actions under the respondeat superior theory:

1. Was the negligent individual an employee?
2. Was the employee acting within the scope of her employment? That is, was the employee performing duties required by her job during working hours?

The courts consider the following elements in deciding whether the employee was acting within the scope of her employment:

1. Did the employer give permission for the act of the employee?
2. Was the act one that was regularly performed by employees within that job description?
3. Were the interests of the employer advanced?
4. Did the employer furnish the resources to perform the act, such as a machine or vehicle?
5. Where and when did the act occur?
6. Did the employer control the act of the employee?

If these items are proven in a tort action against the employer, she will be held liable for the actions of the employee.

In some cases, the courts must distinguish between an employee and an independent contractor to determine which one is liable for negligence in a tort action. Some considerations used to make this determination include the following:

1. Is the person completing the effort in a different field from that of the employer?

2. Does the employer have direct supervision over the worker's actions, or does the worker act independently to perform the desired result?

3. Is the person hired for this particular job, or does she work for a long period of time for the employer?

4. Are special skills needed to perform this task?

5. Does the worker possess her own tools?

6. How is the worker paid?

A worker who has her own company and is hired to perform a specialized job for the employer would usually be considered an independent contractor. Many businesses have contracts with independent contractors to perform tasks not normally done by employees. For instance, a law firm might hire a cleaning company to provide maintenance and cleaning services, or a plant service company to provide plants for the office and to take care of the plants. The firm may have its own messengers who are employed by the law firm, or it may employ an outside firm under contract to provide delivery services. These are all examples of independent contractors who would usually be liable for their own negligence in performing acts for the benefit of the business.

GOVERNMENT REGULATIONS

The power to regulate business is given to the federal government in Article I, Section 8, of the United States Constitution, more commonly known as the Commerce Clause. This clause enables the government to regulate foreign commerce and interstate commerce (commerce between the states). These powers have been broadened significantly by court cases.

State governments regulate local commerce within their individual states. When conflicts between state and federal powers arise, the courts examine whether specific state or federal laws regulate the specific type of activity.

Taxes

The Internal Revenue Service has the power to administer the federal tax laws related to income tax. The various states may also impose a state income tax on income received. Some states, however, do not impose a state income tax on earnings. Complete the information in the following box for your state.

> STATE-SPECIFIC INFORMATION
>
> The state of _____ (imposes / does not impose) a state income tax on earnings.

Each state may also impose other taxes as it deems proper. Property taxes on owned property are imposed by the state and by individual counties within the state. Retail establishments may be taxed by the imposition of sales tax, which is passed on to the consumer. The state may also tax manufacturers of certain items, such as gasoline and tobacco products. These taxes are then passed on to the consumer.

Unfair Competition

The Federal Trade Commission (FTC) was created to protect against unfair competition and business practices that may be fraudulent or misleading. Certain rights and responsibilities have been given to the FTC to prevent or discourage these unfair or fraudulent practices.

1. The FTC may issue an order to stop the violation.
2. The FTC may take more drastic action, such as obtaining a court order requiring the business to stop engaging in the activity or to dissolve the business.
3. A consent decree may be obtained from the company to stop the questionable activity without penalty.
4. Media releases may be distributed to let the public know about the forbidden activities of the business.

People who have been injured by these activities may sue the business in court either individually or in a class-action case.

Antitrust/Monopoly Regulations

The Sherman Antitrust Act was passed because of public concern over the problem of corporations that were monopolies. Several recent cases in the computer industry illustrate this concern. The courts have held that monopolies should be forbidden only if they are unreasonable, a concept known as the "Rule of Reason."

However, the Supreme Court has held that certain activities violate the law because they harm the general public. For instance, when several companies in the same industry conspire to establish a uniform price for their products, a practice known as *price fixing,* the courts have held that the practice harms the public and must be forbidden. Companies are also forbidden to get together and establish geographic boundaries for the sale of each of their products. Franchise operations are allowed, however. Similar violations occur when companies conspire to limit the amount of a certain product that they will supply to the public in order to raise prices because the products would be in lower supply.

Individuals or factions that are damaged by these violations may sue the involved company or companies and obtain treble damages (three times the amount of their actual damages). The Department of Justice may also impose criminal penalties through its Antitrust Department, including fines, prison time, and court injunctions.

EMPLOYEE RELATIONS

The earliest law that protected the right of employees to protest unfair labor practices was the Norris-LaGuardia Act, which was passed in 1932. The act protected employees from injunctions by the government for peaceful protests and picketing as long as there was no violent or illegal activity. In 1935, the National Labor Relations Act (NLRA) was passed to allow employees to form unions and to support collective-bargaining agreements. Employers were prohibited from forbidding unionization or discriminating against employees who joined unions. The act required employers to participate in collective-bargaining agreements.

The NLRA also established the National Labor Relations Board (NLRB) to manage the elections of union representatives. In addition, the NLRB investigates and corrects unjust employment practices by employers.

Minimum wages were established in 1938 by the Fair Labor Standards Act (FLSA). This act also establishes minimum work standards for employees. Exempt from the minimum wage were certain categories of professional employees, such as management and some sales employees. Some companies develop categories for this purpose, using the terms *exempt* (straight salary) and *non-exempt* (minimum hourly pay).

Over the next several years, several additional laws were passed to protect the employees and employers from unfair union practices. The Taft-Hartley Act of 1947 included terms that protected employers from certain unfair union practices, including requiring the employer to pay employees for work that was not done (featherbedding), forcing the employer to fire nonunion employees by striking the employer's place of business, and refusing to bargain with the employer in good faith. The act also restored the courts' power to stop certain practices in labor disputes if the NLRB demanded it. Although the *closed shop* (which required all individuals to join the union in order to get a job) was made illegal, the practice of requiring employees to join the union after a set time period on the job was allowed. This latter practice was left to the individual states to enforce. The states were given the power to pass laws that made the practice of requiring union membership illegal.

Discrimination in the Workplace

Several federal laws were established after the civil rights movement of the 1960s to ensure that employees and prospective employees were not discriminated against because of their age, color, race, religion, or sex. This was later extended to handicapped individuals as well. Minorities were further protected by the Civil Rights Act of 1964, which bans discrimination in pay, employment, promotion, or firing of employees.

The Equal Employment Opportunity Act was enacted to administer and regulate violations. It established the Equal Employment Opportunity Commission (EEOC) to investigate claims of discrimination by employers and attempt to reach mutually beneficial settlements with the employer and employee. In this capacity, the EEOC institutes guidelines and regulations for employers to eliminate discrimination.

The employee must prove her case by guidelines established by the United States Supreme Court:

1. membership in a minority category
2. application and qualification for an open position
3. rejection
4. continued action by the employer to seek qualified candidates

If the individual is able to prove her case on its face (prima facie case) using these four guidelines, the employer must then prove that it did not discriminate against the person. She may do so by establishing that the discrimination is reasonable for the operation of the business if the discrimination was based on religion, nationality, or sex.

The protected classes have been extended to include age discrimination. In 1967, the federal government passed the Age Discrimination in Employment Act (ADEA), which prohibits both public and private employers from discriminating against individuals over age 40 because of their age. However, the employer can show that age is a bona fide qualification that is reasonably necessary for the business's standard operations.

In 1973, the federal government endeavored to protect people with disabilities by passing the Rehabilitation Act. All employers with government contracts of more than $2,500 must hire and promote people with disabilities who were qualified for the positions. As a part of this law, employers are also required to provide rehabilitation training and access to their facilities.

In 1978, pregnancy was added to the protected classes. Employers may not fire or refuse to hire a woman because she is pregnant. They are also forbidden from not promoting a woman who is pregnant. Pregnant women may work until they decide to leave unless they are physically unable to continue to work. The firm may establish a mandatory time for pregnancy leave.

Many employee suits have been filed because of the sexual harassment policy of the firm. Federal law forbids employers from engaging in activities in which sexual advances are made and are unwelcome, whether or not actual involvement was voluntary. For instance, if a legal assistant has an illicit affair with her employer because she feels pressured to do so at the risk of losing her job, this could be considered sexual harassment if the conduct unreasonably interferes with the work performance of the individual or creates an intimidating, hostile, or offensive work environment. Many of these types of cases have been filed based on the employer's intimidation of the employee. Any unwelcome sexual advances, requests for sexual favors, or other verbal or physical conduct of a sexual nature may be considered prohibited sexual harassment if the behavior interferes unreasonably with one's work performance or creates an intimidating, hostile, or offensive work environment. Thus, if Mr. X makes sexual remarks to Ms. Y in Ms. Z's presence, Ms. Z may be able to prevail in a suit for sexual harassment if she can prove that the remarks created a hostile work environment and/or interfered unreasonably with her work performance.

Many states have passed laws that prohibit employers from firing an individual without reasonable cause. Since these laws vary so much from state to state, you should research the laws related to wrongful discharge in your state and complete the following box.

STATE-SPECIFIC INFORMATION

Employers in the state of _____ may not fire employees without reasonable cause or for the following reasons:

_____

_____

_____

_____

_____

_____

Workers' Compensation

State laws have been established to protect workers who are injured while working on the job. These laws create liability on the part of the employer when an employee is injured or becomes ill as a result of her employment. Employers may purchase private insurance or insurance from the state. In order to establish liability, the injured worker must show that the injury occurred during the course of her employment. Only the costs of the actual injury are compensable, and the employee may not sue the employer to establish liability until the workers' compensation board has made a decision on the employee's compensation. If it is proven that the injury occurred during the course of employment, the employee will receive costs of medical care, time lost from work, and, in some cases, rehabilitation costs. The employee is precluded from filing a negligence lawsuit against the employer.

Find the laws related to **workers' compensation** from your state and complete the following box.

STATE-SPECIFIC INFORMATION

The laws for workers' compensation in the state of _____ are as follows:

_____

_____

_____

_____

_____

_____

---

workers' compensation laws   state laws established to pay funds to workers injured on the job

Occupational Safety and Health Act (OSHA)

OSHA was passed by Congress to protect employees from being hurt or getting an illness while they are on the job. The purpose of the law was to guarantee that all workers would work in a safe and healthy environment. The law establishes safety and health standards to which the employer must adhere. The federal Department of Labor administers and enforces OSHA regulations. The states must meet the minimum standards established by the federal government and may establish stricter standards for their own state.

Each industry has different standards, depending on the type of business. OSHA requires employers to eliminate recognized hazards in the workplace. These standards may include provisions for air quality, noise, and safety.

Find the OSHA regulations for your state and fill in the following blanks.

STATE-SPECIFIC INFORMATION

OSHA regulations established by the state of _____ are as follows:

_____

_____

_____

_____

_____

_____

ENVIRONMENTAL PROTECTION

Much has been written about studies that have been performed to determine how various pollutants destroy the environment and cause illness and death among the population. The Environmental Protection Agency (EPA) is a federal organization that was established to make and enforce standards to control pollutants involving air, water, noise, toxins, pesticides, and radiation.

Congress passed the National Environmental Policy Act (NEPA) to solve the problems of pollution, but the act did not establish standards. However, the act requires an organization to prepare an Environmental Impact Report (EIR) before undertaking any new project that will affect the quality of life of the people. When a company wants to build a manufacturing plant that may pollute the environment, when a county wants to build a new airport that may create excessive noise for its nearby neighbors, or when a contractor wishes to build a large residential development in a city, an EIR is required.

Several subsequent acts of Congress have imposed standards for pollution involving air (Clean Air Act), water (Clean Water Act), toxic substances (Toxic Substances Control Act), hazardous waste and chemical products (Resource Conservation and Recovery Act), ocean dumping of hazardous waste (Marine Protection, Research, and Sanctuaries Act), nuclear power (Nuclear Regulatory Commission), dangerous pesticides (Environmental Pesticide Control Act), and excessive noise (Noise Control Act). Further regulations have been imposed by the Endangered Species Act, which authorizes the secretary of the interior to protect wildlife threatened with extinction after consulting with the state's representatives. All of these acts impose monetary penalties on violators.

Corporations that operate in many different states often find it difficult to determine the controlling regulations for each state. Therefore, in order to comply with the many environmental regulations placed on businesses, most companies hire attorneys who specialize in environmental law to keep them in compliance.

INTERNATIONAL BUSINESS

International business involves importing goods and services from foreign-based businesses as well as exporting products to other countries. United States–based corporations are becoming increasingly international in their direction and operate in many different countries. These corporations must learn the laws of the various countries in which they operate. A full discussion of all international laws is beyond the scope of this textbook. However, individuals who are employed in law firms that specialize in international law are encouraged to review reference materials and books to learn these laws.

Many Web sites provide information on international law. One of the most comprehensive sites was developed by the American Society of International Law. The site (**http://www.eisil.org**) provides links to many topics, including basic sources, treaties, international organizations, international environmental law, economics, human rights, criminal law, and dispute settlement. The site's home page is shown in Exhibit 4-7. This database of authenticated primary and other materials provides a depth of resources for legal research.

International Court of Justice

The International Court of Justice has been established by the Charter of the United Nations as the principal judicial organ of the United Nations. It hears cases that are brought before it by the member states of the United Nations. This court has jurisdiction in the following types of legal disputes:

1. the interpretation of a treaty
2. any question of international law
3. the existence of any fact that, if established, would constitute a breach of an international obligation
4. the nature or extent of the reparation to be made for the breach of an international obligation

EXHIBIT 4-7 Eisil Web Site of International Law Sources

Reproduced with permission from EISIL 2005 © The American Society of International Law.

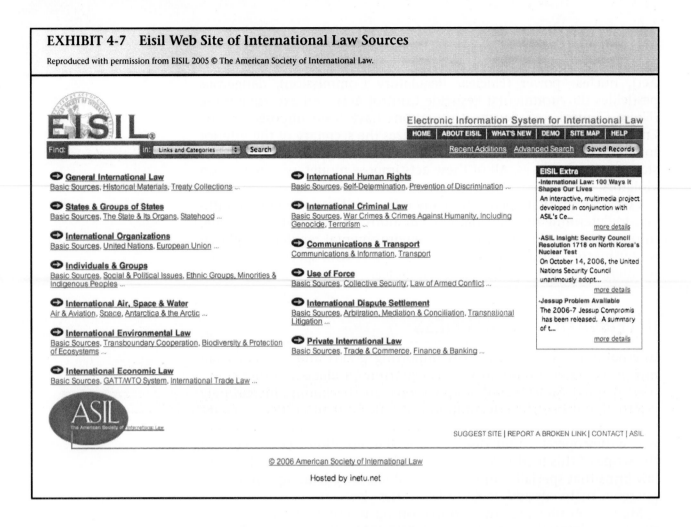

The full statute of the International Court of Justice may be found on the United Nations International Law Web site at

http://www.un.org/law

This site provides links to the various bodies that deal with international law, including the International Court of Justice. Procedures for dealing with the various courts and organizations are described. The site's home page is shown in Exhibit 4-8.

The Web site of the International Court of Justice, also known as the World Court, contains information on statutes, treaties, court decisions, advisory opinions, the United Nations charter, resources for students, and international law Web sites.

Several other sites provide information on international law, which involves legal relationships and interactions between different countries, or legal relations between individuals or corporations from different countries, as well as international trade agreements, treaties, and contracts.

Some countries have their laws online, as well as trade agreements and treaties, along with links to branches of their governments. Included in this list are the following:

1. British Parliament   **http://www.parliament.uk**

EXHIBIT 4-8 United Nations International Law Web Site

Reprinted with permission of United Nations Publications.

2. Australia   http://austlii.law.uts.edu.au

3. Canada: http://www.washlaw.edu/forint/
                       america/canada.html

4. International Links   http://www.law.nyu.edu/library/
   Including France   foreign_intl/france.html

5. The Library of Congress maintains a Web site for the Global
   Legal Information Network (**http://www.glin.gov**), which provides a database of laws from countries throughout the world.
   It is often the best place to start when doing research into international law.

Some Web sites also list lawyers who specialize in international law and
those who practice in foreign countries. A comprehensive list may be
found on the FindLaw Lawyer Directory page, practice area section,
which is available at

http://lawyers.findlaw.com/lawyer/practice.jsp

This site lists lawyers who specialize in international law by state as
well as those who practice in other countries.

The Martindale-Hubbell Lawyer Locator (**http://martindale.com**)
lists lawyers who practice in many different countries as well as those
who specialize in international law in the United States.

International Contracts

When contracts for the sale of goods are made between businesses in the United States, the law of contracts of this country and the Uniform Commercial Code apply. However, when contracts are made with businesses in other countries, the parties must choose whether to follow the law of the importer's or the exporter's country. This should be specifically stated in the contract and is known as the *choice-of-law clause*. Many countries have entered into treaties with the United States to specify the terms of international trade agreements. These treaties are accessible via the United Nations Web pages discussed previously. Two of the most well known treaties are the following:

1. United Nations Convention on Contracts for the International Sale of Goods (CISG)—This agreement sets out uniform rules to govern international sales contracts and the rights and obligations of both parties. It was patterned after Article 2 of the Uniform Commercial Code. Many countries, including the United States, are parties to this agreement.

2. The General Agreement on Tariffs and Trade (GATT)—This treaty, subscribed to by many countries including the United States, is based on nondiscrimination in trade and protection through tariffs. Each country is bound by this agreement to treat each country with which it trades the same as each other country, with no preferential treatment.

American businesses conduct their sales overseas directly via export sales or indirectly by a number of other methods. Under direct sales, the United States firm sells to customers in other countries subject to the tariff imposed by the foreign country. In other situations the local manufacturer appoints a foreign agent who operates on a commission for sales made for the American company. In most of these cases, the local firm must pay taxes imposed by the foreign countries. If the American company wishes to retain control over the operation, then a wholly owned subsidiary may be formed. In most cases, the company is relieved from double taxation by the United States and the foreign government by treaties granting them this relief.

Barriers to Foreign Trade

The tariff placed on goods as they move in and out of a country is the most widespread manner in which foreign countries restrict the importation of foreign goods. The tariff placed on foreign imports may make an item produced in the domestic market more reasonably priced and therefore more advantageous. Tariffs raise the total costs of products and may be a deterrent to purchasing foreign manufactured goods.

In addition to barriers placed by tariffs, other barriers to foreign trade may be instituted by restrictions that restrain the movement of goods among countries. A quota that a country imposes on imports will restrict the number of that particular item that can be imported. For instance, if the United States had a quota on the number of automobiles that could be imported from foreign countries, the price of foreign automobiles would go up and more people would likely buy American-made automobiles.

The controls that the United States places on exports have been used in establishing foreign policy. For instance, in recent years certain military supplies and weaponry have been forbidden from exportation to unfriendly nations. Under the Export Administration Act of 1979, export controls were placed on certain goods and technical information. The president and the Department of Commerce have the power to implement the provisions of the act.

Other laws protect the United States from receiving foreign goods at less than fair value, unfair import competition, and unreasonable or discriminatory acts by foreign governments. A major fear of American businesses is the risk of the taking of their assets by a foreign government, known as *expropriation.* Treaties with these countries generally protect the firms from this practice. Companies may purchase insurance that protects against foreign expropriation of the firm's assets.

● KEY TERMS

agency	franchise
agent for process	merger
articles of incorporation	nonprofit corporation
bylaws	partnership
close corporation	pre-incorporation agreement
consolidation	professional corporation
corporation	sole proprietorship
derivative suit	subchapter S corporation
dissolution	workers' compensation laws
Fictitious Business Name Statement	

● SELF TEST

1. What are the types of business organization? Define each.
2. Explain the advantages and disadvantages of each type of business organization.
3. How are new corporations formed from corporations that are dissolved?
4. List two laws that protect workers and explain the purpose of each.
5. How are business protected from losses when they operate in foreign countries?

● NOTEBOOK PROJECTS

1. Prepare articles of incorporation for a business that you would like to create. Follow the format in the text.
2. Prepare a Fictitious Business Name Statement for this business.
3. Using the Web sites listed in the chapter, research the methods for filing a lawsuit in the International Court of Justice. Write a memorandum to your instructor setting forth the procedures to follow.
4. Complete all State-Specific Information boxes in this chapter and include them under appropriate headings in your notebook.

  For additional resources, visit our Web site at **www.paralegal.delmar.cengage.com.**

CHAPTER 5

CIVIL LAW AND PROCEDURES

CHAPTER OUTCOMES

After studying this chapter, the student will understand

1. the principles of tort law.
2. beginning the process of filing a suit.
3. the pretrial process.
4. trial procedures.

TORT LAW

A *tort* is defined as a civil wrong that causes harm to another's person or property. In order to commit a tort, one must have a legal duty and breach that duty, thus causing harm to the other individual. The individual who commits the tort is known as the *tortfeasor*. Some of the more common tort categories include negligence, strict liability, product liability, intentional torts, and defamation.

Negligence

Most tort actions are based on *negligence*. Negligence has been defined as a requirement that all individuals have a duty to conduct themselves so as not to create an unreasonable risk of harm to others. In other words, we must conduct our activities with reasonable care so as not to injure another's person or property. If we breach that duty, we may be held liable in a negligence action. To prevail in this type of lawsuit, the plaintiff (the individual or entity filing the lawsuit) must prove all of the following elements:

1. *Duty.* The defendant (the individual against whom a lawsuit is filed) owed a duty of due care to the plaintiff.
2. *Breach.* The defendant breached that duty.
3. *Causation.* The breach actually caused the plaintiff's injuries.
4. *Damages.* The plaintiff suffered measurable damages.

For example, assume that Jane Hart drove through a red light and hit Sam Ford's automobile, causing damages to the car and injuries to Sam. Here, Jane had the *duty* to drive her automobile in a careful manner so as not to cause an unreasonable risk of harm to Sam. She *breached* that duty by driving through the red light. By so doing, she *caused* injuries to Sam and damages to his car. The measurable *damages* can be proved by the bills from the body shop for fixing Sam's automobile and by the medical expenses he incurred. A plaintiff who can prove all four elements of negligence is said to have established a *prima facie case.*

Violation of Statute.   In some states, negligence actions are easier to prove when the defendant has violated a statute or local law. If the defendant violates speeding regulations by operating his motor vehicle at an excessive speed, and he hits the plaintiff walking in a crosswalk because he is going too fast to stop his car, then the defendant violated the statute and may have caused the accident by his excessive speed. The following must be proven:

1. The defendant caused the accident.
2. The statute was violated, and that violation caused the injury to the plaintiff.
3. The plaintiff was within the group that the statute was intended to protect.

States vary as to the degree of negligence that can be imputed to the defendant based on these circumstances. Some states consider the violation to be negligence on its face, while others merely apply the standard that the statute violation may be a degree of negligence. Research your state's laws to determine its standards for violation of a statute and record them in the following box.

STATE-SPECIFIC INFORMATION

The state of _____ imposes the following standard on the defendant for the violation of a statute:

_____

_____

_____

_____

_____

_____

Product Liability Actions.   *Product liability actions* are a special kind of tort action. In these actions, a lawsuit is brought against a merchant or manufacturer because of a defective product. The defect may be in the product itself, in the product's design, in the product's packaging, or in the manner in which the product was manufactured. In most cases, the lawsuit is instituted against the seller, the manufacturer, or both. For example, if a new automobile tire blows up, causing an accident in which the plaintiff is injured, he may be able to sue the manufacturer of the tire by proving that the tire blew up because of a defect in its manufacture. In another example, a person who is injured when a bottle of juice explodes as it is being opened may initiate a lawsuit for a defect in the product's packaging. The three types of product defects are as follows:

1. *Design defects*—The design of the product is defective and this defect causes injuries. An example would be a small item on a baby's toy that may be readily removed and swallowed by the baby. Although all of the toys were made in this manner, they were designed in a defective manner.

2. *Product manufacturing defect*—Although the design of the product is not defective, the manufacture or distribution of the product rendered it dangerous. For example, if the tires on an automobile were not fastened to the rim correctly, a tire may fall off and cause an accident that injures someone. Examples of product manufacturing defects are a foreign substance inside the package and the previously mentioned exploding juice bottle.

3. *Defect in warning*—Certain products may be made with no manufacturing or design defects, but may be defective because no warning labels are affixed to them. For instance, some medications should not be taken if the consumer is taking certain other types of medication. A warning label should be affixed to the medication. Some cleaning products are dangerous if ingested and should be kept out of the reach of small children. Warning labels should be affixed to these products.

Most product liability actions are brought under a theory of negligence. The plaintiff must prove all elements, including duty, breach, causation, and damages. The duty to make safe products is required of all manufacturers. The plaintiff must prove that the defendant breached the duty of due care in the manufacture of the product. He must prove that this type of injury was foreseeable. The plaintiff must prove that the defective product caused the injury and that he suffered damages as a result.

The plaintiff may be one who buys the product, uses the product, or is a bystander when the defective product causes injury. The plaintiff may establish a **cause of action** against the manufacturer, the supplier, or the merchant who sold the product.

The theory of *res ipsa loquitur* simplifies the process for a plaintiff who is attempting to prove negligence against the manufacturer. The following elements must be proven to prevail using this theory:

1. The type of accident that occurred would not have happened without someone's negligence.
2. The instrumentality that caused the accident was in the exclusive control of the defendant.
3. The plaintiff did not contribute to his own injuries.

cause of action facts or legal theory on which the case is based

Thus, the scissors left in the patient after the operation, the new car whose brakes fail as the new owner drives it away from the dealer's lot, and the drug containing improper dosage may all follow the *res ipsa loquitur* doctrine for recovery. A person who is under anesthesia during the operation is not aware of who left the scissors in his body, but if they are found by an X-ray after the surgery, this theory may be used to establish liability.

In *Honeycutt v. State Farm Fire and Casualty Co.,* 39,301 La. App. 2d Cir. (2004), the court held that

> [t]he trial court could apply *res ipsa loquitur* doctrine and infer cow owners' negligence in motorist's suit arising out of collision with cow; absent negligence, a cow confined within fencing of proper height and maintenance will not wander into the center of the roadway in the middle of the night, owner offered no plausible explanation except to testify that neither he nor any member of his family left the gates open and that he observed no open or drooping areas in his fence, and motorist testified that she had noticed areas of fence that drooped significantly, . . .

And further:

> The "res ipsa loquitur" doctrine is a rule of circumstantial evidence, which is appropriate for those situations involving accidents that normally do not occur, absent negligence.

Strict Liability

The theory of *strict liability* states that when injuries are caused by certain activities, the defendant will be held liable despite any excuses or justifications. The courts have consistently held that some activities are so inherently dangerous that they are forbidden under any circumstances. A defendant who commits one of the strict-liability torts may be found liable for damages without any proof of intent or negligence. Strict (or absolute) liability is imposed for the following activities:

1. *Keeping wild animals as pets.* Any damages caused by these animals are charged to the defendant-owner. If you have a pet tiger in a locked cage and the tiger escapes and injures someone, you may not claim that you are not liable because the animal was in a locked cage. Just keeping the tiger as a pet makes you liable for any injuries it causes.

2. *Ultrahazardous activities.* Any activity that involves a substantial risk of harm to others or their property is forbidden. This includes the use, sale, and manufacture of explosive devices. An activity that cannot be performed safely and is not commonly performed in the community is considered ultrahazardous. If you are using dynamite to demolish a building and someone is injured by flying debris, you cannot claim that you were using the utmost care and caution in the blasting activity. Just using the dynamite makes you liable for any injuries it causes. However, the courts would be more likely to establish liability if the blasting occurs in your backyard next to a school than if it were conducted in the middle of the desert with no homes for several miles.
   In *Green v. Ensign-Bickford Company,* 595 A.2d 1383 (Conn. App. 1991), the defendant was conducting experiments with explosive chemicals at its manufacturing facility. The court held that

. . . the defendant's experiment with a highly explosive chemical created an unavoidable risk of damage, and that the risk was not alleviated by the fact that the research was conducted in a specially designed building . . .

and further

. . . the defendant was engaged in the perilous activity of conducting research with a highly volatile chemical for use in its explosive manufacturing business. The fact that the defendant did not intend to cause an explosion with this research does not justify relieving it of liability.

The court held in this case that under the doctrine of strict liability imposed on a person who engages in ultrahazardous activity, the plaintiff is not required to show that the defendant's negligence caused his loss but only that defendant engaged in the ultrahazardous activity that caused the loss.

Intentional Torts

The more common intentional torts include assault, battery, false imprisonment, conversion, trespass to chattel, trespass to land, intentional infliction of emotional distress, and wrongful death. Each of these torts must be committed by the defendant with the intent to commit them and must cause the plaintiff damages that are caused by the commission of the tort against him.

Assault.   A civil *assault* is an intentional act that causes the plaintiff to have an apprehension of a harmful or offensive touching or contact. Note that the plaintiff does not have to be afraid of the commission of the act, but he must anticipate the act with some discomfort, anxiety, or uneasiness. This act may be actionable if it reasonably causes apprehension on the part of the plaintiff even if the defendant does not actually have physical contact with the plaintiff. The defendant may be held liable for injuries to the plaintiff in addition to any mental suffering or apprehension the plaintiff experiences.

Battery.   If the defendant intends to cause a harmful or offensive touching of the plaintiff, and actually does have harmful or offensive contact with that individual, then the tort of *battery* has occurred if the defendant actually caused the contact. The most obvious case occurs when the defendant beats the plaintiff and injures him. However, a battery may also involve offensive contact that offends the personal self-respect of a reasonable person. It makes no difference if the person hit is not the one the defendant intended to hit (*transferred intent*) or if the contact benefits the plaintiff (for example, a doctor giving medication forcibly to one who refuses treatment). The battery also may occur if the plaintiff is not aware of it at the time, such as if he is asleep. However, if the defendant can prove that the plaintiff consented to the contact, then no battery has been committed.

False Imprisonment.   *False imprisonment* occurs when the defendant intentionally commits an act that completely confines the plaintiff within fixed boundaries and the plaintiff was conscious of the confinement or was harmed as a result of it. For instance, if a librarian leaves the library knowing that Jack is still there, locking the door behind her, and Jack tries to leave but can't, she could be liable for false imprisonment. But if she comes back and unlocks the door before Jack is aware of the confinement, the elements of the tort are not met. However, in the latter case, if a fire ensues and Jack is injured, the librarian may be held liable for his injuries even if she was gone for only a short period of time.

Conversion and Trespass to Chattel.   Only a minor distinction exists between the torts of conversion and trespass to **chattel**. A minor interference with possession of the chattel would represent *trespass to chattel,* while a more severe interference would substantiate an action for *conversion.* Both of these torts involve interference with the plaintiff's possession of his personal property (chattel). The conversion tort requires that the defendant intended to exercise dominion and control over the property, while the trespass to chattel tort requires that the defendant wished to deprive the plaintiff of the property or intermeddle with his possession of it Therefore, if the defendant steals the plaintiff's car, a suit for conversion would be appropriate. However, if the defendant takes an item belonging to the plaintiff and returns it in a short period of time, the tort of trespass to chattel would have occurred.

Trespass to Land.   The intentional tort of *trespass to land* requires that the defendant interfere with the possession of the land by intruding on the land in another's possession with the intent to intrude on it. This may include actually going onto the land and/or remaining on the land beyond the time allowed. It may also include failure to remove items from the land. The plaintiff must have possession of the land in order for this tort to occur. The plaintiff does not have to prove that the defendant damaged the land but merely that he entered the land. In the latter case, the court may award nominal damages.

Intentional Infliction of Emotional Distress.   In order to be liable for *intentional infliction of emotional distress,* the defendant must have committed an outrageous act intending to cause extreme emotional distress to the plaintiff, who suffered extreme emotional distress. Some courts have extended this tort to include *reckless infliction of emotional distress.* The defendant's outrageous act must be the cause of the plaintiff's injuries. The plaintiff's damages may include compensation for physical or emotional injuries or illness. If the defendant's actions were malicious, the plaintiff may also recover *punitive damages* (extra compensation to punish the defendant for a particularly malicious act and to prevent the act from occurring again).

Wrongful Death.   *Wrongful death* has been defined as the death of an individual who is the victim of a tort. The death must be a result of the tort. For instance, if John commits a battery against Sally and Sally dies of her injuries, most states allow Sally's heirs and/or estate to institute a wrongful death action against John. State laws vary on the method of

chattel an item of personal property

recovery for wrongful death. The most common methods of recovery are as follows:

1. *Survival statute*—The tort action survives the death of the victim and covers any damages that ensue up to the time of the victim's death. The original lawsuit may be continued by the victim's legal representative and may include the victim's medical bills, funeral expenses, lost accumulated earnings based on life expectancy, and pain and suffering up to the time of his death.

2. *Wrongful death statute*—A new cause of action may be instituted by the victim's family, including the spouse and children. The legal representative brings a new action for the benefit of the family. In this case, the victim's losses are not recoverable. Recoverable damages include the family's loss of support and services of the victim, as well as any monetary sums that the family would have received had the victim lived to his life expectancy. A few states, however, have allowed family members to collect for mental anguish.

3. *Both survival statute and wrongful death statute*—In some states that have both a survival statute and a wrongful death statute, the surviving family may institute both actions at the same time.

Research the law in your state to determine which of the preceding methods is used, and note your findings in the following box.

STATE-SPECIFIC INFORMATION

The state of _____ allows the following types of recovery for the death of the victim:

Survival statute:

_____

_____

_____

Wrongful death statute:

_____

_____

_____

Both survival statute and wrongful death statute:

_____

_____

_____

Statute of Limitations

Most states require that personal injury and tort actions be filed within a year of the time the injury occurred. The time is generally lessened if the claim is being filed against a government entity. In some states this requirement is lessened to six months from the accrual of the cause of action. Determine the **statute of limitations** for your state and complete the following box.

STATE-SPECIFIC INFORMATION

The state of _____ requires that a personal injury or tort action must be filed within _____ of the time the injury occurred. Actions against government entities must be filed within _____ of the accrual of the cause of action.

Defenses

Consent.   **Consent** may be used as a defense for assault, battery, and/or false imprisonment. If the plaintiff consents to the touching or imprisonment, then the defense is valid. Consent may be actual (a direct statement by the plaintiff giving his consent), express (consent by action, such as when a person enters a boxing match), or implied (inferred by the circumstances). The defense of implied consent is often used when the defendant aided the plaintiff at an accident scene but worsened his condition. This type of consent is not valid in all states; research the law in your state and complete the following box.

STATE-SPECIFIC INFORMATION

The following types of consent are valid defenses in the state of _____:

_____

_____

_____

---

statute of limitations   a law that sets a maximum amount of time after something happens within which it can be taken to court

consent   a defense to assault, battery, and/or false imprisonment; if the plaintiff consents to the touching or the imprisonment, then the defense is valid

Self-Defense.   A person may defend himself against another's battery as long as the degree of force used is no greater than the perpetrator's. For instance, if someone slaps you with his hand, you may not shoot him.

Defense of Others.   A person may use the same degree of force defending another that would be allowed if he were the one being attacked. In the preceding self-defense example, if another person comes to your aid, he also may not use a gun, because you (the individual being attacked) may not use a gun.

Defense of Property. If someone steals your property, you may use reasonable force to protect the property but may never use lethal force.

Intent. A person may defend himself against an intentional tort action by proving that there was no intent to commit the act. For instance, if a librarian leaves the library and locks the door, not knowing that a library patron is in the rear section of the library, the patron has not been falsely imprisoned because there was no intent to do so. Similarly, the individual must be aware of his false imprisonment at the time. If the librarian comes back and unlocks the door before the patron is aware of the incident, no false imprisonment has occurred.

Several other defenses to intentional torts are available in many states. The descriptions in this book are necessarily brief and may be expanded upon in a course in tort law. Determine your state's defenses for intentional torts and complete the following box.

STATE-SPECIFIC INFORMATION

The following defenses to intentional torts are valid in the state of
_____:

_____

_____

_____

_____

_____

_____

RULES OF CIVIL PROCEDURE

Initial Client Interview

The client interview is the first contact made in a civil case. A sample form for conducting the client interview in a personal injury case is shown in Exhibit 5-1.

If the legal assistant conducts the initial client interview, he should stress the importance of confidentiality to assure the client that none of the information provided during the interview will be divulged outside the office.

After the interview, it is appropriate for the legal assistant to write a letter to the client thanking him for hiring the law firm and reiterating any special instructions given at the interview. The letter should include any additional requests for information from the client. In some firms, this letter is signed by the attorney. A sample letter is shown in Exhibit 5-2.

EXHIBIT 5-1   Client Interview Form

Name _____   Social Security No. _____

Telephone No.: (cell) _____ (work) _____ (home) _____

Birth Date: _____ Place of Birth: _____

Address: _____

Former addresses: _____
_____
_____
_____

Married _____ Single _____ Divorced _____ Date of marriage: _____
Date of Divorce: _____

Employer: _____ Job title: _____
Duties and responsibilities: _____
Address of Employer: _____
Present occupation: _____

Previous employers (10 years) with Name, Address, Telephone Number, Job Title , Duties:
_____
_____
_____
_____

Education: Graduated high school _____ Year _____
Colleges attended and degrees received with dates:
_____
_____
_____

Technical or other trade schools: _____
_____

Economic losses from this injury, including salary and others: _____
_____

Spouse: _____   Address if different from client: _____
_____

Telephone Numbers: (cell) _____ work _____ home _____

Former Spouses if any and dates of marriage and divorce: _____
_____

continued

Exhibit 5-1   *continued*

Natural or adopted children:

1. Name: _____ Date of Birth: _____
   Address: _____
   Telephone: (home) _____ (work) _____ (cell) _____
   Social Security Number _____ Place of Birth: _____
      Name, address, and telephone number of other parent: _____
   _____
   _____

2. Name: _____ Date of Birth: _____
   Address: _____
   Telephone: (home) _____ (work) _____ (cell) _____
   Social Security Number _____ Place of Birth: _____
      Name, address, and telephone number of other parent: _____
   _____
   _____

3. Name: _____ Date of Birth: _____
   Address: _____
   Telephone: (home) _____ (work) _____ (cell) _____
   Social Security Number _____ Place of Birth: _____
      Name, address, and telephone number of other parent: _____
   _____
   _____

4. Name: _____ Date of Birth: _____
   Address: _____
   Telephone: (home) _____ (work) _____ (cell) _____
   Social Security Number _____ Place of Birth: _____
      Name, address, and telephone number of other parent: _____
   _____
   _____

Others supported by client:

1. Name: _____ Date of Birth: _____
   Address: _____
   Telephone: (home) _____ (work) _____ (cell) _____
   Social Security Number _____
   Relationship _____ % income spent on this person _____

continued

Exhibit 5-1   *continued*

2. Name:_____ Date of Birth:_____
   Address:_____
   Telephone: (home)_____ (work)_____ (cell)_____
   Social Security Number_____
   Parent:_____
   Relationship_____ % income spent on this person_____

Father of client _____ Living or deceased _____
If living, address: _____
Telephone number: (work) _____ (cell) _____ (home) _____
Date and place of birth: _____
Date of death if deceased:_____ Place of death: _____

Mother of client _____ Living or deceased _____
If living, address: _____
Telephone number: (work) _____ (cell) _____ (home) _____
Date and place of birth: _____
Date of death if deceased: _____ Place of death: _____

Client's Siblings:
1. Name: _____ Date and place of birth: _____
   Address: _____
   Telephone: (home) _____ (cell) _____ (work) _____
   Date and place of death if deceased: _____

2. Name: _____ Date and place of birth: _____
   Address: _____
   Telephone: (home) _____ (cell) _____ (work) _____
   Date and place of death if deceased: _____

3. Name: _____ Date and place of birth: _____
   Address: _____
   Telephone: (home) _____ (cell) _____ (work) _____
   Date and place of death if deceased: _____

4. Name: _____ Date and place of birth: _____
   Address: _____
   Telephone: (home) _____ (cell) _____ (work) _____
   Date and place of death if deceased: _____

EXHIBIT 5-2   Sample Thank-You Letter to Client

Law Firm Letterhead

Date

Client Name

Address

RE: *Client v. Defendant*

Dear Mr. Client:

Thank you for the opportunity of serving your legal needs in your upcoming civil litigation case. We appreciate your hiring our firm, and we will do our best to meet your requirements in this action.

As requested at your interview, please provide this office with the following documents within the next week:

1. Police report of the accident on December 2, 2007.
2. All of your medical bills to date.
3. Bills from the body shop for car repairs.

Be sure to keep an ongoing diary of any pain you might experience as a result of your injuries. Note any time lost from work and additional expenses incurred as a result of the accident such as automobile rental while yours was being repaired.

Please call or e-mail me if you have any questions about your case. My e-mail address is Helpu@lawyer.com.

Very truly yours,

Your Name

Your Title

Guardian ad Litem

Many states require that a **guardian ad litem** be appointed for a **minor** or incompetent who is a party to the action. The court in which the action is pending appoints the guardian upon petition by the attorney. The legal professional must file the appropriate documentation with the court to appoint the guardian ad litem before commencing the lawsuit. In most cases, a parent applies on behalf of the minor plaintiff and is appointed the guardian ad litem by the court.

> STATE-SPECIFIC INFORMATION
>
> Forms required for appointment of a guardian ad litem in the state of _____ are as follows:
>
> _____
>
> _____
>
> _____
>
> The person who must make the application is:
>
> _____

Defendant minors must apply for a guardian ad litem within 10 days after service of the summons in most states. The documentation varies by state, but a typical application for appointment of a guardian ad litem is shown in Exhibit 5-3.

> STATE-SPECIFIC INFORMATION
>
> In the state of _____, minor defendants must apply for appointment of a guardian ad litem within _____ days of being served with the summons. Other requirements include the following:
>
> _____
>
> _____
>
> _____

COMMENCING THE LAWSUIT

Documents filed with most courts are prepared on lined and numbered pleading paper or court forms. In states that use court forms, prepackaged software programs are available. Each state has its own formatting rules, and court rules are available to learn these regulations. Some states

guardian ad litem a guardian for a minor for a particular lawsuit

minor an individual who has not reached the age of majority

EXHIBIT 5-3   Petition and Order for Appointment of Guardian ad Litem

Reprinted with permission from *Office Procedures for the Legal Professional*, Judy Long, 2005: Thomson/Delmar Learning.

1   John P. Evans

2   Attorney at Law

3   1122 Main Street

4   Torrance, CA 90503

5

6   LOS ANGELES COUNTY SUPERIOR COURT

7

8   NORTHEAST SUPERIOR COURT DISTRICT

9

10   KATHERINE AGNESS SPRINGER,   ) Case No.: PI-95-CC81

11   )

12   A Minor, By and Through   ) PETITION FOR APPOINTMENT OF GUARDIAN

13   ) AD LITEM, AND ORDER APPOINTING

14   MARGARET MARY SPRINGER, Her Guardian   ) GUARDIAN AD LITEM

15   )

16   ad Litem,   )

17   )

18   Plaintiff,   )

19   )

20   vs.   )

21   )

22   JOHN Q. MARTINEZ,   )

23   )

24   Defendant   )

25   _____   )

26   Petitioner, KATHERINE AGNES SPRINGER, alleges that she is a minor of the age of twelve (12) years, born April 15, 1995.

27   Petitioner has a cause of action arising out of an automobile accident on September 25, 2006, where she

28   sustained physical injuries.

1

continued

Exhibit 5-3 *continued*

1 Petitioner has no general Guardian, and no previous Petition for Appointment of a Guardian Ad Litem has

2 been filed in this matter.

3 MARY MARGARET SPRINGER is the mother of Petitioner and is competent to act as Guardian Ad Litem.

4 WHEREFORE, Petitioner prays that MARY MARGARET SPRINGER be appointed as Guardian Ad Litem for

5 Petitioner.

6 I declare under penalty of perjury under the laws of the State of California that the foregoing is true and correct.

7 DATED: July 9, 2007

8

9 _____

10 KATHERINE AGNES SPRINGER

11

12 CONSENT OF NOMINEE

13 I, MARY MARGARET SPRINGER, the nominee of Petitioner, consent to act as Guardian Ad Litem for the

14 minor Petitioner in the above action.

15 DATED: July 9, 2007

16

17 _____

18 MARGARET MARY SPRINGER

19

20 ORDER APPOINTING GUARDIAN AD LITEM

21 The court, having considered the petition of KATHERINE AGNES SPRINGER for the appointment of a

22 Guardian Ad Litem for petitioner, a minor, who is the plaintiff in the above action, and good cause appearing,

23 IT IS ORDERED that MARY MARGARET SPRINGER be appointed Guardian Ad Litem for KATHERINE AGNES

24 SPRINGER in the above action.

25 DATED: July 20, 2007

26

27 _____

28 JUDGE OF THE SUPERIOR COURT

2

no longer use lined and numbered legal pleading paper. Determine the rules for your state and complete the following box.

STATE-SPECIFIC INFORMATION

In the state of _____, documents filed with state courts must be prepared in the following manner:

_____

_____

_____

_____

_____

_____

Complaint

The first pleading filed to commence the lawsuit is the **complaint.** The plaintiff indicates in the complaint the facts constituting the cause of action and a demand for relief (*prayer for damages*). The *caption* must include all information identifying the case, including the attorney's name, address, and telephone number; the names of the parties; the name and address of the court; and the nature of the complaint (such as "Personal Injury"). The case number is assigned by the court and is also stamped in the caption under "Case Number."

The complaint must contain a statement of jurisdiction and venue. Many states have two levels of trial courts for civil actions, with a monetary cutoff determining the appropriate court for filing. For instance, if the state has a lower court system with a maximum amount of damages of $25,000 and a higher court system for suits of more than $25,000, the statement of jurisdiction would affirm which of the courts has proper **jurisdiction.**

Venue refers to a court's proper geographical location in which to hear the case. Although the jurisdiction may be correct, the attorney must also determine which location of that particular court would be appropriate. Considerations involve where the incident occurred, the domicile of the defendant, and the domicile of the plaintiff.

Each cause of action in the complaint must be numbered consecutively. The prayer for damages includes the following:

complaint the first pleading filed to commence a lawsuit

jurisdiction the power of a court to hear a case

venue an appropriate geographical location to hear the case

1. *Special or compensatory damages* covering actual out-of-pocket expenses, such as medical bills and car repairs.
2. *General damages* to compensate the plaintiff for pain and suffering and any permanent injuries resulting from the incident.
3. *Punitive damages* if the defendant's actions were intentional or grossly negligent.

Service of Summons

The summons should be prepared and filed with the court along with the complaint. Most states have a court form for this purpose. Enough copies for each defendant and a copy for the office file should be presented to the court clerk at the same time so that the original will be signed and copies conformed for service on the defendant(s). The defendant(s) must then be served with a copy of the complaint and a conformed copy of the summons.

Methods of Service

Personal Service.   The most common method for serving the defendant is by *personal service,* which is accomplished by handing the complaint and summons to the defendant and telling him what they are. If the defendant refuses to accept the documents, you may drop them at his feet. They must be given to the defendant personally, however, and not left in a mailbox, on a front porch, or on a desk. The time and date served must be noted on the *proof of service,* described later.

Service by Mail.   *Service by mail* is accomplished by sending the documents to the defendant by certified mail with return receipt requested. The date received must be noted, because the response will be due 30 days from the date the receipt is signed, plus an additional five days for mailing. This time period may vary in a few states; review your state's court rules and complete the following box.

> STATE-SPECIFIC INFORMATION
>
> In the state of _____ , if the defendant is served by mail, the response is due _____ days from the date the receipt is signed, plus an additional _____ days for mailing.

Substituted Service.   If the defendant cannot be served personally or by mail, another individual may be served in place of the defendant. At the defendant's home, an adult member of the household may be served. At a business, an adult who is in a management capacity at the business may be served. A copy must then be sent to the defendant at the address served.

Service by Publication.   As a last resort, the defendant may be served by publication in a newspaper of general circulation. However, the plaintiff must prove that the defendant could not be served by any other means. The attorney must make a motion to the court with accompanying affidavits indicating how service was attempted on the defendant. The court then issues a ruling on the motion, allowing or denying service by publication. The service may then be published in a newspaper in the town or county of the defendant's last known residence.

Agents for Process

If a corporation is a defendant, the authorized agent for the organization must be served. Corporations are required to designate agents for process in each state in which they operate. This information may be obtained from the state secretary of state's office.

Proof of Service

A proof-of-service form must be prepared by the individual who served the summons and complaint on the defendant. In most states, this form is attached to or part of the summons. The date, place, and time served must be indicated, along with the method of service.

Of particular importance is the date of service, which should be noted in the tickler file with the date on which responding documents are due. The date is usually 30 days from the day after the complaint and summons have been personally served, or 35 days if service is accomplished by mail.

Defendant's Responses to the Complaint

The defendant may respond to the complaint in the amount of time specified previously with one or more of the following documents:

1. answer
2. cross-complaint
3. demurrer
4. motion to strike

In some states, attorneys may grant the opposing counsel an extension of time in which to file these documents. Some states, however, have adopted new *fast-track* rules that have changed the number of time extensions that may be granted. One should review local court rules to determine whether extensions are allowed.

Affirmative Defenses.   In some cases, the defendant raises an issue not covered in the plaintiff's complaint that would defeat the plaintiff's complaint even if he is able to prove all elements. For example, some state statutes stipulate that if the plaintiff contributes to the negligence, the defendant is not liable. In that case, the defendant would claim contributory negligence as an affirmative defense.

Request to Enter Default.   If the defendant fails to answer the complaint in the allotted time, the plaintiff may file a **default judgment** by preparing a *request to enter default,* along with accompanying documentation. The court generally issues a judgment in favor of the plaintiff if the defendant fails to appear at the default hearing.

Answer.   The *answer* includes factual issues in response to the complaint. The plaintiff must prove these issues at the time of trial. In many cases, the defendant issues a *general denial* to all issues raised in the complaint, thereby compelling the plaintiff to prove all of his allegations.

By filing an answer, the defendant submits to the court's jurisdiction. Therefore, a defendant who wishes to object to the court's jurisdiction over him must file and serve a *motion to quash service of summons* before answering the complaint.

In some cases, the defendant may wish to admit to some allegations in the complaint and to deny others. In those situations, he should

default judgment a judgment taken when the defendant fails to respond to the complaint submit *specific denials* to those numbered allegations in the complaint and *admissions* to others.

A defendant who wishes to bring up additional issues or facts constituting a defense must do so in the answer. If additional facts constituting a defense are presented, each one must be explained separately and must be listed in numbered paragraphs. Examples of defenses include the following:

1. Expiration of the statute of limitations, which bars the plaintiff from filing a complaint.
2. Comparative negligence, if the plaintiff was partially at fault.
3. Assumption of the risk of injury by the plaintiff.
4. Asserting that the proper remedy is a workers' compensation action because the plaintiff was acting within the scope of his employment at the time of the incident.
5. Immunity, such as a public officer may have.
6. Other defenses that may be asserted by the attorney for the defendant.

Cross-Complaint

If the defendant has a claim against the plaintiff or third parties arising from the same or a related transaction, a **cross-complaint** may be filed with the answer. The terminology used for the parties is as follows:

1. *cross-complainant*—the party filing the cross-complaint
2. *third-party defendant*—a third party against whom the cross-complaint is filed
3. *cross-defendant*—the party against whom the cross-complaint is filed
4. *third-party plaintiff*—a defendant who files the cross-complaint against a third party

When many different parties are involved in the case, it is possible to have a number of cross-complaints filed against parties to the action as well as third parties. In those cases, the legal assistant must pay particular attention to who is filing against whom and to the due dates of responsive pleadings. Each time a cross-complaint is filed, the responsive pleading is subject to the same 30-day answer requirements described earlier.

The heading of the cross-complaint should contain two separate captions:

1. the names of the parties in the initial action
2. the names of all cross-complainants and cross-defendants

The body of the cross-complaint must include the facts constituting the cause of action and a precise demand for damages. A defendant who fails to file a cross-complaint against the plaintiff in a related or the same transaction may be barred from filing it at a later time. In some states, a claim filed by the defendant against the plaintiff is known as a *counterclaim.*

cross-complaint a complaint by the defendant against the plaintiff or a complaint by one defendant against another defendant

Demurrer

If the defendant feels that the plaintiff has filed a complaint with no legal grounds, the defendant's attorney files a **demurrer,** a pleading that maintains that the plaintiff's complaint has no legal basis. **Points and authorities** (P&As) supporting the defendant's contentions must accompany the demurrer. These include a statement of the issue or argument along with the citation of the case or statute from which it was obtained. For example, if the defendant objects on the ground that the plaintiff does not have the legal capacity to sue, the points and authorities must include the statute number or code section that states what constitutes legal capacity to sue.

The court holds a hearing on the demurrer. Both attorneys present their oral arguments to the judge, who then issues a ruling. If the court rules that the demurrer is *sustained without leave to amend,* the defendant wins the lawsuit. In some cases, the court allows the plaintiff to amend the complaint. If the court overrules the demurrer, the defendant must file an answer within the allotted time period.

Response to Demurrer. The party against whom a demurrer was filed may respond either by amending the complaint to alleviate the insufficiencies raised by the demurrer or by filing points and authorities in opposition to the demurrer. Papers opposing the demurrer must be served and filed at least five court days prior to the hearing in most states.

Motion to Strike

In some cases, the complaint may be legally sufficient, but some of its allegations may be legally objectionable. In that event, the defendant may file a **motion to strike** asking that the objectionable allegations be removed. The motion must set forth the objectionable wording along with points and authorities to support the defendant's contentions. The exact page and line number(s) of the objectionable words must be noted on the motion. The court holds a hearing on the motion.

Motion for Summary Judgment

Either party may file a motion for **summary judgment.** The plaintiff files such a motion to assert that there is no defense that the defendant can claim in the action. The defendant files the motion to claim that the action has no merit. In either case, affidavits of witnesses or parties to the action must be filed with the motion. The court holds a hearing at which attorneys present oral arguments and a decision is rendered.

Discovery

The period of time in a lawsuit during which both sides formally exchange facts and information is known as the **discovery** phase. Legal assistants draft discovery documents and keep track of all documents filed. Important parts of discovery are document control, summarizing documents, and cataloging. The most common discovery devices are the following:

demurrer a document stating that the other side does not have a legitimate legal argument in the case and that the propounding party should prevail

points and authorities cases and statutes used as an argument in a memorandum to the court

motion to strike a motion to the court to strike legally objectionable language from a pleading

summary judgment a judgment based on a motion that there are no disputed facts to be decided at trial and there is no defense that can be claimed

discovery a formal exchange of information by both parties

1. depositions
2. written interrogatories
3. requests for admission
4. demand for inspection
5. demand for physical examination

Any requests by the adverse party for information or material that is covered by the attorney-client privilege or work-product privilege is not discoverable. Additional privileges include the following:

1. privilege against self-incrimination
2. spousal privilege
3. physician or psychotherapist privilege
4. clergy-penitent privilege

Only the holder may waive these privileges. A claim of privilege should be made upon being served with the discovery request, by an objection setting forth the nature of the privilege along with a refusal to respond.

Deposition.   The **deposition** is a pretrial examination of a party or a witness to a lawsuit. The party whose statement is taken, called the **deponent,** makes a declaration under oath. The rules of civil procedure for each state govern the location and time line for taking the deposition. Typically it is scheduled at the law office of the attorney who is requesting it. A court reporter is present to take the transcript and administer the oath.

Deposition Summaries.   Because depositions often elicit considerably more information than is required, the legal assistant is often asked to summarize the deposition testimony. The summary should point out any discrepancies in the witness's testimony. The most common types of summaries are as follows:

1. topical summary
2. page/line summary
3. issue summary
4. index to a video deposition

Exhibits 5-4, 5-5, 5-6, and 5-7 show samples of each type of summary. Exhibit 5-8 shows instructions for their completion.

Written Interrogatories.   Written questions asked by one party of another party are known as **written interrogatories.** Each state has its own service requirements. Written interrogatories are the most-used discovery tool as well as the least expensive. All evidentiary information within the party's knowledge may be obtained except that covered by a privilege. Some states restrict the number of written interrogatories that may be propounded on each party. Other states have other restrictions on the format of written interrogatories.

Most states require the responding party to answer the interrogatories within 30 days. Unless an objection is submitted, all questions

deposition   a pretrial in-person examination of a party or a witness to a lawsuit

deponent   an individual whose deposition is taken

written interrogatories   written questions asked by one party of another

EXHIBIT 5-4 Topical Deposition Summary

Reprinted with permission from *Office Procedures for the Legal Professional*, Judy Long, 2005: Thomson/Delmar Learning.

(1)

FIELD V. RIVERS

Case No. 42196

Deponent Name: Lucelly Oso

Date of Deposition: May 1, 2007

Deposition Volume: No. 1

Topic/Subject	Transcript Page/Line	Summary Page
Personal	2/15	1
Employment history	3/5	1
Medical history	8/2	1
Psychiatric treatment	10/4	1
Psychiatric treatment	14/5	2
Educational history	17/19	2

(2) (3) (4)

EXHIBIT 5-5 Page/Line Deposition Summary

Reprinted with permission from *Office Procedures for the Legal Professional*, Judy Long, 2005: Thomson/Delmar Learning.

Morgan v. Castillo

Case No. 33333

Deponent Name: Linda Stoner
Date of Deposition: March 6, 2007
Deposition Volume No. 1

(1)

(2) Page/Line	(3) Subject	(4) Summary
2/15	Personal	Resides at 222 Western Avenue, Akron, Ohio, phone: (999) 222-1111
3/5	Procedures	Explanation of deposition procedures
6/4	Employment	Currently employed by Ross Enterprises, 435 Irvine Boulevard, Akron, Ohio, as accountant for 6 months. Prior to that, accountant for Attorney Deanna Caudillo, 123 Broad Street, Akron, Ohio, 8 months
8/2	Medical	No present medication. Treated for back pain and psychiatric problems last three years.
10/4	Psychiatric	Saw Dr. Danielli for one year in Akron.
14/5	Psychiatric	Denies seeing psychiatrist for emotional or psychiatric problems.
16/9	Psychiatric	Dr. Danielli's office located on Madison Street but can't remember address. Deponent's attorney will provide.
17/19	Education	Completed Whittier School in Whittier, Ohio, 1992. Completed paralegal classes in 1994. CPA 1995.

EXHIBIT 5-6   Issue Deposition Summary

Reprinted with permission from *Office Procedures for the Legal Professional*, Judy Long, 2005: Thomson/Delmar Learning.

Morgan v. Guerrero

Case No. 55555

Deponent Name: Susan Dawson

Date: May 1, 2007

Deposition Volume No. 1

①

Subject/Issue	Page(s)
Personal/background	
Personal information	2
Employment history	6
Educational history	9
Medical history	
Current status	8
Psychiatric history	11, 16

②   ③

EXHIBIT 5-7   Index to a Video Deposition

Reprinted with permission from *Office Procedures for the Legal Professional*, Judy Long, 2005: Thomson/Delmar Learning.

Daniels v. Kenell—Case No. 11111

Deponent: William Minot

Date: December 26, 2007

Volume No. 1

①

Time/Date No.*	Page/Line	Summary
00:40:08	5/9	Identification of parties and attorneys
01:38:00	7/14	Witness William Minot sworn in
01:55:20	8/25	Attorney Melissa Chan begins direct examination
02:22:07	9/20	Exhibit 1 identified and authenticated by deponent (contract between Minot and Daniels dated 7/17/92)
02:50:03	10/25	Personal background of witness
03:30:02	12/5	Educational history of witness

* Times and dates are indicated as they appear on the video display.

EXHIBIT 5-8   Instructions for Preparing Deposition Summaries

Reprinted with permission from *Office Procedures for the Legal Professional*, Judy Long, 2005: Thomson/Delmar Learning.

Use the following instructions to prepare a topical deposition summary:

1. *Heading.*   Type the name of the case, the case number, the name of the individual being deposed, the date of the deposition, and the volume number being summarized.

2. *Topic/subject.*   Separate the deposition by subject matter and indicate each topic covered.

3. *Transcript Page/line.*   Indicate the page and the line number of each individual topic in the deposition. This shows the attorney where the material appears in the deposition transcript.

4. *Summary Page.*   Indicate the page number on which each individual topic appears in the deposition summary.

Use the following instructions to prepare a page/line deposition summary:

1. *Heading.*   This includes the case name and number, the deponent's name, the date of the deposition, and the volume number.

2. *Page/line.*   This shows at what page and line number in the transcript the material under "subject" and "summary" appear.

3. *Subject.*   What is the general subject area?

4. *Summary.*   This provides a brief summary of the information contained on that line and page and about that general subject. This summary should necessarily be brief but should indicate any discrepancies in the testimony. For example, see the summary of psychiatric information in Exhibit 4-14.

Use the following instructions in preparing an issue deposition summary:

1. *Heading.*   This includes the title of the summary, the case name and number, the name of the individual whose deposition is being taken, and the date and volume number.

2. *Headings.*   List here each individual subject or issue discussed in the deposition.

3. *Page.*   Indicate here the page number on which the discussion of each individual subject or issue appears in the deposition transcript.

These instructions will help in preparing an index to a video deposition:

1. *Heading.*   This includes the type of index, the case name, the client's name, the name of the person whose deposition is being taken, the date of the deposition, and the volume number.

2. *Time/date.*   Because this is a videotaped deposition, it is advisable to indicate the numbers that appear on the video display at the point where this portion of the testimony appears. It is necessary to have a VCR player with a display for time and date.

3. *Page/line.*   Here you will list the page number and line number at which this portion of the testimony appears in the transcript.

4. *Summary.*   This provides a summary of what appears in the deponent's testimony at this point in the transcript and videotape.

must be answered within this time period. Proper grounds for objecting to questions follow. Individual objections must be stated for each question that is unacceptable.

1. If the question is irrelevant to the case or will not lead to the discovery of admissible evidence, then the question exceeds the scope of discovery and will not be allowed.

2. If the question seeks to obtain information covered by attorney-client privilege, it will be objectionable.

3. Questions about the contents of documents are not allowed; however, questions about the identity or location of documents may be obtained.

4. If the question would take an extraordinary amount of time and effort by the respondent, it is said to be burdensome and oppressive and will not be allowed.

Some states have further grounds for objections.

STATE-SPECIFIC INFORMATION

Special requirements for written interrogatories in the state of _____ are as follows:

_____

_____

_____

_____

_____

_____

Challenging Objections.   If the answering party objects to answering questions propounded (asked) in the interrogatories, the propounding party must first meet with opposing counsel to work out the dispute. If this is not possible, he may file a *motion to compel further answers* with the court, in which the court is asked to order the respondent to provide answers. The court decides whether the answers previously provided are adequate and, if not, what additional information the answering party must provide.

Responses to Written Interrogatories.   Paralegals may be asked to help the client answer written interrogatories that have been propounded to them. The client may answer each question or object to it. Some attorneys list the interrogatory question and then the response when responding to written interrogatories.

Objections to Questions.   If the individual objects to a question based on any of the allowed privileges, the responding party must specifically claim each privilege separately. The responding party's attorney and the party must sign any answers in which objections occur. If no objections are raised in the answers, the party responding must sign under oath.

Requests for Admission.   A **request for admission** is served only on a party to the action. The request asks the opposing party to admit any points that are not in dispute and do not have to be litigated. The plaintiff may serve a set of requests asking the defendant to admit each and every allegation in the complaint. For example, the party may be asked to admit that a document is genuine, that relevant facts or opinions are true, or that the law is applied to the facts truthfully.

Requests for admission have their own time lines. Review the law in your state to determine when these requests must be filed, the number of requests allowed, and the number of days the other party has to answer, and complete the following box.

STATE-SPECIFIC INFORMATION

In the state of _____, requests for admission must be filed at least _____ days after the summons is served. Each party may prepare up to _____ requests to the other party. The other party has _____ days to answer.

Other rules for this state for requests for admission follow:

_____

_____

_____

Demands for Inspection (or Requests for Production).   **Demands for inspection** allow parties to examine physical evidence that is within the other party's control. This may include documents or other items. There is usually no limit to the number of demands that may be served. Parties may examine and copy documents or inspect, photograph, and perform tests on other tangible evidence. Real property may be entered, measured, photographed, or otherwise tested pursuant to a demand for inspection. Responses to a demand for inspection must be served within a specified number of days of the date of service, usually 20 to 30. In some states, the demand for inspection is called a *request for production*.

Demands for Physical Examination

Demands for physical examination are typically made by defendants of personal-injury plaintiffs. Only one examination is usually allowed, and it must be scheduled within a set distance of the plaintiff's residence. The plaintiff has a certain number of days to comply with the defendant's demand as well as to respond to the defendant's demand.

Some states require a motion to be filed with the court requesting an examination. Additional requirements may be found in each state's laws; research the law in your state and complete the following box.

request for admission   the request of a party to admit points not in dispute

demand for inspection   one party's demand on the other party to inspect records or documents relevant to the case

STATE-SPECIFIC INFORMATION

In the state of _____, the plaintiff has _____ days to comply with the defendant's demand for medical examination and _____ days to respond to the defendant's demand. A motion must be filed with the court requesting this examination under the following circumstances:

_____

_____

_____

Subpoenas

To force a party or witness to appear at a deposition or other proceeding, you may issue a **subpoena**, which is signed by the judge and orders the person to appear at the designated time and place. Because a subpoena is a court-issued document, a person may be held in contempt of court for failure to appear and may also be required to pay damages. The witness is usually paid witness fees and mileage. Most states require the subpoena to be served in person, and proof of service must be filed with the court. If the individual is required to bring any items to the proceeding, the subpoena is called a *subpoena duces tecum*. Materials must be listed on the form and may be letters, documents, payroll records, or any other tangible items that may be used as evidence. A subpoena that is issued to require the individual to appear at a deposition is known as a *deposition subpoena*.

Stipulations

Stipulations are agreements made between the attorneys and binding on the parties to the action. A stipulation may be in the form of a written document or may be made in open court. The most common stipulations relate to extending time or amending pleadings.

Arbitration and Mediation

Many states either encourage or require the parties to submit to arbitration or mediation to attempt to settle the case without a trial. *Arbitration* involves the appointment of a third party to hear both sides of the issue and reach a judgment on behalf of the parties. In most such cases, the parties agree to mandatory arbitration and the ruling of the arbitrator is final. *Mediation* involves the appointment of a neutral third party to help the plaintiff and the defendant reach a settlement of their disputes that will be agreeable to both parties.

Mandatory Settlement Conference

Most states have some sort of settlement conference among the attorneys and judge before the trial. At these conferences, the judge helps

subpoena   a formal court document issued by the court to order a person's appearance

the attorneys resolve as many issues as possible. Many cases actually settle at this time.

If the case reaches final settlement, it is *dismissed with prejudice,* meaning that the plaintiff may not file a suit in the same action at a later date. If the case is *dismissed without prejudice,* the plaintiff may file the suit again later within the statute of limitations.

TRIAL PROCEDURES

During the trial phase, the legal assistant prepares of the *trial book,* which contains all pertinent information on the case. Exhibit 5-9 shows a sample trial book for a civil case. Notebooks with tabs may be purchased from vendors that specialize in litigation materials. Additional tabs may be added for key documents and expert witnesses.

One item not noted in the trial book is a jury selection chart, shown in Exhibit 5-10. This chart consists of a blank page with space for 12 self-stick notes to use when selecting the jury. The attorney and legal assistant may make notes on each prospective juror being questioned for later approval or challenge.

AFTER THE TRIAL

Enforcing Judgments

If the plaintiff wins the suit but is not aware of the defendant's assets, a supplementary proceeding known as an *examination of judgment debtor* may be held, at which the defendant appears and testifies about his assets.

After the hearing a *writ of execution* or *writ of possession* may be filed against the defendant's assets notifying the defendant that unless he pays the judgment within the specified time frame, the sheriff or marshal will take possession of the property and sell it at a public sale. The proceeds will be used to pay the judgment. Any money left over will be returned to the defendant. This writ may be filed against real or personal property.

If the defendant has no attachable assets, the plaintiff may file a *garnishment* against the defendant's wages. A certain percentage of the defendant's salary will be paid to the plaintiff each pay period until the judgment is satisfied.

Appeals

The losing party in a civil action may appeal the decision to a higher court. The individual or entity that appeals is known as the *appellant;* the individual or entity against whom the appeal is taken is known as the *appellee.*

Strict guidelines apply to the filing of appellate briefs, which are usually prepared by a printing company that specializes in this service. Local and state court rules should be examined and followed. The legal

EXHIBIT 5-9   Sample Trial Book—Civil Case

Reprinted by permission from Bindertek.

LawFiles Civil Trial Notebook™

——————— *Contents* ———————

Section 1: Trial Preparation

- White tabs for research, briefs, orders, trial administration and strategies

- Green tabs for pleading, discovery and damages

Section 2: Trial

- Purple tabs for motions in limine, jury selection and opening statement

- Yellow tabs for testimony; includes witness and exhibits lists, plaintiff's and defense witnesses

- Pink tabs for trial motions, closing argument, jury instructions and verdict

10 Write-on Tabs are provided for witness names or to add supplemental categories of information.
Use ball point pen, pencil or Sharpie marker

6 Trial Forms are to assist in preparation and through trial:

- Deadlines/To Do
- Witness Address and Phone List
- Deposition Summary
- Juror Profile
- Jury Selection Chart
- Exhibits List

These forms are to be kept as masters. Photocopy as needed.

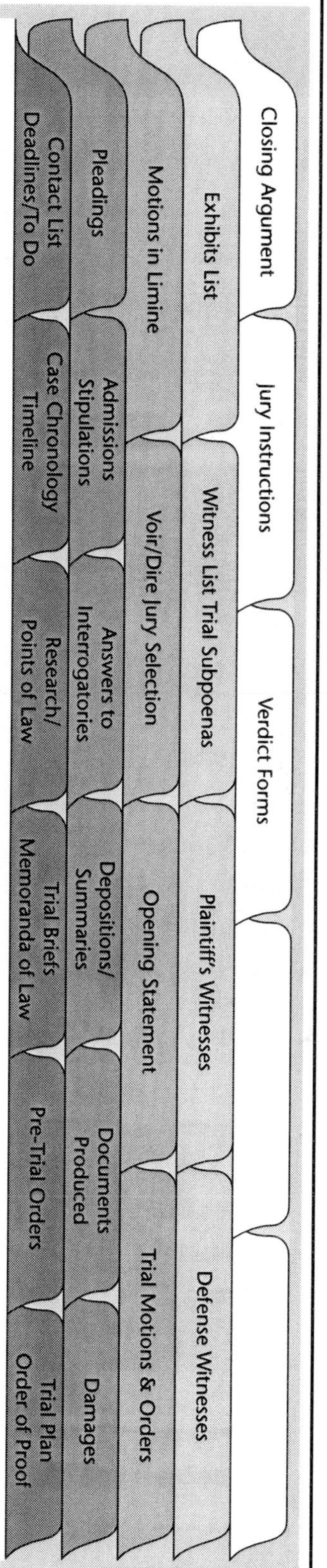

Tabs (right side):
- Contact List Deadlines/To Do — Case Chronology Timeline
- Pleadings — Admissions Stipulations — Research/Points of Law — Trial Briefs Memoranda of Law — Pre-Trial Orders — Trial Plan Order of Proof
- Motions in Limine — Voir/Dire Jury Selection — Answers to Interrogatories — Depositions/Summaries — Documents Produced — Damages
- Exhibits List — Witness List Trial Subpoenas — Opening Statement — Plaintiff's Witnesses — Trial Motions & Orders — Defense Witnesses
- Closing Argument — Jury Instructions — Verdict Forms

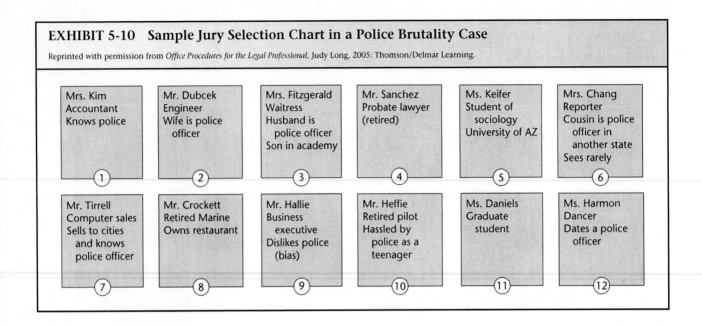

EXHIBIT 5-10   Sample Jury Selection Chart in a Police Brutality Case

Reprinted with permission from *Office Procedures for the Legal Professional*, Judy Long, 2005: Thomson/Delmar Learning.

assistant should proofread the brief carefully when the printer returns the first draft. Especially significant is checking all citations to be sure they are correct. All cases used in the brief should be Shepardized to be certain none of them have been overruled.

● KEY TERMS

cause of action	guardian ad litem
chattel	jurisdiction
complaint	minor
consent	motion to strike
cross-complaint	points and authorities
default judgment	request for admission
demand for inspection	statute of limitations
demurrer	subpoena
deponent	summary judgment
deposition	venue
discovery	written interrogatories

● SELF TEST

1. What are the major discovery documents, and why is each of them used?
2. Explain the responsibilities of the legal assistant during the discovery phase.
3. List the items that are included in the trial book.

● NOTEBOOK PROJECTS

1. Interview a local civil litigation attorney and obtain samples of documents used in a civil case for your notebook.

2. Write a memorandum to your instructor explaining the time lines for all discovery documents in your state.

3. Prepare a list of items included in the trial book. Use additional items not listed in the text.

4. Complete all State-Specific Information boxes in this chapter and include them in your notebook under the appropriate headings.

For additional resources, visit our Web site at **www.paralegal.delmar.cengage.com**.

CRIMINAL LAW

CHAPTER OUTCOMES

After studying this chapter, the student will understand

1. the difference between civil and criminal law.
2. the elements of a crime.
3. the different types of crimes.
4. the rights of defendants and defenses to crimes.
5. the basic procedures followed from arrest to trial and sentencing.

DIFFERENCES BETWEEN CIVIL AND CRIMINAL LAW

Civil law deals with the rights and responsibilities of individuals when dealing with others. *Criminal law* deals with wrongs against society in general. When an individual is prosecuted for committing a crime, the case is called *The People v. Samuel Jones,* whereas in a civil lawsuit, the case is called *Joan Sanchez v. Samuel Jones.* Although Joan Sanchez may be the victim in the criminal case, she is not considered the plaintiff because the crime exists against society as a whole. For example, suppose Samuel Jones beat Joan Sanchez and injured her severely. The criminal action against him may result in punishment that includes time in prison, while in the civil action Joan Sanchez would sue for money damages for her injuries.

In a civil action, private attorneys represent both the plaintiff and the defendant. Criminal actions are prosecuted by district attorneys or prosecuting attorneys who are employed by the state in which the crime occurred. In some cases, the defendant is prosecuted for committing a federal crime, which would be prosecuted by the federal prosecuting attorney. The defendant in a criminal action is represented by a private attorney or a public defender (if she cannot afford to pay for a private attorney).

Criminal law also has a different objective from civil law. The purpose of prosecuting individuals for committing crimes is to prevent behavior that society has determined is unacceptable and to punish individuals who commit these unacceptable acts. However, the objective of civil law is to compensate individuals who are injured by another's wrongful act.

CRIMINAL LAW AND CRIMINAL PROCEDURE

The various areas of law are distinguished by whether they are substantive or procedural. *Substantive law* defines rights and obligations; *procedural law* determines the procedures followed to enforce those rights and obligations. For instance, the substantive criminal law defines the elements of the individual crimes and determines what acts are prohibited and what the punishment is for committing those acts. Criminal procedure defines the procedures followed to bring defendants to justice. It commences with the police investigation of the criminal act and continues through the justice process of arrest, arraignment, preliminary hearing, trial, and sentencing.

Many of the laws of criminal procedure are established by the United States Constitution as well as the various state constitutions. Many of these laws relate to the rights of the accused and the obligations of the police to protect these rights. For instance, an individual may not be subjected to unreasonable search and seizure, which is a right protected by the United States Constitution.

ELEMENTS OF A CRIME

Criminal acts can be divided between felonies and misdemeanors, depending on the nature of the crime itself. *Felonies* are serious crimes that expose the defendant to imprisonment for more than one year, generally in state prison. If the felony violates federal law (for example, drug trafficking), the defendant may be incarcerated in federal prison. Murder, manslaughter, kidnapping, robbery, arson, rape, and burglary are all felonies.

A *misdemeanor* is a less serious crime that is punishable by incarceration in the county jail for up to one year. Petty theft, malicious mischief, and simple assault are examples of misdemeanors.

Most crimes consist of two elements: the criminal intent and the act itself. If you have the desire to steal an automobile but never commit the act of stealing the car, then no crime has occurred. Mere intent does not constitute a crime. Some crimes, however, do not require intent; for example, statutory rape, or sexual intercourse with a minor, is a crime even if the defendant did not know the individual was a minor.

Not all offenses are considered crimes. An *infraction* is an offense that does not constitute a crime and is punishable by a fine. Many traffic violations are considered infractions. For example, if you park your car in a no-parking zone, you may get a ticket and pay a fine, but you will not go to jail unless you fail to pay the fines to the point that a warrant is issued for your arrest.

CATEGORIES OF CRIMES

Crimes are categorized by crimes against the person, the public, the public order, or property. The most serious crimes are those against the person.

Crimes against the Person

Crimes directed against an individual are known as *crimes against the person* and include the following:

Homicide. *Homicide* is the unlawful killing of another without justification. It can be broken down into first-degree murder, second-degree murder, and manslaughter. *First-degree murder* is an intentional killing or a death under the *felony murder rule* doctrine. Under the felony murder rule, if a death occurs during the commission of a serious felony, all defendants involved in the felony may be found guilty of first-degree murder, regardless of which of them caused the death. Premeditated murder, poisoning, and murder by torture are examples of first-degree murder. Other crimes that may be included by different states in the felony murder rule include kidnapping, torture, and robbery. *Second-degree murder* includes any intentional killing not classified as first-degree murder. *Manslaughter* generally involves killing someone without actual criminal intent, such as during a fight or during the "heat of passion."

Special Circumstances Rule. Some states have adopted the *special circumstances rule* for capital punishment cases. If the victim died during the commission of a kidnapping, torture, or other enumerated felony, the defendant may receive capital punishment for the commission of the crime. The circumstances for this rule vary by state, and it is used only in states that allow capital punishment. Some states also follow the special circumstances rule for defendants who aided or abetted the commission with the intent to kill or with reckless indifference to human life if they were major participants in the crime. These rules vary considerably from state to state. Research the rules for your state and complete the following box.

STATE-SPECIFIC INFORMATION

Definition of murder in the _____ state statutes:

_____

_____

_____

Felony murder rule:

_____

_____

_____

Special circumstances rule:

_____

_____

_____

> The state of _____ (allows / does not allow) capital punishment. The crime must have the following elements to be eligible for capital punishment:
>
> _____
>
> _____
>
> _____

Mayhem. Most states define *mayhem* as the permanent disfigurement of another. It includes the loss of a limb, eye, or other part of the body. The act must be purposeful and intentional; that is, one must have the intent and actually commit the act.

Rape or Sexual Assault. A forcible sexual attack constitutes *rape* in most states. Some states use the term *sexual assault* instead of rape. It may be further defined as sexual intercourse with a person without consent. Most state laws consider any sexual activity with a minor to be statutory rape, even if the minor consented to the act. All states have instituted laws against child molestation. Sexual activity with children is forbidden, even if no rape occurred.

Assault and Battery. An **assault** is an attempted battery in criminal law. Once the battery is successful, the perpetrator may be charged with both. **Battery** is the harmful or offensive touching of another without consent. Most states consider battery with a weapon a more serious crime than battery without a weapon. If an individual is deliberately attacked with a weapon but not killed, the crime may escalate to attempted murder. A defendant who attempts a battery but does not succeed may be charged with assault. In some states, once the battery is completed, the assault merges into the battery and the defendant is charged only with battery.

Kidnapping. The transportation of an individual from one place to another against her will is *kidnapping*. In many states, transporting the victim only a few feet may be sufficient to constitute the crime. If an individual is taken across state lines, the kidnapping escalates to a federal crime.

Crimes against the Public

Crimes against the public are categorized into two groups: crimes against public morality and crimes against public order. Examples of crimes against public morality include the following:

Prostitution. *Prostitution* is the providing of sexual favors in exchange for money. It is illegal in all states except certain counties in Nevada.

Indecent Exposure. The intentional exposure of private parts of the body in a public place constitutes *indecent exposure*. Nude dancing is an example.

assault an attempted battery

battery harmful or offensive touching of another without consent

Obscenity. Although purveyors of pornography use their First Amendment rights to challenge charges of *obscenity,* the United States Supreme Court has consistently held that it is not protected speech. In a landmark case in California in 1973,[1] the Court established the following definition for obscenity; it uses these standards when cases are appealed based on free speech issues.

In order to be considered obscene, the material in question must

1. appeal to the prurient interest.
2. show offensive sexual conduct as defined by applicable state law.
3. lack serious literary, artistic, political, or scientific value.

All elements must be present for the material to be considered obscene.

The laws against child pornography are considerably more stringent. All exploitation of children is prohibited.

Crimes against the Public Order

Offenses that disturb the orderly running of society are considered crimes against the public order and include the following:

Rioting. When a group of individuals behave in a disorderly manner, their actions may constitute a *riot.* In most states a riot must involve a large number of people who refuse to disperse when commanded to do so by the police. The rioters may be arrested and charged with rioting.

Disorderly Conduct. A less serious crime than rioting and one that is not as outrageous is *disorderly conduct.* It may include playing loud music late at night, being very loud in a public place, or committing an act that disturbs the peaceful environment of others.

Drug Sales. The sale and use of illicit drugs is illegal in all states. *Drug trafficking* has become a serious problem in today's society. The federal government has enacted drug-trafficking statutes in an attempt to stop drug smuggling. As of the writing of this text, some states have enacted laws that allow medicinal distribution of marijuana. A considerable amount of controversy exists in the medical community about these new laws, which may be overturned by the time this book is published. Research the law in your state to determine whether such a statute exists.

STATE-SPECIFIC INFORMATION

The state of _____ (has / has not) enacted legislation allowing the use of marijuana for medicinal purposes. Medical use of marijuana is permitted under the following circumstances:

_____

_____

_____

---

[1] *Miller v. California,* 413 U.S. 15 (1973)

Crimes against Property

Most crimes against property involve unlawfully taking the property of another by stealing, force, fire, or deceit. The most serious crime against property is **arson**, which is the unlawful and intentional burning of another's property. In many states, the property must be a house or other building. Arson has been extended in most states to include burning one's own house or building if the purpose is to defraud an insurance company.

Burglary is the unlawful entry of another's building with the intent to commit a felony within the building. In some states, unlawful entry with intent to commit a misdemeanor is also considered burglary.

Robbery is the taking of another's property from her person by threat or force. A person who threatens a storekeeper in order to get money from the cash register may be committing a robbery.

Other types of theft are also considered criminal acts. These crimes may also lead to imprisonment. Students who are interested in learning more about specific criminal acts are encouraged to enroll in a course in criminal law and procedures.

Federal Crimes. Title 18 of the United States Code describes the federal crimes. An individual may be prosecuted in federal court if she commits a violation of federal law or a crime on federal property. Some of the more common federal crimes involve controlled substance violations, immigration law violations, mail or wire fraud, bank robbery, violation of gun laws, postal offenses, child pornography, counterfeiting, and crimes that occur on federal property or in federal buildings. Other significant federal crimes include terrorism, cybercrime, public corruption, civil rights violations, organized crime and racketeering, and white-collar crime. Procedures in federal court differ somewhat from those used in the various state courts. Federal court procedures may be found on the United States courts Web site:

http://www.uscourts.com

DEFENSES

Although a defendant may have committed the crime of which she is accused, a number of defenses provide an excuse for the commission of the crime. Of course, the most common defense is that the defendant did not commit the crime of which she is accused. Other common defenses include the following.

Self-Defense

A defendant who pleads self-defense must prove that she was actually defending herself from the victim. She may not use more force to defend herself than is reasonable or more than was used by the other

arson intentional burning of another's home, structure, or building

burglary unlawful entry of a building of another with the intent to commit a felony therein

party. For instance, if Joan slapped Chris, Chris may not shoot Joan and claim self-defense. One may use deadly force only to defend one's person and not her property, and only if the deadly force is also used by the other party.

Defense of Others

The defendant must prove that the individual being defended was not the aggressor. A person may not use more force than was being used by the other person and may not use deadly force unless deadly force was being used against the person being defended. Deadly force may not be used in defense of property.

Insanity

The insanity defense and its parameters vary by state. In general, the defendant must prove that when the crime was committed, she was not capable of understanding the nature of the criminal act or that it was wrong. Determine the rules in your state and complete the following box.

> STATE-SPECIFIC INFORMATION
>
> In the state of _____ , the defendant must prove the following elements to prevail with an insanity defense:
>
> _____
>
> _____
>
> _____

Temporary Insanity

In general, the defendant must prove that she was legally insane at the time the crime was committed but later regained her sanity. The rules for temporary insanity vary greatly by state; research the rules for your state and complete the following box.

> STATE-SPECIFIC INFORMATION
>
> In the state of _____ , the defendant must prove the following elements to prevail with a temporary insanity defense:
>
> _____
>
> _____
>
> _____

Coercion

The defendant must prove that she committed the crime only under compulsion from another, who used threats or force to compel her to commit the crime. She must show that had it not been for the threats or force, she would not have committed the criminal act.

Entrapment

This defense is similar to the coercion defense, but the coercion must have been committed by a police officer. For the defense to succeed, the crime must have been initiated by the officer and not the defendant. A person may also be entrapped by someone who was directed to do so by a police officer. The defendant must show that had it not been for this coercion, she would not have committed the crime.

Constitutional Defenses

Several defenses arise from the United States Constitution, and from the state constitutions as well. A few of the most critical defenses are described next.

Double Jeopardy.   The Fifth Amendment to the United States Constitution prohibits a second trial or punishment for the same offense, provided that the defendant has entered a guilty plea that has been accepted by the court, or the first witness has been sworn in at the trial. Note that if the judge has declared a mistrial, double jeopardy does not occur. For instance, if at the conclusion of the presentation of evidence, the jury deliberates and cannot reach a unanimous verdict, the judge may declare a mistrial and the defendant may be retried. Although the Fifth Amendment applies to the states through the Fourteenth Amendment, the defendant may be punished by two different jurisdictions for the same crime. For instance, the defendant may be tried in federal and state court for a bank robbery.

Ex Post Facto Law.   If a law is passed after the defendant committed an act that was not unlawful prior to the passage of the law, the defendant may not be punished. Likewise, the defendant may not receive a more severe punishment if a new law is passed making her crime a more serious one after she commits the crime.

First Amendment—Free Speech.   The First Amendment protects people in their speech and religious practices. The government may not interfere with the exercise of free speech unless an individual is inciting to riot. Several types of statements are not protected, however, such as slander, libel, and fighting words.

First Amendment—Freedom of Religion.   The government may not make a law that establishes religion or one that interferes with an individual's right to practice the religion of her choice. Certain acts will not receive government protection, however, based on a balancing act of the nature of the government's interest in prohibiting the act and the degree of intrusion against the individual. For instance, the Mormon practice of polygamy has been prohibited, as has the use of illegal drugs as part of a religious ceremony. Again, the courts use a balancing act weighing government interest against infringement of the rights of the individual.

CRIMINAL PROCEDURES

Various procedures exist in the criminal justice process once an individual commits a crime. The procedures from arrest through trial and sentencing are described next. Legal assistants may be involved in a number of procedural issues as the case is moved through the criminal justice system.

Arrest

In most cases, a police investigation determines whether an individual is arrested for the commission of a crime. If the police officer actually sees the perpetrator commit the crime, the officer may arrest the person without a warrant because probable cause exists; that is, the police officer has cause to reasonably believe the individual committed the criminal act because she personally saw it being committed.

Once the police have enough evidence to arrest a suspect, that person is taken into custody, transported to the police station, fingerprinted, photographed, and charged with the crime (booked).

Interview and Investigation

Before interrogating a suspect, the police must inform her that she has a right to have her attorney present. At this point, defendants usually call their attorneys. Paralegals or legal assistants employed by criminal defense attorneys may be required to interview clients who are in custody. Paralegals or legal assistants employed by the prosecution may be required to investigate the defendant's background, prior arrests and/or convictions, and alibi. You may have to search out witnesses to the crime, possibly visiting the neighborhood where the crime was committed.

Arraignment

arraignment a hearing in which the defendant is brought before a judge to hear the charges against her and to enter a plea

The defendant attends an **arraignment,** in which she is brought before a judge to hear the charges against her and to enter a plea of guilty, not guilty, or *nolo contendere* (a plea in which the defendant does not admit guilt but also does not contest the charges). If the defendant cannot afford an attorney, the court appoints a public defender to represent her. The judge may allow the accused to post bail to get out of jail or may allow an *OR* (own recognizance) *release* if the defendant has ties to the community and is not accused of a violent felony.

Burden of Proof

The prosecution has the burden of proving "beyond a reasonable doubt" that the defendant is guilty. Note that this is a much heavier burden than the proof required in a civil trial, which is "a preponderance of the evidence."

In a civil trial, the plaintiff must prove that the defendant is liable for the act of which she is accused by a preponderance of the evidence. This means that the jury must be satisfied that it is more likely that the defendant committed the act than that she did not commit it. Therefore, if a jury member is 51 percent sure that the defendant in a civil case committed the act, she may find her liable and rule in favor of the plaintiff. If the majority of the jury rules in this manner, the defendant will be found liable.

Criminal cases, however, are more difficult to prove because of the higher burden of proof "beyond a reasonable doubt." This means that the jury must acquit if there is sufficient doubt of the defendant's guilt that a reasonable person would question whether she is guilty. A guilty verdict does not mean that there is no doubt in the jury's mind that the defendant is guilty, because there is always some doubt. The standard is difficult to quantify, but it has been said to be greater than the 51 percent required in a civil trial but not quite the 100 percent required if there is no doubt.

A criminal defendant is presumed to be innocent until she is proven guilty. The criminal defendant is not required to prove her innocence and cannot be required to testify at her own trial. The prosecution may not make reference to the jury that the defendant did not testify. However, if the accused chooses to testify, then the prosecuting attorney may subject her to full cross-examination.

Plea Bargaining

Because many states have overcrowded prisons, a defendant may be given the opportunity to plead guilty to a lesser offense and have the charges reduced from a serious felony to a less serious one or from a felony to a misdemeanor. This process is known as **plea bargaining.** Plea bargaining may also occur if the prosecuting attorney does not think the evidence is strong enough to sustain a guilty verdict, or if the defendant has information that is more critical to the prosecution and the prosecution wishes to trade this information for a plea to a lesser charge. The defendant may then receive a shorter sentence in state prison, less time in county jail, or even probation.

Plea bargaining has been the subject of considerable debate. Proponents say it saves money and helps alleviate the court's workload by reducing the number of cases that must go to trial. It also enables a defendant to be found guilty without the prosecution having to prove her guilt at trial. In addition, in some cases the defendant may implicate

plea bargaining   pleading guilty to a lesser offense with less jail time than the original offense

others in exchange for a plea bargain. Then the prosecution can bring charges against the other perpetrators.

Opponents of plea bargaining say that it allows repeat offenders to be freed more quickly and, in some cases, to commit the same crimes again. Whatever its advantages and disadvantages, plea bargaining is used in most states, especially those with high crime rates and crowded prisons.

To plea-bargain effectively, both the prosecutor and the defense attorney must be well prepared for the discussions. The more evidence the prosecution has amassed against the accused, the better the prosecutor can argue that the defendant should plead guilty to a more serious charge. Similarly, the more thoroughly the defense attorney has prepared her case, the better the plea bargain she can get for her client. In most cases, plea bargains are used with guilty defendants.

Grand Jury

Some states have *grand juries* instead of **preliminary hearings** to determine whether the prosecution has sufficient evidence to hold the defendant over for trial. The prosecutor presents evidence to the grand jury, but the defendant is not present and is not given an opportunity to present a defense. The prosecutor can call witnesses, who usually must appear before the grand jury without an attorney. After hearing the evidence, the grand jury decides whether to hand down an *indictment*. If it does so, the defendant is held over for trial. Some states call a grand jury only in cases of major significance that have been well publicized.

Constitutional Trial Rights of the Accused

The United States Constitution protects criminal defendants and gives certain rights to the accused. The Sixth Amendment grants many rights to the defendant; these rights are extended to the states by the Fourteenth Amendment. These rights are enumerated next.

Right to Counsel. The Sixth Amendment guarantees the *right to counsel* to all criminal defendants. This is one of the most basic rights guaranteed to the accused. Present-day defendants who cannot afford to pay for a private attorney may obtain the services of the public defender. In cases as early as 1923[2] the Supreme Court recognized the constitutional right to appointed counsel for indigent defendants. However, in this case the Court ruled that the absence of counsel deprived the defendants of a fair trial and violated their due process rights under the Fourteenth Amendment. However, this case was applicable only to capital cases with indigent defendants. The right was extended to include all state felony prosecutions in 1963[3] and again in 2002 to include defendants whose prison sentences are reduced to probation.[4]

Not only are defendants guaranteed the right to counsel, but they are also entitled to the effective assistance of counsel as well. A defendant

preliminary hearing
a hearing in court to determine whether there is enough evidence to hold the defendant over for trial

[2]*Powell v. Alabama*, 287 U.S. 45 (1923)
[3]*Gideon v. Wainwright*, 372 U.S. 335 (1963)
[4]*Alabama v. Shelton*, 122 S. Ct. 1764 (2002)

who is convicted and claims that she received ineffective representation must prove on appeal that the attorney was extremely inadequate and that the defendant was harmed by this representation. Most of these cases fail unless the defendant can prove that she was actually convicted because of this inadequate counsel.

The Supreme Court gave defendants the right to represent themselves in 1975.[5] The Court held that the defendant's right to choose is more critical than having attorney representation. The judge at trial generally queries the defendant to be sure that she is representing herself voluntarily and that she has not been coerced into doing so. The judge explains to the defendant all of the disadvantages of representing herself. In most cases, the judge appoints an attorney to assist the defendant in her defense or to assume responsibility for the case if the defendant engages in unruly behavior in the courtroom.

Right to Public Trial by Jury.   The United States Constitution guarantees defendants the *right to a public trial*. The judge, however, may exclude individuals who become unruly or disrupt the proceedings. On rare occasions, the judge may exclude the public from the trial.

The Sixth Amendment guarantees the defendant the *right to a jury trial* in felony cases. Some states have extended this right to misdemeanor cases as well. Exceptions include military trials and juvenile court. Although most states require a unanimous verdict of the jury in a criminal case, there is no constitutional requirement for this unity. Most states require twelve jurors in criminal matters, along with unanimous verdicts. However, the Supreme Court has held that agreement of nine jurors of a twelve-person jury is adequate for conviction in a criminal case.

Speedy Trial Rights.   The defendant is guaranteed the *right to a speedy trial*. However, the constitution does not enumerate the exact time frame required. Many states require that the defendant be tried within six months of being charged with a crime. The federal statute requires that the defendant be formally charged within thirty days from the date of arrest and tried within seventy days of the later of indictment or the defendant's initial appearance before the court. Several exceptions to this rule exist, including the postponement of the trial by the defendant's attorney. Determine the requirements in your state and complete the following box.

STATE-SPECIFIC INFORMATION

The defendant's rights to a speedy trial in the state of _____ are as follows:

_____

_____

_____

---

[5]*Faretta v. California*, 422 U.S. 806 (1975)

Protection from Self-Incrimination. The Fifth Amendment of the United States Constitution protects individuals from incriminating themselves. No person on the witness stand can be forced to incriminate herself; *pleading the fifth* means that the defendant (or witness in court) is refusing to answer a question because of her right not to incriminate herself.

Trial and Sentencing

The defendant has the opportunity to choose whether to have the case heard by a judge or jury. A few states allow only the prosecuting attorney to seek a jury trial. In order to prove the defendant guilty, the judge or jury must find that the evidence shows guilt beyond a reasonable doubt, which is a very high standard. In most states, the verdict must be unanimous (all twelve jurors must agree on the defendant's guilt). Oregon allows a guilty verdict if ten out of the twelve jurors agree, while Louisiana allows a guilty verdict if only nine of the twelve agree.

The prosecution presents its *case in chief* first. The prosecution witnesses testify, and each witness may be *cross-examined* by the defense attorney. The defense attorney may cross-examine the witness only about the matters brought up during *direct examination* by the prosecuting attorney. After the cross-examination, the prosecution may conduct *redirect examination* of the witness, but only about matters brought out during cross-examination. The defense attorney may then conduct *recross-examination,* in which she asks questions about only what was brought out during redirect examination. Think of this testimony of witnesses as a series of boxes that get smaller and smaller each time that witness is asked questions (Exhibit 6-1). The largest box is direct examination.

After the prosecution has questioned all of her witnesses, it is the defense's turn to put on her case in chief. The defense attorney calls

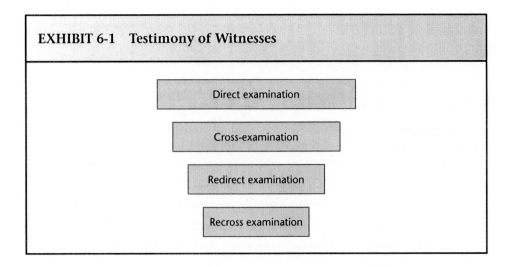

EXHIBIT 6-1   Testimony of Witnesses

Direct examination

Cross-examination

Redirect examination

Recross examination

each defense witness to the stand for questioning just as the prosecuting attorney did previously with the prosecution witnesses.

During the witness testimony on both sides, the attorneys introduce items into evidence by having them *authenticated* by the witness. That is, the witness must be able to say that the evidence is what it purports to be. For instance, a police officer who is a prosecution witness in a murder case might be asked to identify a weapon that she found at the scene. Once the weapon has been properly identified, the attorney will ask the judge if she can offer it into evidence as an *exhibit.* No evidence may be introduced at trial unless there is some method of authentication through a witness.

In addition to authenticating an item for evidence, the witness might be asked to prove the *chain of custody* of that item. For instance, if the police officer placed the weapon into a sealed container, then initialed and dated the container, it would be an appropriate method of proving chain of custody. But if the police officer carelessly placed the weapon in her desk drawer without preserving it in some manner, the court generally does not allow the evidence to be introduced into the trial because chain of custody has not been proven.

Once all witnesses have testified and all evidence has been introduced, each attorney gives closing arguments to the jury or judge. If there is a jury, the members go into the jury room to deliberate their decision and render a verdict. In a judge trial, the judge either renders a verdict immediately or adjourns until she has reached a verdict.

The sentencing phase follows a guilty verdict. If the verdict is *not guilty,* the defendant may be released unless the judge overrules the jury and renders a *judgment notwithstanding the verdict,* which is very rare. In this situation, the judge overrules the jury's verdict because she does not think that the jury applied the law properly to the case. In most states, the judge hands down the sentence to the guilty defendant. However, some states allow juries to impose the sentence. At the sentencing phase, the defendant may present character witnesses in an attempt to persuade the judge to impose a lighter sentence. A report indicating whether the defendant might successfully be released on probation may also be submitted as part of the sentencing recommendations.

Hung Jury.   If the jury is divided and cannot agree on a verdict (or, in states that allow nonunanimous verdicts, less than the required number agree), a *hung jury* results. In this case, the defendant is found neither guilty nor not guilty. States use various procedures when a hung jury results, but usually the district attorney or prosecuting attorney has the option of retrying the defendant. In that case, a new trial is conducted with a new jury.

Double jeopardy does not attach in a case that has a hung jury because the case did not reach a final conclusion, which would have been a verdict by the judge or the jury. If the defendant had been found not guilty, she could not have been retried because double jeopardy would result.

Appeals

Only death penalty cases are automatically appealable to the state's highest court, which is usually called the *state supreme court.* Some states have different names for their highest court. Find out your state courts' names and complete the following box.

STATE-SPECIFIC INFORMATION

The court names for the state of _____ are as follows:

Trial courts:

_____

Appeals courts:

_____

Highest state court:

_____

● KEY TERMS

arraignment

arson

assault

battery

burglary

plea bargaining

preliminary hearing

● SELF TEST

1. List five felonies in your state.
2. Define the felonies listed in question 1.
3. What is the difference between burglary and robbery?
4. Why do defendants enter into plea-bargain agreements?
5. List the steps in the trial process.

● NOTEBOOK PROJECTS

1. List the procedures that are followed at each stage after the defendant is arrested and define each one.

2. Interview a prosecuting attorney about her use of a legal assistant. Ascertain the duties and responsibilities of the legal assistant in the prosecuting attorney's office, and write a report to your instructor about the interview.

3. Interview a criminal defense attorney about her use of a legal assistant. List the duties and responsibilities of the legal assistant.

4. Complete all State-Specific Information boxes in this chapter and file them in your notebook.

   For additional resources, visit our Web site at **www.paralegal.delmar.cengage.com.**

FAMILY LAW

CHAPTER OUTCOMES

After studying this chapter, the student will understand

1. the requirements for a valid marriage.
2. how to draft documents required for divorce and dissolution.
3. the terminology and definitions for divorce and dissolution.
4. the law surrounding adoptions.

INTRODUCTION

Family law encompasses a broad area that includes domestic relations issues such as annulment, divorce, dissolution, and adoption. However, most family law offices specialize in divorce or dissolution and the various issues surrounding them, such as abuse, support, custody, and visitation. Although earlier courts usually awarded custody of the children to the mother when a couple obtained a divorce or dissolution, many courts offer some type of joint custody: joint legal custody, joint physical custody, or both.

BEFORE MARRIAGE

Before individuals marry, they may wish to enter into an agreement that provides for the disposition of the property of the two individuals if they obtain a divorce or dissolution, or upon the death of one of the parties. These contracts, called *prenuptial agreements,* must be signed by both parties to be valid. If the parties enter into the contract after they are married, it is called a *postnuptial agreement.* A sample prenuptial agreement is shown in Exhibit 7-1.

MARRIAGE

marriage the legal union of a man and a woman as husband and wife in most states and of a couple of either sex in other states

In most states, **marriage** is the legal union of a man and woman as husband and wife in a formal ceremony. However, some states allow civil unions between partners of the same sex. The ceremony may be performed by a minister, priest, rabbi, judge, or justice of the peace. A marriage license is issued and becomes a binding agreement between the parties. Each state has different requirements for a valid marriage. Many

EXHIBIT 7-1   Prenuptial Agreement

This Prenuptial Agreement is entered into this 27th day of June, 2007, by and between DANIELLA MARIE GALLO and WILLIAM JEFFREY MICHAELS, of San Francisco, California, in contemplation of the marriage of the parties. This agreement shall become effective upon the date of the contemplated marriage of the parties.

This agreement is being made on the basis of the parties' contemplated marriage on December 20, 2008. Neither party has been previously married. Both parties wish to define their rights and responsibilities regarding property and finances.

In consideration of the contemplated marriage between the parties and other consideration enumerated below, the parties agree:

1. REVOCATION

   If the parties wish to revoke this agreement, they must prepare a writing signed by both parties.

2. RELATED INSTRUMENTS

   Additional instruments required to accomplish the intent of this agreement shall be promptly delivered, executed, and acknowledged, at the request of the other party on a timely basis.

3. DISCLOSURES

   Each of the parties to this agreement is of lawful age and competent to enter into a contract. Neither party knows of any reasons why he or she may not enter into the contemplated marriage. Both parties enter into this agreement voluntarily and without duress or coercion.

   Both parties are fully aware of all terms and provisions of this agreement. Each party has disclosed to the other prior to signing this agreement the extent and value of their individual property interests described herein. Each party has fully divulged to the other party the extent of their financial holdings and the respective value of each holding described herein. All properties described herein represent a full and complete enumeration of their respective property interests as of this date.

4. TAX LIABILITY

   No clause in this agreement shall waive the right of either party to report income for federal or state tax purposes in the manner permissible for any other spouses. No rights are hereby waived under the Federal Gift Tax Laws or the Federal Estate Tax laws regarding any transfers of property.

5. BINDING CLAUSES

   This agreement shall be binding upon and benefit both parties and their heirs, assigns, administrators, executors, and personal representatives.

6. COMPLETE AGREEMENT

   This agreement is complete in its entirety with respect to the rights of the individuals herein. All prior agreements and representations regarding the subject matter of this agreement are waived or merged into this agreement.

continued

Exhibit 7-1 *continued*

7. VALIDITY

If any of the clauses of this agreement shall be invalid or unenforceable, then the remaining provisions shall continue to be effective.

8. ASSETS

A. All assets of DANIELLA MARIE GALLO that shall remain her separate property after the contemplated marriage to WILLIAM JEFFREY MICHAELS are enumerated below:

2005 Porsche 918 automobile, California License No. DANI

Bank account in the First National Bank of San Francisco, Account No. 1234567

One-carat emerald-cut diamond solitaire ring

B. All assets of WILLIAM JEFFREY MICHAELS that shall remain his separate property after the contemplated marriage to DANIELLA MARIE GALLO are enumerated below:

Home located at 4545 Sunset Lane, in the City of Prescott, State of Arizona

One-acre parcel of land located at 222 Forest Trails Road in the City of Prescott, State of Arizona

4-carat diamond man's ring with initials "WM" in rubies

2004 burgundy Rolls Royce, Arizona license "BRDY"

9. LIABILITIES

All liabilities listed below are considered to be the separate property responsibility of each of the parties and are not to be paid from community funds:

A. DANIELLA MARIE GALLO shall be responsible for the following debts:

1. Automobile loan with ABC Financial Corporation of $22,354

2. Visa card No. 555666777 in the amount of $2,555

B. WILLIAM JEFFREY MICHAELS shall be responsible for the following debts:

1. Visa card No. 888999000 in the amount of $1,234

2. Automobile loan with ROB Corporation for $55,333

Signed this 27th day of June, 2007, in the City of San Francisco, County of San Francisco, State of California.

_____

DANIELLA MARIE GALLO

_____

WILLIAM JEFFREY MICHAELS

states require a waiting period after the marriage license application; others require that the couple be tested for various diseases. Most states require that the parties be residents of the state in which the marriage occurs. Check the rules for your state and complete the following box.

STATE-SPECIFIC INFORMATION

The following rules for marriage apply in the state of _____:

Waiting period for license:

_____

Blood tests required:

_____

Other requirements:

_____

_____

_____

Common-Law Marriage

When a man and woman agree to enter into a marital-type relationship without going through a marriage ceremony and live together, a **common-law marriage** may exist. Many states recognize common-law marriage. Some states that do not permit common-law marriage recognize one that was undertaken in another state that allows them. Complete the following box for your state.

STATE-SPECIFIC INFORMATION

The state of _____ (does / does not) recognize common-law marriage.

The state (will / will not) recognize a common-law marriage that was undertaken in another state that allows them.

The elements of common-law marriage in states that allow it include the following:

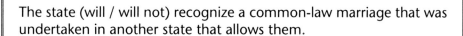

1. Both parties must agree to enter into a marital relationship.
2. Both parties must be legally competent to marry.
3. The parties must have an oral or written agreement, preferably written. In some states, the agreement may be implied by the parties' behavior.
4. The parties must live together as husband and wife (cohabit) and represent themselves to the outside world as being married.

common-law marriage
the condition that exists when a man and a woman agree to enter a marital relationship and live together as if married but without a formal marriage ceremony

Void and Voidable Marriage

Some marriages are **void** at the outset and may never be made valid. These include marriages between ancestors and descendants (such as mother, father, grandmother, grandfather, son, daughter, or grandchild); marriages between brothers and sisters (including adoptive siblings); and marriage to an aunt, uncle, first cousin, niece, or nephew. Note that an adopted person becomes a member of the adoptive family and may not marry any of the adopted prohibited family members listed here.

A **voidable marriage** has certain defects that make it possible for one of the parties, generally the innocent party, to have the marriage annulled. The marriage is not automatically void, however, and may become valid if certain events occur. Defects that can lead to a voidable marriage include the following:

1. One of the parties was not of legal age at the time of the marriage and did not have parental consent.
2. At the time of the marriage, one of the parties had a spouse from a former marriage who was still alive, although the party had believed the spouse was dead.
3. An incurable physical incapacity of one of the parties prevents the consummation of the marriage.
4. One of the parties was forced to consent to the marriage.
5. The consent of one of the parties was obtained by fraud.
6. Either party was of unsound mind at the time of the marriage.

In most cases, if the parties continue to live together as husband and wife for a specified period of time after the defect ceases to exist, the marriage will be considered valid and may not be voided at a later date.

COHABITATION

void marriage a marriage that is not legal; includes marriage between close relatives

voidable marriage a marriage that may be voided by one of the parties or may be made legal on the occurrence of certain events

cohabitation living together without a marriage contract

palimony support paid to one party after a relationship ends based on an implied contract between the couple while they lived together

Cohabitation occurs when a man and a woman live together without the benefit of a marriage contract and without the intent to enter into a common-law marriage. Some cohabiting couples draw up a *cohabitation agreement,* which is written in the same format as a prenuptial agreement (see Exhibit 7-1). This contract should set forth property arrangements and financial arrangements if the couple terminates the relationship; it may also deal with other issues such as payment of expenses, separate property, child support, and child care. The primary difference in these two documents is that in the case of a cohabitation agreement, the couple does not intend to marry.

Some courts have awarded **palimony** upon the breakup of these relationships. The party seeking support must show that there was an oral or written agreement that one person would keep house and run the household while the other party would pursue a career outside the home. In such cases, the working party may have to pay support to the person who stayed home as compensation for services rendered. The courts may not award compensation for sexual services, however, because this would represent an illegal contract based on prostitution.

ANNULMENT OR NULLITY OF MARRIAGE

The grounds for **annulment** are the same as for voidable marriages in most states. However, in an action for nullity of marriage (or annulment) the marriage is treated as never having existed. No property division takes place, and no support payments are allowed. Some couples obtain a divorce or dissolution of marriage even though they may have grounds for annulment.

LEGAL SEPARATION

Although a *legal separation* does not terminate the marriage, the results and procedures are very similar. The primary difference between a divorce or dissolution and a legal separation is that the couple may not remarry when they have had a legal separation. All other issues are resolved, such as property division, child support, and child custody. Other differences between legal separation and divorce or dissolution that are present in most states include the following:

1. There are no minimum residency requirements for a legal separation.
2. Both parties must consent to a legal separation.
3. There is no waiting period for the legal separation to become final.
4. Each spouse can receive health insurance benefits on the other's policy under a legal separation, as they are still considered legally married.
5. Inheritance rights continue under legal separation.
6. A woman may not restore her maiden name in a legal separation.
7. If one spouse dies during the legal separation, the other spouse is entitled to receive pension or other death benefits payable to a spouse.

DIVORCE AND DISSOLUTION ACTIONS

Divorce proceedings are adversarial, and the parties are known as the *plaintiff* and *defendant*. The plaintiff must have grounds for a divorce, and these grounds must be proven in court. If the grounds are not proven, then the divorce will not be granted by the court.

Dissolution is a form of no-fault divorce. The breakup of the marriage is treated as similar to a dissolution of a partnership. Because it is not an adversarial proceeding, the parties are known as the *petitioner* (the spouse who initiates the action) and *respondent* (the other spouse). Neither party is held responsible for a dissolution. If one party wishes to obtain a dissolution, the other party may not object to the procedure. However, the respondent may dispute the property settlement, support issues, and child custody.

Table 7-1 shows the terms used in divorce and the corresponding terms in dissolution.

annulment the act of making a marriage void; nullity

divorce an adversary proceeding to end a marriage; requires grounds in most states

dissolution no-fault divorce; no grounds are required, and either party may file a petition

TABLE 7-1 Terminology for Divorce and Dissolution	
Divorce	**Dissolution (No-Fault Divorce)**
Divorce	Dissolution
Complaint	Petition
Answer	Response
Plaintiff	Petitioner
Defendant	Respondent
Alimony	Spousal support
Johnson v. Johnson	*IN RE Marriage of Johnson*

Many states have begun to use the dissolution action instead of the divorce to eliminate the adversarial aspects. Determine your state's laws and complete the following box.

> STATE-SPECIFIC INFORMATION
>
> The state of _____ uses
>
> _____ dissolution.
>
> _____ divorce.

Divorce

Grounds for Divorce. Each state that uses the divorce proceeding has its own **grounds for divorce.** The most common ones are listed here.

Physical or Mental Cruelty. Extreme physical or mental cruelty of one spouse toward the other is grounds for divorce in most states. The injured spouse must prove the abuse by testimony of witnesses, police reports, pictures, or other forms of physical evidence.

Incurable Insanity. The spouse bringing the action must be able to prove that the other spouse is incurably insane. Proof may take the form of medical reports, expert testimony, or other physical evidence.

Abandonment. One spouse must depart from the family home for a period of time, such as a year, without any intention of returning. Other forms of abandonment allowable in some states are *constructive abandonment,* in which one spouse refuses to engage in sexual relations with the other spouse continuously for a period of time such as one year, and *lockout,* in which one spouse refuses to allow the other spouse into the home continuously for a set period of time.

Imprisonment. If the defendant is imprisoned for three consecutive years after the marriage, a divorce action may be commenced in some

grounds for divorce
reasons for which the state allows a couple to obtain a divorce

states if the defendant is still in prison. Other states require that the defendant must have been imprisoned for a felony.

Adultery. If the defendant voluntarily performs sexual intercourse with a person other than the spouse during the marriage, a divorce action may be filed on the grounds of adultery. Proof must be obtained in the form of witness testimony or physical evidence. However, admission in court by the guilty spouse is generally sufficient to prove adultery.

Separation Agreement. In some states, both parties may choose to live apart for more than one year based on the terms of a separation agreement signed by both parties. The agreement must be signed before a notary public and filed in the county where one party resides. If the parties decide to obtain a divorce after the year is up, they may do so in states that recognize the separation agreement as grounds for divorce.

Research your state's laws and complete the following box.

STATE-SPECIFIC INFORMATION

The following grounds for divorce are applicable in the state of
_____:

_____

_____

_____

Residency Requirements. Before filing for divorce, a couple must have lived in the state for at least the minimum time allotted by that state to establish residency. In some states, only one of the parties must establish residency in that state in order to file for divorce or dissolution. Determine your state's residency requirements and complete the following box.

STATE-SPECIFIC INFORMATION

In the state of _____, the plaintiff must be a resident of the state for _____ (years / months) and the county for _____ (years / months) before filing a divorce action in the state. The defendant must be a resident of the state for _____ (years / months) and the county for _____ (years / months).

Divorce Procedures. Because a divorce is an adversarial proceeding, it begins with the filing of a summons and complaint by the plaintiff. These documents are similar to those used in a civil action. They are filed with the county clerk and served on the defendant. Most states require that the defendant be personally served by a resident of the state who is not a party to the action and who is not a minor. Therefore, the plaintiff may not serve the complaint and summons on the defendant.

In many cases, the defendant agrees to the divorce and the action is considered *uncontested*. In many states, the defendant must sign an affidavit stating that he agrees to the divorce and does not contest it. This document is filed with the court.

However, in a *contested* divorce, a number of other items must be completed and the process is considerably more complicated. The defendant must file an *answer* that states the reasons why the divorce should not be granted. It may include *affirmative defenses* such as the following:

1. *Condoning misconduct.* If the plaintiff is asking for the divorce based on the defendant's misconduct, the defendant must prove that the plaintiff accepted this misconduct. For example, if Sandra wishes to divorce John because he has committed adultery, John may contest the divorce by stating that Sandra had been aware of the adultery for some time and accepted it.

2. *Mental impairment.* The defendant must prove that the behavior that provided grounds for the divorce was caused by a mental defect.

3. *Connivance.* The defendant must prove that the plaintiff lured him into the misconduct that provided the grounds for divorce.

4. *Recrimination.* If the defendant can prove that the plaintiff was also guilty of the misconduct that established the grounds for the divorce, the court may deny the divorce. This defense is based on the English common-law theory of "clean hands"; that is, an individual who seeks relief from the court cannot also be guilty of the same wrongdoing in the situation, but must come into the court with "clean hands."

In many cases, the defendant agrees to the divorce but contests the support, property division, custody, or visitation rights offered by the other party. If the parties cannot agree on those issues, the court will decide the most equitable settlement.

Exhibit 7-2 shows a sample divorce complaint from the state of New York using the couple's separation agreement as grounds for the divorce.

Dissolution (No-Fault Divorce)

Many states have simplified the process of divorce by treating the dissolving of a marriage as similar to the dissolution of a partnership. Rather than having to prove grounds for the divorce, one spouse may merely file a document called a *petition* and serve it on the other spouse to commence the action. Several states allow some form of no-fault divorce, especially when the parties have lived apart under a separation

EXHIBIT 7-2   Divorce Complaint with Separation Agreement (New York)

SUPREME COURT OF THE STATE OF NEW YORK

COUNTY OF WESTCHESTER

SUSAN SANCHEZ: Index No. _____

:

Plaintiff:

:

-against-:

:

WILLIAM SANCHEZ

:

Defendant:

_____

The plaintiff, complaining of the defendant, by her attorneys, BURNS & DAILY, alleges:

1.   That on or about the 20th day of June, 1989, plaintiff and defendant were married in Peekskill, New York.

2.   That for a continuous period of at least two years, immediately preceding the commencement of this action, the plaintiff and defendant were and still are residents of the County of Westchester, State of New York.

3.   That there are two infant issue of this marriage, to wit: JULIE MARIE, born the 25th day of October, 2000; and MICHAEL ALAN, born the 5th day of March, 2002.

4.   After their marriage, as aforesaid and until the 20th day of May, 2004, the plaintiff lived with defendant as man and wife, in various places in the State of New York, and during all that period of time, plaintiff was a true and dutiful wife to the defendant and duly performed all of her duties and obligations as such.

5.   That during the course of their marriage, plaintiff and defendant encountered irreconcilable differences which led to their separation and subsequent agreement, entered into the 22d day of May, 2004, and that the parties have lived separate and apart pursuant to this written agreement for a period of more than one year.

WHEREFORE, plaintiff asks judgment against the defendant dissolving the bonds of matrimony existing between the plaintiff and defendant herein, for custody of the minor children of the marriage, and child support; and for such other and further relief as this court may deem just and proper.

DATED at Peekskill, New York, this 20th day of June, 2007.

Yours, etc.

BURNS & DAILY
Attorneys for Plaintiff
112233 Main Street
Peekskill, New York 19007
(914) 555–1111
BY: _____

agreement for a specified period of time. In most cases, the respondent may not contest the dissolution, and no grounds are required.

Residency Requirements.   All states require that the petitioner must have lived in that state long enough to establish residency before filing for a dissolution. Some state statutes require that the respondent be a resident of the state for a specified period as well. In California, for example, the petitioner must have been a resident of the state for six months and the county for three months to initiate a dissolution proceeding. In contrast, Florida allows immediate residency by the filing of a *Declaration of Domicile* with the clerk of the court. Determine whether your state allows no-fault divorce or dissolution and its residency requirements and complete the following box.

> **STATE-SPECIFIC INFORMATION**
>
> The state of _____ (allows / does not allow) no-fault divorce or dissolution actions.
>   In a dissolution action, the petitioner must have been a resident of the state for _____ (years / months) and the county for _____ (years / months) before filing a petition in the state. The respondent must have been a resident of the state for _____ (years / months) and the county for _____ (years / months).

PROPERTY

In states that recognize the concept of **community property**, the laws are simplified. Basically each party retains half of the community property upon dissolution. Determine whether your state recognizes the concept of community property and complete the following box.

> **STATE-SPECIFIC INFORMATION**
>
> The state of _____ (recognizes / does not recognize) the concept of community property in the division of assets upon a divorce or dissolution.

community property
property acquired during the marriage that is not separate property; the concept is used in community property states

separate property
property acquired before marriage or after separation, or during marriage by gift or inheritance

Community property includes all property acquired during the marriage that is not separate property. **Separate property** is property acquired before marriage or after separation, or property that was acquired by the individual as a gift or an inheritance during the marriage. For instance, if Jack receives an inheritance from a relative during the marriage, he retains this inheritance after the divorce, and its value is not deducted from his share of the marital assets. The issue sometimes arises as to whether certain property that was given during the marriage was a gift to the individual or a gift to the couple.

Courts have consistently held that wedding gifts are community property, whether given by the parents of the wife or husband. In one case, the bride's parents gave the couple a house for a wedding gift. Upon obtaining a dissolution, the wife claimed that the house was her sole and separate property. But the court held that the house was given to both spouses as a couple and not as an individual gift to the wife, and ruled that the house was community property.

In states that do not have community property, the property acquired during the marriage is divided based on that particular state's formula. While most states provide for a division of half of the marital assets to each spouse, a few states award a higher percentage of the assets to the husband. Determine your state's division formula and report the results in the following box.

STATE-SPECIFIC INFORMATION

The state of _____ divides marital assets by the following formula upon divorce or dissolution:

_____ to the wife

_____ to the husband

The courts have consistently held that which spouse holds title to the marital property is irrelevant to proving that this is marital property that must be divided between the parties. Even in states that do not recognize the concept of dissolution and community property, the courts have consistently held that the breakup of a marriage is tantamount to the dissolution of a partnership.

Property that is acquired by both parties during the marriage, to which both parties retain title, is the easiest to trace and is generally considered community or marital property. However, the courts are divided as to separate property that has become commingled with marital property. When the separate property melds with the community property to a point at which it cannot be traced, that property has been transformed into marital or community property. This melding of the two properties is known as **transmutation**. It is important that the spouse who has commingled his property with the marital property is able to trace its origins back to separate property in order to claim it.

For example, suppose that the couple has a joint bank account. On June 5, 2003, the husband receives a $100,000 inheritance and deposits it into the account. When the couple obtains a divorce on February 15, 2006, no money is left in this account. The issue then becomes whether the husband actually made a gift of his separate property to the community. It would be difficult to argue for the husband's right to retain $100,000 of assets from the community unless he had a written document that stated he was making a loan to the community and not a gift.

transmutation melding of separate property with community property to a point at which it cannot be traced

Once the issue of separate and community (marital) property has been decided, a list of each should be made with a value placed on each piece of property. Generally one would use the **fair market value**, which is the price the seller could obtain for the property if he sold it. On items of property that have outstanding loans or liens against them, the costs of the encumbrances are deducted from the fair market value to determine the equity in the property.

In some cases the couple cannot agree on the market value of the property and an expert must be retained to appraise the property. For instance, the couple may have purchased a home several years ago and its value may have increased considerably.

Property Division

Once the total assets and their values have been determined, the couple must decide how the community property should be divided. Courts have consistently held that an uneven distribution is allowable as long as both parties have had adequate legal representation and one party is not taking advantage of the other party. A *marital settlement agreement* is prepared, both parties sign it, and the property is divided. When the couple cannot agree on the division of property, the court must resolve the dispute.

In states that do not use the community property method of property division, an *equitable distribution* system may be used. In equitable distribution states, property is divided based on fairness and equity and not based on which spouse holds title to the marital property. The ultimate decision of the division of property falls on the court if the couple cannot agree.

Quasi-Community Property

In states that recognize community property, *quasi-community property* is property owned in another state that would be community property if it were located in the state where the couple resides. Although this property is considered community property in the state of the couple's residence, the laws related to property ownership may be different in the state in which the property is located. If the state where the property is located is not a community property state, the court would award the property to one party but would offset that property with other property in the settlement agreement. For instance, suppose a husband and wife live in a community property state and own land worth $200,000 in a non-community property state. In the case of a divorce, the court may award the property to the husband, and the wife would receive other property worth $100,000 to offset the award to the husband.

Pensions

The spouses' pensions are often difficult to evaluate when dividing marital property. Employees with pensions are entitled to either a lump-sum payment or a periodic monthly payment upon their retirement. An employee who has not worked for the employer for the required number of years and leaves the job will be entitled to receive

fair market value the price a seller could obtain for property if he sold it

his *nonvested interest,* which is the amount of money he has invested into the pension fund. However, an employee who has worked the required number of years will be entitled to the amount contributed by the employer and himself. In a long-term marriage, the pension is often one of the greatest assets of the marriage. The federal Employee Retirement Income Security Act (ERISA) statute and its amendment, the Retirement Equity Act (REA) passed in 1984, determine how a pension may be divided upon the couple's divorce or dissolution.

Because the funds are not taxed initially, a large amount of taxes would be deducted if the pension were cashed in upon divorce. Therefore, the parties may agree to have the pension evaluated to determine its value. The value of the pension may be offset against other marital assets. If enough assets are not available, the employee spouse may choose to buy out the other spouse by paying him a sum of money in exchange for retaining the pension.

As a general rule, the division of the pension benefits is based on the period of time the individual has been paying into those benefits during the marriage. The longer the marriage, often the greater the share of pension benefits the other spouse receives.

Professional Degrees and Practices

In most cases, if the professional degree is obtained during the marriage, the courts place a value on this degree and consider it marital property. Some courts have extended this property to contracts of sports figures. In some states, the spouse who obtained the degree or has the contract for future funds must pay the other spouse a form of alimony or spousal support. States vary greatly on their method of treating these degrees and contracts, however.

Many states consider the goodwill of a professional practice a marital asset that should be divided between the spouses upon divorce or dissolution. The goodwill is evaluated and the other spouse is paid a lump-sum payment for a portion of its value.

Complete the following box with the rules for your state.

STATE-SPECIFIC INFORMATION

In the state of _____ , professional degrees are treated in the following manner:

_____

_____

_____

Goodwill of a professional practice is evaluated as follows:

_____

_____

_____

Alimony/Spousal Support

Some spouses may be required to pay for the support of the other spouse upon divorce or dissolution, paying **alimony.** The court considers whether both parties are capable of making a living and whether one spouse may lack job skills. In that case, the court may order a vocational rehabilitation counselor to interview the nonworking spouse to determine whether a training period should be established to enable that individual to become self-supporting. In that case, the court may award temporary support until the training period is over.

Other factors that the court considers in awarding support include the following:

1. the ages of the parties
2. the length of the marriage
3. the standard of living of the couple
4. the ages of the children (if any)
5. the salaries of both spouses

In general, older individuals with long-term marriages are more likely to be awarded support, especially if the working spouse earns a considerable income. This support may be required until the spouse receiving the support dies or remarries.

CHILD CUSTODY

Although in earlier times mothers were usually awarded custody of minor children, in recent years the courts have held that both parents have an equal right to custody of their children. The court uses the principle of "the best interests of the child" in determining which spouse gets custody. In some cases, the court may award *joint physical custody,* in which each parent retains custody of the child or children for part of the time; each spouse has equal physical custody of the child. In some cases, one spouse has custody during the week and the other on weekends; one spouse may have custody during the school year and the other on holidays and during summer vacation. The couple may, on its own, agree on an amenable custody arrangement. However, if there has been a history of abuse by one of the spouses, the court may grant sole physical custody to the nonabusing parent and supervised visitation to the abusing parent. In extreme cases, the abusive parent may not receive visitation rights.

Some courts award *joint legal custody* and not joint physical custody. In this type of arrangement, both spouses have equal rights to make decisions for the welfare of the child, such as those involving education, medical care, or religion.

CHILD SUPPORT

alimony support of the other spouse upon divorce or dissolution

Both spouses are legally required to support their children. In general, the noncustodial parent pays child support to the custodial parent. The amount of support is based on the best interests of the child.

The court looks at the age of the child, the salaries of both parents, the manner in which the child has been living, the number of children, and any significant health issues. Child support payments may not be discharged in bankruptcy proceedings.

In addition to the necessities of life, the parents may be required to provide the following items to the minor child:

1. medical, vision, and/or dental insurance
2. education expenses
3. medical and hospital expenses

ADOPTION

Adoption is the process whereby *birth parents* give up their rights to a child and *adoptive parents* assume all rights to the child. Once the birth parents relinquish their rights to the child in an adoption proceeding, they no longer have any rights to see or have contact with the child. The adopting parents become the child's legal parents, and all former relatives of the child also relinquish any rights to him. The adopting parents' relatives become the relatives of the child. For example, the birth mother's mother would be the child's grandmother. Once the child is adopted, the adopting parents' parents become the child's grandparents.

Many states have a waiting period before the adoption becomes finalized, and some states allow the birth parents to take the child back during this time period. In most cases, however, a good reason must be shown to enable the birth parents to retain custody of the child.

TERMINATION OF PARENTAL RIGHTS

Most states have statutes setting forth the circumstances under which one parent may request the termination of the parental rights of the other parent. The ability to terminate parental rights generally stems from abandonment of the child by one of the parents, including lack of child support payments. The parent who is trying to terminate the other's parental rights must prove that the other parent has had no contact with the child for a set period of time. State statutes vary on the time period and the exact circumstances necessary for parental rights termination.

STATE-SPECIFIC INFORMATION FOR THE STATE OF _____:

In the state of _____, parental rights may be terminated under the following conditions:

_____

_____

_____

adoption   a legal proceeding whereby an individual or a couple become parents to a child who was not born to them

● KEY TERMS

adoption	divorce
alimony	grounds for divorce
annulment	marriage
cohabitation	palimony
common-law marriage	separate property
community property	void marriage
dissolution	voidable marriage

● SELF TEST

1. What is palimony and when is it awarded?

2. Is community property divided in annulments?

3. What does the court consider when awarding child custody?

4. Which parent is responsible for paying child support?

5. What factors are considered when requiring the payment of child support?

● NOTEBOOK PROJECTS

1. Acquire the papers required to obtain a divorce or dissolution in your state.

2. Prepare the documents required for an adoption in your state using the following set of facts:

   Olivia and Robert Munoz wish to adopt a child, Virginia Medina, whose parents are Stephen and Rosa Medina. The child was born on July 30, 2005, in your state. The Medinas will consent to the adoption. Virginia's new name will be Virginia Munoz.

3. List the grounds for divorce that are recognized in your state. Describe the procedures for filing for divorce or dissolution in your state.

4. Complete the State-Specific Information boxes in this chapter for your notebook.

For additional resources, visit our Web site at **www.paralegal.delmar.cengage.com.**

ESTATE PLANNING

CHAPTER OUTCOMES

After studying this chapter, the student will understand

1. the governing law for will preparation.
2. how to prepare a will.
3. the elements of a trust.
4. the parties to a trust agreement.
5. other estate-planning tools, such as the advance directive.

INTRODUCTION

Estate planning involves the active planning, during one's lifetime, of how the person's property will be distributed upon her death. In some cases, the individual transfers some property to the heirs during her lifetime for tax purposes. A person who has a very large estate should hire the services of a professional in the area of estate planning to ensure that the person and her heirs retain the maximum amount of property allowable without being required to use a large amount of estate assets to pay taxes.

PROBATE

Upon an individual's demise, her estate must go through the *probate* process. This involves appointing a personal representative for the decedent and processing the estate through the probate court to allow distribution to the heirs. Even individuals with a trust also have a will for assets that have not yet become a part of the trust. Some attorneys establish an *estate plan* for the client, with the goal of avoiding probate entirely, while others feel that the probate process is more effective in distributing the decedent's assets as she requires. A more detailed explanation of the probate process may be found in Chapter 9.

WILLS

Terminology Used in Wills

A **will** is a written document that sets forth the manner in which a **decedent's** estate will be distributed upon her death. The person

estate planning the process of creating a plan during one's lifetime regarding how the person's property will be distributed upon her death

will a written document setting forth the manner in which a person's estate will be distributed upon her death

decedent an individual who dies

137

making the will is known as the **testator,** who is said to have died *testate* if she had a will. A person who dies without having made a will is said to have died *intestate.* In a few states, a female who dies with a will is known as a *testatrix.* However, most states have given up the gender definition. Anyone who receives the decedent's property under the will is known as a **beneficiary.**

STATE-SPECIFIC INFORMATION

In the state of _____ , a female who makes a will is known as a
_____ testator.
_____ testatrix.

When an individual dies, she is known as the *decedent.* The person or entity charged with overseeing the distribution of the decedent's estate is known as the *executor* if there is a will and the *administrator* if there is no will. Again, in a few states a female personal representative is known as an *executrix* or an *administratrix.*

STATE-SPECIFIC INFORMATION

In the state of _____ , a female personal representative of one who dies with a will is known as an
_____ executor.
_____ executrix.
A female personal representative of one who dies without a will is known as an
_____ administrator.
_____ administratrix.

The process used by the courts to distribute the assets of the decedent to the beneficiaries is called *probate.* If an executor is not named in the will, the court appoints an administrator to administer the estate subject to that state's probate laws.

A gift of real or personal property by will is known as a *bequest.* A *devise* is a gift of real property by will. The manner in which property is distributed by will depends on whether it is a *general bequest* or a *specific bequest.* The *residuary estate* is the property that is left after distributing all general and specific bequests.

Because the decedent's debts must be paid prior to the distribution of the property, occasionally all property will not be available for division. Therefore, the courts have created a specific order in which property is distributed. The first property distributed is the **specific bequest,**

testator one who makes a will

beneficiary one who receives property under a will

specific bequest a gift of a specific item made in a will which is a selected piece of property or designated amount of money that is named in the will. A general bequest is a general gift that is not specifically designated. Some examples of specific bequests include the following:

1. $200,000 in cash
2. my 2006 silver Lexus ES-330
3. my three-carat marquise-shaped diamond engagement ring

Some general bequests include the following:

1. my car
2. my house
3. my jewelry

The residuary estate is not mentioned in the will as specific pieces of property, but as "the rest and residue of my estate."

If a specific bequest is no longer a part of the estate, then that gift lapses and the beneficiary does not receive a substitute gift. For example, if the decedent sold her Lexus described previously, the beneficiary would not receive whatever car the decedent owned at the time of her death. A general bequest does not lapse because it is not specifically described. However, if the estate has more debts than assets, the residuary estate is disposed of first to pay the debts, and the general bequests are used to pay any debts not covered by the residuary estate.

Thus, each type of gift has both advantages and disadvantages. Although a specific bequest will be sold last to pay debts, it is often not available at the time of the testator's death, particularly if several years have passed since the decedent made her will. Although general bequests are usually more readily available at the distribution of the estate, they will be used to pay debts if the residuary estate is not sufficient to cover the decedent's bills.

Who May Make a Will?

In order to make a valid a will, the testator must be *competent,* which is defined as being 18 or more years of age and of sound mind. Some states consider younger people who are serving in the armed forces competent to make a will. Research the definition of competence in your state and complete the following box.

STATE-SPECIFIC INFORMATION

The state of _____ defines competence to make a will as follows:

_____

_____

_____

In addition to being competent to make a will, the testator must have *testamentary capacity* to make a will. The testator must understand the nature of the act she is performing, that of signing her will. The testator must know the nature of the property being distributed and to whom she is distributing it. Lack of testamentary capacity is generally established by proving one of the following:

1. The testator made the will under duress, defined as being forced or threatened in order to influence her to act in a certain way.
2. The testator was under the undue influence of someone with a special relationship.
3. The testator lacked the mental competence necessary to make the will due to a mental incapacity.

Testamentary capacity is proven by the testimony of witnesses who witnessed the signing of the will. Unless the will is contested, the capacity of the testator will not likely be questioned.

Types of Wills

Formal Wills. A **formal will** is a typed will with between one and three witnesses, depending on the laws of the state in which the will is prepared. The witnesses to the will must attest to the fact that the testator signed the will in front of each of them, that the signature is the true signature of the testator, and that she signed the will voluntarily. A formal will must be typed and witnessed. If the will is formal, then all subsequent codicils to the will must also be formal. That is, the codicils must be typed, signed, and witnessed.

STATE-SPECIFIC INFORMATION

The state of _____ requires that a formal will must have _____ witnesses.

In most cases, it is advisable to have witnesses to the will who are younger than the testator to increase the likelihood that they will still be alive upon the testator's death. The individuals who witness a will may not be named in the will. Therefore, an executor to a will may not be a witness to the will. Nor may any beneficiary named in the will be a witness to the will.

Certain clauses are present in all wills and are described next. The first clause of the will usually states the testator's name and her revocation of former wills. The spouse and children are identified in the will, as well as their locations at the time the will is written. Later clauses distribute the decedent's property. A sample formal will is shown in Exhibit 8-1.

formal will a formally typed and witnessed will

EXHIBIT 8-1   A Sample Formal Will

Reprinted with permission from *Office Procedures for the Legal Professional*, Judy Long, 2005: Thomson Delmar Learning.

LAST WILL AND TESTAMENT

of

JANE MARIE ROBERTSON

I, JANE MARIE ROBERTSON, of 559 Sunset Drive, Cordova, Texas, being of lawful age and of sound and disposing mind and memory and not acting under fraud, duress, menace of the undue influence of any person or thing, do hereby make, publish and declare this instrument to be my Last Will and Testament, and I do hereby revoke all other Wills and Codicils to Wills heretofore made by me as follows:

FIRST: I direct that all my just debts and expenses of last illness and funeral expenses be paid from my estate as soon after my demise as can lawfully and conveniently be done.

SECOND: I declare that at the time of the execution of this Will, I am married to JEFFREY WILLIAM ROBERTSON and have three children as follows:

JONATHAN MICHAEL ROBERTSON, date of birth: June 20, 2000
DANIELLE MARIE ROBERTSON, date of birth: December 19, 2003
JEFFREY MICHAEL ROBERTSON, date of birth: September 2, 2005

THIRD: I nominate and appoint as Executor Of my Last Will and Testament, my husband, JEFFREY WILLIAM ROBERTSON, of Cordova, Texas, to serve without bond. In the event JEFFREY WILLIAM ROBERTSON cannot or will not serve for any reason whatsoever, I then appoint MARC DAVID TIGER, of Memphis, Tennessee, to serve without bond.

FOURTH: I declare that all of my property is community property and from my share thereof, I bequeath all of my property to my husband JEFFREY WILLIAM ROBERTSON. In the event my said husband shall predecease me or shall not be alive at the time of the distribution of my estate, I then direct that my estate be divided equally among my children JONATHAN MICHAEL ROBERTSON, DANIELLE MARIE ROBERTSON, and JEFFREY MICHAEL ROBERTSON, in equal shares.

FIFTH: In the event any of my said children shall predecease me or shall not be alive at the time of the distribution of my estate, I then direct that his or her share shall lapse and shall be distributed in toto to the surviving child or children.

SIXTH: In the event my said husband shall predecease me or shall not be alive at the time of the distribution of my estate, and if any of my children, or all of them, are minors under the law at that time, I hereby appoint MARY ELIZABETH GALWAY, my sister, of Memphis, Tennessee, to serve as their guardian, with full authority to support them from the proceeds of my estate, until they reach the age of majority. If MARY ELIZABETH GALWAY shall be unable or unwilling

continued

Exhibit 8-1   *continued*

to serve, then I appoint my brother, JAMES ALLEN ROBERTSON, to serve as their guardian, with full authority to support them from the proceeds of my estate, until they reach the age of majority.

SEVENTH: I have intentionally and with full knowledge failed to provide for any other persons living at the time of my demise except as otherwise provided herein. If any person, whether a beneficiary under this Will or not, shall contest this Will or object to any of the provisions hereof, I give to such person so contesting or objecting the sum of One Dollar ($1.00) and no more in lieu of the provisions which I have made herein or which I might have made herein to such person or persons so contesting or objecting.

EIGHTH: I give, devise, and bequeath the rest, residue, and remainder of my estate to my above-named spouse, JEFFREY WILLIAM ROBERTSON. If my said spouse shall predecease me, then I give, devise and bequeath the residue of my estate to my above-named children in equal shares.

IN WITNESS WHEREOF, I have hereunto set my hand this 9th day of June, 2008, at Cordova, Texas.

_____

The foregoing instrument, consisting of two (2) pages, was at this date hereof, by JANE MARIE ROBERTSON signed as and declared to be her Will, in the presence of us who, at her request and in her presence, and in the presence of each other, have subscribed our names as witnesses thereto. Each of us observed the signing of this Will by JANE MARIE ROBERTSON and by each other subscribing witness and knows that each signature is the true signature of the person whose name was signed. Each of us is more than twenty-one (21) years of age and a competent witness and resides at the address set forth after his or her name. We are acquainted with JANE MARIE ROBERTSON. At this time she is over the age of eighteen (18) years, and to the best of our knowledge, she is of sound mind and not acting under duress, menace, fraud, misrepresentation, or undue influence.

_____

_____

Name

_____

_____

Name

Witnesses. Most states require two witnesses to a formal will. These individuals must observe the signing of the will by the testator and sign in the presence of the testator and each other. Generally the legal assistant arranges for all parties to be present at the will signing; that is, the attorney, the testator, and the witnesses. The witnesses must be disinterested parties who are not named in the will and who are not beneficiaries of the estate. In most cases, the attorney will ask two members of the office staff to witness the signing of the will.

In order to make the will *self-proving,* the will must be signed in front of a *notary public,* who witnesses the signing of the will by the testator and the witnesses. The notary signs an attached affidavit attesting to the signing. States vary as to the number of witnesses required and the requirements for a self-proving will. Determine your state's requirements and complete the following box.

STATE-SPECIFIC REQUIREMENTS

Formal wills in the state of _____ require _____ witnesses to sign after the testator signs the will. A self-proving will in this state has the following requirements:

_____

_____

_____

Holographic Will. A **holographic will** must be written entirely in the handwriting of the testator. If any part of the will is not in the testator's handwriting, it will not be considered a valid will. In most states, the handwritten will does not have to be witnessed. However, upon the testator's death, someone who can identify the testator's handwriting must testify as to the will's authenticity. The testator must also have signed the will. If the will is holographic, any codicils to the will must also be holographic.

Nuncupative Wills. **Nuncupative wills,** or spoken wills, are valid in very few states and only under very narrow circumstances. They were originally used by military personnel dying on the battlefield, telling someone how they wanted their property distributed. Only a few states recognize nuncupative wills. Determine whether your state recognizes this type of will and complete the following box.

STATE-SPECIFIC INFORMATION

The state of _____ (does / does not) recognize nuncupative wills.

The state recognizes nuncupative wills under the following circumstances:

_____

_____

_____

---

holographic will a will totally in the handwriting of the maker

nuncupative will an oral will; valid in a few states

Joint Wills. Some married couples execute a **joint will** whereby they leave all of their property to each other and, if the spouse is not alive at the time of death, then to the same individuals. Attorneys often discourage this type of arrangement because each spouse may not wish to dispose of his or her property in the same manner. If the surviving spouse wishes to make changes to his or her will, it would not be possible with a joint will.

Instead of preparing a joint will, the attorney may prepare separate wills for both spouses with similar provisions. Each spouse would be able to make changes to this type of will individually, and may make gifts to different beneficiaries.

Changing a Will

Wills should be reviewed and possibly updated yearly or whenever the status of the testator changes. For instance, a person who obtains a divorce or dissolution should write a new will. If one's spouse or child dies, the will should be rewritten. Although a **codicil** may be used to make changes to a will, writing a new will is generally more advantageous if more than one change is being made. For example, a codicil may be used to change the executor to a will. However, if the testator divorces her spouse, more than one change will probably be required and a new will should be made.

Multiple Wills. Some people make several wills throughout their lifetime. When a new will is made, the old one should be destroyed. If more than one will is found upon the individual's death, the will with the most recent date is considered the latest will.

The original will should be kept in a safe place where another responsible person knows of its whereabouts. Some attorneys keep the original of the will; others feel that the testator should keep the original in case the attorney is no longer available. Although many people keep copies of a will, they are not valid if the original is lost. Also, when one keeps copies of the will and the original is destroyed, the copies tend to "muddy the waters" when trying to probate an estate where there are multiple copies of different wills.

Revoking a Will. A person may write a new will that revokes the prior will. Language in the will itself should indicate that this will revokes all former wills and codicils made prior to this will. Destruction of the old will revokes it. For example, if the testator rips up or burns the old will, it is considered revoked. The purposeful destruction of a will is considered a revocation of that will.

The courts have determined that in order to be considered a revocation, the will must be substantially destroyed. Several cases have been brought regarding what the courts mean by "substantial destruction." In general, if the majority of the will has been destroyed, it is considered revoked. If just a small corner of one page has been torn off, the revocation is usually not considered valid.

joint will a will made by a married couple leaving property to each other and, if one dies before the other, leaving property to the same individuals

codicil a formal document making changes to a will

Divorce or Dissolution.   States vary as to the effect of divorce or dissolution on a will. Some states require that the testator draw up a new will upon divorce or dissolution. Other states treat the divorced spouse as having predeceased the testator, so their gifts under the will are voided. Research your state's laws to determine the procedure to follow in the case of divorce or dissolution and complete the following box.

STATE-SPECIFIC INFORMATION

In the case of divorce or dissolution, the following procedures are required in the state of _____ to remove the former spouse as a beneficiary under the will:

_____

_____

_____

Heirs

Minor Children.   The testator should provide for minor children in her will. At least one *guardian* should be appointed for the minor children, preferably someone who is younger than the testator to increase the likelihood that the guardian will be alive at the time of the testator's death. The guardian will make decisions on behalf of the minor or an incompetent adult that would have been made by the testator had she been living. The testator should obtain permission from each guardian before putting her name in the will, and should also arrange in the will for the guardian to use the proceeds of the estate to care for the minor children.

A *conservator* may also be appointed for either minor children or an incompetent adult. The court administers the *conservatorship proceeding* appointing the individual to manage the assets and affairs of the minor or incompetent adult. The conservator must report to the court periodically on the status of the property.

Adopted Children.   Adopted children are entitled to all rights given to natural-born children under the law. The adoptive parents gain legal rights to the child and the child gains all of the legal rights of a natural child. Therefore, adopted children have the same inheritance rights as natural children. Adoption places both the adoptive parents and the adopted child in the same position that they would have been in had the child been born to these parents. The biological parents likewise give up all rights to the adopted child, and that child gives up all inheritance rights with the biological parents. Once the adoption is finalized, the child has different parents and relatives, and the adoptive parents have an additional child.

Pretermitted-Heir Statute. The **pretermitted-heir statute** requires that any child not mentioned in the will may take "against the will." Such a child may take the share she would have received if the parent had mentioned her. For example, if the mother is deceased and the father leaves his property to his two children even though he has a third child, the third child may take her one-third share against the will. The courts hold that if the child's name is completely left out of the will, the parent must have forgotten to include her inadvertently. Sometimes this situation occurs when the parents have additional children after the will has been written.

In order to leave a child out of the will and avoid the pretermitted-heir statute, the parents should mention all children's names in the will and specifically state that they are not leaving any of their estate to the child they wish to disinherit.

Methods for Distribution of Assets

In the case of a testator with children and/or grandchildren, the estate may be distributed either *per stirpes* (by right of representation) or *per capita*. If the decedent wishes each child to receive an equal share of the estate, and if the child is deceased to have the grandchildren share equally in the parent's share, then the distribution would be per stirpes or by right of representation. In that case, each child (or his or her heirs, as a group) would receive an equal share of the estate. If the testator wishes each descendant to receive an equal (per capita) share of the estate, then equal shares of the estate would be distributed to all living children, grandchildren, great-grandchildren, and other descendants.

For example, suppose Mary dies, leaving two living children. The third child is deceased but has three children surviving. In the per stirpes method of distribution, each of Mary's living children receives one third of Mary's estate. The deceased child's children each receive one third of the one third of the estate allocated to the deceased parent, or one ninth of the estate. If the per capita method of distribution is used, there would be five living descendants of Mary, and each would receive one fifth of the estate.

Testators should decide which method works best for their situation. If another method of distribution is preferred, then the testator/client must decide how the estate will be distributed. Perhaps the testator has a favorite grandchild to whom she wishes to leave a higher percentage of the estate. Perhaps the testator wishes to leave one child out of the will entirely. In that case, all children must be mentioned in the first part of the will for identification purposes. Otherwise, if the child left out contests the will, the courts may hold that the parent forgot to include the child, who will collect the amount she would have collected had there been no will. This is known as *collecting against the will*.

Dying without a Will

A person who dies without a will is said to have died *intestate*. Laws of the various states determine how property will be divided upon one's

pretermitted-heir statute
a statute requiring that a child not mentioned in the will may take the share she would have received had there been no will

death. These laws are known as the *laws of intestate succession.* The court appoints an administrator as the personal representative of the estate. That individual must collect the assets of the estate, pay the estate debts and expenses, and distribute the decedent's property according to the laws of intestate succession of that particular state. The laws of intestate succession are also used if a will is invalid. Find the laws of intestate succession for your state and complete the following box.

STATE-SPECIFIC INFORMATION

Under the laws of intestate succession for the state of _____, property is divided in the following order:

_____

_____

_____

A typical method of intestate succession might leave all property to the surviving spouse, or a percentage to the surviving spouse and a percentage to the children.

TRUSTS

The establishment of a **trust** creates a **fiduciary relationship** in which property is held by one party, known as the *trustee,* who has legal title to the property. The property is held for the benefit of the *beneficiary,* who has equitable title to the property. The individual who establishes the trust with her own assets is known as the *trustor* or *settlor.* The trustee manages the trust. Individuals who receive any of the trust proceeds or assets are known as the beneficiaries.

A trust is established by the preparation of a *trust agreement* that sets out its terms and conditions. The trustor transfers her assets, known as the *corpus,* into the trust to establish it. Any moneys earned on the trust are called the *trust income* and may be the proceeds from investing the initial corpus. For example, suppose the corpus consists of stocks and bonds that earn dividends. The dividends are considered trust income. If a piece of rental property is included in the corpus, then the net income received from the rent minus the expenses is considered trust income.

Individuals with large incomes might establish a trust while they are living for the benefit of their heirs after their death. Trusts are not subject to probate or inheritance taxes. They represent a private method for distributing one's assets.

The attorney draws up the trust instrument based on the requirements of the trustor or settlor. Perhaps the trustor wishes to maintain large sums in the trust and provide a monthly income for her spouse

trust   a fiduciary relationship in which property is held by one party (the trustee) with legal title for the benefit of another with an equitable title (the beneficiary)

fiduciary relationship   a relationship founded on trust and dependence in which an individual dominates or influences the other, generally by managing her money or property and children upon her death. In some cases, one child may be a spend-thrift and there may be a provision requiring the child to attain a certain age before obtaining trust income. Any number of situations may be addressed in the preparation of the trust agreement.

Types of Trusts

Several different kinds of trusts exist. Some may be made effective during the maker's lifetime; others take effect when the maker dies. Some trusts are set up so that the maker may change their terms during her lifetime; others are made irrevocable. A person may create a trust for the benefit of her heirs, or for the assistance of charitable organizations.

Testamentary Trust.   A **testamentary trust** is established in the testator's will to take effect upon the death of the maker. The maker of the will may make changes to the trust by means of a codicil to the will. No provisions of the trust may be effective until the testator's death.

The testamentary trust is often set up for the benefit of the family of the decedent. Rather than give the family the entire estate in a lump-sum payment, the trust terms may allow for them to receive monthly payments from the trust for a period of time, and then to receive the remainder of the estate at a later date. This provides a particularly effective method of ensuring that funds will be available to care for the family for years to come.

Inter Vivos Trust: Revocable or Irrevocable.   The **inter vivos trust** is made and takes effect during the settlor's lifetime. This enables the settlor to control the assets of the trust. The trust may provide the settlor with an income for her lifetime, with provisions for the heirs after the settlor's death.

A *revocable trust* may be changed or canceled by the maker during her lifetime. An *irrevocable trust* cannot be altered or revoked by the maker. However, certain states have made specific laws governing the procedure for making changes to the irrevocable trust if the maker and all beneficiaries agree to the changes and the court approves. Determine whether your state allows alteration of an irrevocable trust and complete the following box.

testamentary trust   a trust made in a will that takes effect after the maker dies

inter vivos trust   a trust established during one's lifetime that takes effect while she is alive

---

STATE-SPECIFIC INFORMATION

The state of _____ enables the settlor to make changes to the irrevocable trust under the following circumstances:

_____

_____

_____

The major advantage to the irrevocable trust is that it provides tax advantages for the maker's estate. However, with these tax savings, the settlor gives up control of the estate to others during her lifetime.

Charitable Trusts.   **Charitable trusts** are made for the benefit of charitable organizations. The estate of the maker gains certain tax advantages. Legitimate charities have received tax-exempt status from the IRS and are called *501(c)* or *501(c)(9)* organizations. These numbers refer to the sections of the Internal Revenue Code that describe the tax-exempt status.

Legal Trusts.   Trusts may be established for any legal purpose. Thus, a trust established in the furtherance of the commission of a crime will be deemed illegal by the court. Other requirements have been established by state statutes and generally include most, if not all, of the following:

1. The settlor must be competent. She must be able to understand the trust agreement's terms and must be of legal age. She must be able to ascertain the rights and responsibilities created in the trust agreement.

2. The trust must be written.

3. The property in the trust must have been transferred to the trust's name. In some cases, the settlor creates a trust but does not transfer the property to the trust. In this case, that part of the trust is invalid.

4. The settlor must have the intention to create a trust.

5. The trust requires consideration, just as in a contract. Something of value must be exchanged between the settlor and the trustee.

6. The trustee must accept her responsibilities under the agreement. Obtaining this acceptance in writing is beneficial.

7. A beneficiary other than the settlor must be provided for in the trust agreement. The beneficiary must obtain the right to the property no later than 21 years after a life in being at the time the interest is created, which is known as the *Rule Against Perpetuities*. All states except Alaska, New Jersey, Rhode Island, and South Dakota recognize this rule.

charitable trust   a trust made for the benefit of a charity

Pour-Over Will

When one establishes a trust, a **pour-over will** must be written at the same time to account for assets of the maker that have not yet been transferred into the trust. For example, suppose John buys property after the trust is established but dies before he has transferred the property into the trust. The pour-over will enables all property to be transferred into the trust during the probate process.

pour-over will   a will made at the time a trust is established to account for assets of the maker that have not yet been transferred to the trust

INCAPACITY

Advance directives enable individuals to appoint others to take care of their decision making if they become unable to make decisions for themselves. The state may appoint a guardian to care for a person's physical well-being, or a conservator who makes financial decisions for her. However, the person may choose a guardian or conservator and prepare the documentation for this eventuality while still competent to make her own decisions.

A prospective guardian must petition the court to attain that position. The court usually approves the petition. The same process is used for a conservator, who manages and protects the financial rights of the incapacitated person. However, the individual (*principal*) may appoint another person (*agent*) to make financial or personal decisions for her in the event of incapacitation. The process used in most states is the preparation of a General Power of Attorney for Property, in which the client designates someone to make financial decisions on the client's behalf if she is unable or unwilling to do so. The document must specify when the agent will assume responsibility for the principal's property.

Durable Power of Attorney for Health Care Decisions

If the individual cannot make her own medical and treatment decisions, the agent named in the Durable Power of Attorney for Health Care has the power to make those decisions. For instance, suppose Jane is in a coma and her doctors do not think she will recover. If Jane has a Durable Power of Attorney for Health Care, the person specified therein determines whether to keep Jane alive on life support or "pull the plug."

Living Will

A *living will* often accompanies the Durable Power of Attorney for Health Care. In this document, the individual declares whether she wishes to be kept alive by life-sustaining procedures if her medical condition is incurable and death is imminent. This document is also known as a *declaration relating to life-sustaining procedures*.

In some states, the living will is actually made a part of the Durable Power of Attorney for Health Care. State statutes dictate how these documents must be written. Generally the information and forms may be obtained from the family doctor.

 Find the appropriate forms for a living will and Durable Power of Attorney for Health Care for your state and include them in your notebook. Look up the statute for your state and complete the following box.

STATE-SPECIFIC INFORMATION

The statutes relating to living wills in the state of _____ require the following:

_____

_____

_____

The statutes for Durable Power of Attorney for Health Care Decisions in this state require the following:

_____

_____

_____

In some states, hospital patients over age 65 are given forms for the living will and Durable Power of Attorney for Health Care during their hospital stay.

● KEY TERMS

beneficiary	joint will
charitable trust	nuncupative will
codicil	pour-over will
decedent	pretermitted-heir statute
estate planning	specific bequest
fiduciary relationship	testamentary trust
formal will	testator
holographic will	trust
inter vivos trust	will

● SELF TEST

1. Who may make a will?
2. What is testamentary capacity?
3. Explain the advantages of having a will.
4. What is a living will?

● NOTEBOOK PROJECTS

1. Make a will for yourself or for a fictional person.
2. Prepare a memorandum for your instructor discussing the advantages and disadvantages of a trust.
3. Obtain a copy of the format for a trust agreement from a law office.
4. Complete the State-Specific Information boxes in this chapter for your notebook.

  For additional resources, visit our Web site at **www.paralegal.delmar.cengage.com.**

PROBATE LAW

CHAPTER OUTCOMES

After studying this chapter, the student will understand

1. the terms used in probate.
2. the information that is discussed at the initial meeting with the personal representative.
3. issues related to property transfers during probate.
4. how to open a probate estate.
5. how to determine the method for settling claims against the estate.

INTRODUCTION

The **probate** process involves proving the validity of the decedent's will and transferring the property of the decedent to the beneficiaries named in the will or those who will take the property as legitimate heirs if the decedent died without a will. During this process, many forms must be completed. The first step in the probate process is an interview with the executor (or personal representative) of the estate. If there is no will or if no executor is named in the will, the court appoints an **administrator** to act as the personal representative of the estate.

Initial Interview

Many individuals appoint a close relative, such as a spouse, parent, or sibling, as **executor** of their estate. Therefore, the initial interview may be difficult for a person who has just lost a loved one. The legal assistant should be sympathetic and understanding but at the same time efficient and professional. A considerable amount of information must be elicited at the interview in order to begin the process of probating the estate.

The attorney usually conducts the initial interview of the personal representative, with the legal assistant present to take notes. Matters to be determined at this interview include the following:

1. Did the decedent die with a will?
2. Where is the original signed will?
3. What property items are not part of the probate estate?

probate a court procedure for proving the validity of a will and distributing estate assets

administrator an individual appointed by the court to administer the deceased's estate when there is no will or when no executor is appointed in the will to take care of the distribution of assets

executor an individual appointed in the will by the decedent to administer the estate

4. Does the personal representative have certified copies of the death certificate?
5. Are there any trusts in the decedent's property?

The primary responsibilities of the personal representative are as follows:

1. Find and collect all assets of the estate.
2. Pay any debts or expenses of the decedent, after determining their legitimacy.
3. Dispense the assets of the estate to the heirs.

The personal representative has a fiduciary responsibility to the estate and is responsible for any actions taken on behalf of the estate. A representative who causes losses to the estate because of his negligence is responsible for those losses. Most state probate codes require that the personal representative undertake his responsibilities diligently and that he act in a prudent manner in any financial matters related to the estate. For instance, if an avocado farm is part of the estate and the avocados are ripe, the personal representative is responsible for arranging to have them picked and sold. Allowing them to rot on their trees would not be a prudent action.

Exhibit 9-1 shows a general estate administration checklist. Exhibit 9-2 shows a specific probate checklist for the state of California, which may be adapted to any other state depending on that state's laws.

After the initial meeting with the personal representative, the legal assistant may assemble the file for the probate of the estate. Several certified copies of the death certificate should be obtained and kept in the file for later use. The original signed will should also be acquired, and the location of the witnesses should be ascertained. The list of nonprobate property should also be kept in the estate's file.

NONPROBATE PROPERTY

Some property passes outside the will and is not part of the probate estate. If the decedent owned property with another individual or individuals as a joint tenant, the joint tenancy property passes outright to the surviving joint tenant(s). However, various documents must be prepared depending on the type of property involved.

Joint Property Bank Accounts

Banks and savings and loan institutions require a certified copy of the death certificate, along with the passbook for the bank account, in order to transfer a savings account to the surviving joint tenant(s). In the case of a checking account, the surviving joint tenant should write a check drawn against the balance in the account and should provide a certified copy of the death certificate in order to close the account and claim the funds.

EXHIBIT 9-1   Estate Administration Checklist
Reprinted with permission of the Iowa State Bar Association.

ESTATE ADMINISTRATION CHECKLIST

ESTATE OF _____

DATE OF DEATH _____

PROBATE NO. _____

PRELIMINARY MATTERS

Obtain copy obituary

Open estate administration file

Meet with personal representative and obtain information concerning decedent and beneficiaries

Determine anatomical gift issues

OPENING ESTATE

INTESTATE ESTATE

Petition for administration and appointment of personal representative

Petition for appointment of administrator and administering intestate estate

Court officer's oath (individual)

Court officer's oath (corporate)

Court officer's bond

Waiver of bond by distributees

Order granting administration and appointing personal representative

Waiver of bond by court

Designation of attorney

Letters of appointment

Notice of appointment in intestate estates—publication and mail notice

Proof of publication of notice filed with clerk/referee

Respond to requests for notice

continued

Exhibit 9-1 *continued*

TESTATE ESTATE

Obtain original will

Petition for probate of will and appointment of personal representative, testimony of witness, and designation of attorney

Submit petition and supporting documents to court

Hearing upon petition (if required)

Obtain order admitting will to probate and appointing personal representative

File court officer's oath

File court officer's bond (if required)

Letters of appointment

Notice of probate of will, appointment of personal representative, and notice to creditors

Proof of publication filed with clerk/referee

POST APPOINTMENT MATTERS

Notice to surviving spouse regarding election to take against will

Open estate account

Application for estate federal identification number (Form SS-4)
    Federal income tax fiduciary notice (Form 56)

Request to employer/Social Security Office for information regarding death benefits, social security benefits, or survivor benefits

Change of address for decedent's mail, if applicable

Information and benefit requests to employer of decedent

Settlement of hospitalization, medical, and expenses related to illness

Settlement of funeral expenses

Notify insurance companies of personal representatives and opening of estate

Request to financial institutions regarding account information

Terminate charge accounts and cancel credit cards

Requests for refunds to utilities, magazine subscriptions, and other services provided to decedent

continued

Exhibit 9-1   *continued*

Requests for information on investments and transfer of investments to estate

Address real estate sale and maintenance, if applicable

Obtain information to prepare and file probate inventory

DATE DUE/FILED

Review and address disclaimers, if applicable

Application for support allowance and order for support allowance

Disposition of real property
If no power of sale clause in will:

a. Petition for authority to sell property;
b. Order fixing time and place of hearing and prescribing notice on petition for authority to sell property
c. Notice of petition for authority to sell property to interested parties;
d. Hearing and authority to sell real property

Prepare and file interlocutory report to court, if required

Distributions of specific bequests

Partial distributions of residue, if appropriate

TAXES

Obtain decedent's individual income tax returns for prior three years

Determine if required to file final decedent Form 1040, and if so, prepare and file state and federal returns and pay tax due

Prepare and file initial estate Form 1041 return

   Initial return filed

Prepare and file estate Form 706, if required

Prepare and file state death tax returns, if required

Transfer estate funds to noninterest bearing account

Prepare and file final estate Form 1041

   Prepared
   Filed

continued

Exhibit 9-1 *continued*

ESTATE CLOSING PROCEDURES

Obtain tax clearances to be filed with final report

    State tax clearances received
    Federal clearances received

Obtain final receipts from beneficiaries

Prepare final accounting

Prepare final report

File final report with proposed order

Obtain closing order

Make final distribution and close estate account

Motor Vehicles Held in Joint Tenancy

Automobile or boat registration held in joint tenancy may be transferred to the surviving joint tenant(s) at the state motor vehicle department. In most states, the following items are required:

1. A certified copy of the death certificate
2. A transfer-of-ownership form signed by the surviving joint tenant(s)
3. The vehicle's official registration

The required items may vary by state. Complete the following box for your state's requirements.

STATE-SPECIFIC INFORMATION

In the state of _____, in order to transfer motor vehicles held in joint tenancy after one joint tenant dies, the following items are required to be taken to the following government department:

_____

1. _____
2. _____
3. _____
4. _____

Joint Tenancy Real Property

Real property includes land, buildings, and items permanently attached thereto. In most states, spouses often own property as joint tenants. The transfer of this property from the deceased joint tenant to his survivor

EXHIBIT 9-2   Probate Procedures for California

Reprinted with permission from *California Legal Directory*, Judy Long, 2000: Thomson Delmar Learning.

PROBATE PROCEDURES FOR CALIFORNIA

NAME OF DECEDENT: EXECUTOR OR
                                                     ADMINISTRATOR:
_____
                                                     _____

DATE OF DEATH: _____   List of Heirs:

1. Certified copy of death certificate   _____

2. List of assets and value at date of death   _____

3. List assets passing outside of will

    Community property _____

    Joint tenancy _____

    Insurance policies _____

    Trusts _____

4. Probate Petition   Prepared _____   Hearing: _____

5. Publication   Newspaper? _____   Date: _____

6. Appointment of executor or administrator? _____

7. Letters? _____

8. Creditors' notices? _____   Dates published? _____

9. Creditors' claims filed? _____

    Name of Creditor: *Claim Amount:*   *Accepted?*

10. Inventory and appraisal filed?

    Fee to appraiser: _____

11. Is federal estate tax due? ($600,000 value of estate?)

12. Does property have to be sold?

    a. Notice of proposed action to heirs?

    b. Hearing required?

13. Have all creditors' claims been satisfied and all property disposed of?

14. Final accounting and distribution _____   Hearing? _____

15. Final distribution of:

    a. Attorney fees

    b. Executor fees

    c. Property to heirs

16. Closed file on: _____

is usually accomplished by the preparation of an affidavit regarding the death of a joint tenant. A certified copy of the death certificate must accompany this affidavit, as well as a preliminary change-of-ownership report. The information that must be included on the affidavit may be found on the original deed to the property. The surviving joint tenant should sign the deed in the presence of a notary public.

Determine the requirements in your state for the transfer of real property held in joint tenancy with the decedent and complete the following box.

STATE-SPECIFIC INFORMATION

In order to transfer joint tenancy real property in the state of _____, these procedures must be followed:

_____

_____

_____

_____

_____

_____

Most states require the surviving joint tenant(s) to sign the affidavit in front of a notary public. Once the affidavit has been completed and signed, it must be recorded in the county recorder's office in the county in which the real property is located. The legal assistant should prepare a letter to the county recorder requesting that the affidavit be recorded and returned to the address on the affidavit. A recording fee must accompany the letter. After the affidavit has been recorded, title to the property passes to the surviving joint tenant(s).

If the process is different in your state, complete the following box.

STATE-SPECIFIC INFORMATION

The process for transfer of joint tenancy real property in the state of _____ is as follows:

_____

_____

_____

_____

_____

_____

Transfer of Stocks and Bonds Held in Joint Tenancy

In order to transfer stocks and bonds held in joint tenancy, the original stock certificate must be obtained. A certified copy of the death certificate is also required. The surviving joint tenant(s) must sign and complete forms transferring ownership. The forms may be obtained at a legal stationery store, from a bank, or from a stockbroker. The form is called an "Irrevocable Stock or Bond Power" or a "Stock or Bond Assignment." The signature of the surviving joint tenant(s) must be guaranteed by a bank officer or stockbroker handling the transaction.

Some transfer agents also require an affidavit of residence indicating that the decedent was a resident of the state. The surviving joint tenant(s) must sign this form before a notary public.

Once all of these documents have been completed, they should be sent to the transfer agent with an accompanying letter. The name(s) of the new owner(s) of the stock should be indicated, along with their address(es) and social security number(s).

Note that if the decedent was the last surviving joint tenant, the stocks and/or bonds become a part of the estate and must go through the probate process.

TRUSTS

In the previous chapter, the advantages of making a trust were discussed. Typically the decedent, during his lifetime, would have prepared the trust with himself as trustee and a spouse as beneficiary. All documents of ownership must be examined to determine whether all property has been transferred to the trust. Any items that have not been placed in the trust must go through the probate process.

The transfer of most trust property to the beneficiaries is relatively simple. A copy of the trust instrument and certified copy of the death certificate are required. If real property is held in the trust, the successor trustee must execute a grant deed to the beneficiaries of the trust.

LIFE INSURANCE POLICIES

Life insurance policies pass directly to the beneficiary without having to go through the probate process. The insurance company will require a certified copy of the death certificate.

COMMUNITY PROPERTY

If the decedent died in a community property state with a surviving spouse, any property held by the husband and wife as *community property* passes to the surviving spouse without a formal probate. Community property includes property acquired during the marriage that is not a spouse's separate property. The legal assistant should read the will carefully to determine whether this is the case. In these situations, the surviving spouse must wait a period of time, generally about 40–60 days, before selling any property to enable potential creditors to come forward.

Determine whether your state is a community property state and the waiting period required before this property may be sold, and complete the following box.

STATE-SPECIFIC INFORMATION

The state of _____ (is / is not) a community property state.

The surviving spouse must wait _____ days after the death before selling any property.

Transfer of Community Real Property

An affidavit from the surviving spouse is required to transfer title to real property. The deed to the property must show that the couple held title "as community property" or "as husband and wife" and not "as joint tenants." If the property is held in joint tenancy, the procedures described in that section earlier in this chapter must be followed. A legal description of the property must be included in the affidavit.

Other Community Property Transfers

Other forms of community property may be transferred by filing a spousal property petition with the probate court. A sample petition for California is shown in Exhibit 9-3.

Item 10-a must be completed only if there are assets in addition to community property that require a separate probate proceeding. In this case, the spousal property petition should have the same case number as the petition for probate of the estate. Local court rules determine whether a probate referee should be appointed (item 1-c.) The legal assistant should investigate local practices in the court in which the proceeding is being filed. The remainder of the form is self-explanatory.

These documents should be filed in the county court in which the decedent resided. Extra copies should be included for the court to conform and return to the law office with the case number and hearing date, if one is required. If there is no other probate proceeding in this case, a filing fee must be included. However, if a petition for probate is filed, it should accompany this petition, along with a filing fee.

EXHIBIT 9-3   Spousal Property Petition with Order

Reprinted from *West's California Judicial Council Forms 2006,* with permission of West, a Thomson business.

DE-221

ATTORNEY OR PARTY WITHOUT ATTORNEY *(Name, State Bar number, and address):*	FOR COURT USE ONLY

TELEPHONE NO.:   FAX NO. *(Optional):*

E-MAIL ADDRESS *(Optional):*

ATTORNEY FOR *(Name):*

SUPERIOR COURT OF CALIFORNIA, COUNTY OF

STREET ADDRESS:

MAILING ADDRESS:

CITY AND ZIP CODE:

BRANCH NAME:

ESTATE OF *(Name):*

DECEDENT

CASE NUMBER:

HEARING DATE:

☐ **SPOUSAL** ☐ **DOMESTIC PARTNER   PROPERTY PETITION**

DEPT.:   TIME:

1. **Petitioner** *(name):*   **requests**
   a. ☐ determination of property passing to the surviving spouse or surviving registered domestic partner without administration (Fam. Code, § 297.5, Prob. Code, § 13500).
   b. ☐ confirmation of property belonging to the surviving spouse or surviving registered domestic partner (Fam. Code, § 297.5, Prob. Code, §§ 100, 101).
   c. ☐ immediate appointment of a probate referee.

2. Petitioner is
   a. ☐ surviving spouse of the decedent.
   b. ☐ personal representative of *(name):*   , surviving spouse.
   c. ☐ guardian or conservator of the estate of *(name):*   , surviving spouse.
   d. ☐ surviving registered domestic partner of the decedent.
   e. ☐ personal representative of *(name):*   , surviving registered domestic partner.
   f. ☐ conservator of the estate of *(name):*   , surviving registered domestic partner.

3. Decedent died on *(date):*

4. Decedent was
   a. ☐ a resident of the California county named above.
   b. ☐ a nonresident of California and left an estate in the county named above.
   c. ☐ intestate ☐ testate and a copy of the will and any codicil is affixed as Attachment 4c.
      (Attach copies of will and any codicil, a typewritten copy of any handwritten document, and an English translation of any foreign-language document.)

5. a. *(Complete in all cases)* The decedent is survived by
      (1) ☐ no child. ☐ child as follows: ☐ natural or adopted ☐ natural, adopted by a third party.
      (2) ☐ no issue of a predeceased child. ☐ issue of a predeceased child.
   b. Decedent ☐ is ☐ is not survived by a stepchild or foster child or children who would have been adopted by decedent but for a legal barrier. *(See Prob. Code, § 6454.)*

6. *(Complete only if no issue survived the decedent. Check **only** the **first** box that applies.)*
   a. ☐ The decedent is survived by a parent or parents who are listed in item 9.
   b. ☐ The decedent is survived by a brother, sister, or issue of a deceased brother or sister, all of whom are listed in item 9.

7. Administration of all or part of the estate is not necessary for the reason that all or a part of the estate is property passing to the surviving spouse or surviving registered domestic partner. The facts upon which petitioner bases the allegation that the property described in Attachments 7a and 7b is property that should pass or be confirmed to the surviving spouse or surviving registered domestic partner are stated in Attachment 7.
   a. ☐ Attachment 7a[1] contains the legal description *(if real property add Assessor's Parcel Number)* of the deceased spouse's or registered domestic partner's property that petitioner requests to be determined as having passed to the surviving spouse or partner from the deceased spouse or partner. This includes any interest in a trade or business name of any unincorporated business or an interest in any unincorporated business that the deceased spouse or partner was operating or managing at the time of death, subject to any written agreement between the deceased spouse or partner and the surviving spouse or partner providing for a non pro rata division of the aggregate value of the community property assets or quasi-community assets, or both.

   [1] See Prob. Code, § 13658 for required filing of a list of known creditors of a business and other information in certain instances. If required, include in Attachment 7a.

Page 1 of 2

Form Adopted for Mandatory Use
Judicial Council of California DE-221
[Rev. January 1, 2005]   **SPOUSAL OR DOMESTIC PARTNER PROPERTY PETITION**
(Probate—Decedents Estates)   Family Code, § 297.5;
Probate Code, § 13650

American LegalNet, Inc.
www.USCourtForms.com

continued

Exhibit 9-3 *continued*

ESTATE OF *(Name):*	CASE NUMBER:
DECEDENT	

7. b. ☐ Attachment 7b contains the legal description *(if real property add Assessor's Parcel Number)* of the community or quasi-community property petitioner requests to be determined as having belonged under Probate Code sections 100 and 101 and Family Code section 297.5 to the surviving spouse or surviving registered domestic partner upon the deceased spouse's or partner's death, subject to any written agreement between the deceased spouse or partner and the surviving spouse or partner providing for a non pro rata division of the aggregate value of the community property assets or quasi-community assets, or both.

8. There ☐ exists ☐ does not exist   a written agreement between the deceased spouse or deceased registered domestic partner and the surviving spouse or surviving registered domestic partner providing for a non pro rata division of the aggregate value of the community property assets or quasi-community assets, or both. *(If petitioner bases the description of the property of the deceased spouse or partner passing to the surviving spouse or partner or the property to be confirmed to the surviving spouse or partner, or both, on a written agreement, a copy of the agreement must be attached to this petition as Attachment 8.)*

9. The names, relationships, ages, and residence or mailing addresses so far as known to or reasonably ascertainable by petitioner of (1) all persons named in decedent's will and codicils, whether living or deceased, and (2) all persons checked in items 5 and 6

☐ are listed below   ☐ are listed in Attachment 9.

Name and relationship	Age	Residence or mailing address

10. The names and addresses of all persons named as executors in the decedent's will and any codicil or appointed as personal representatives of the decedent's estate ☐ are listed below ☐ are listed in Attachment 10 ☐ none

11. ☐ The petitioner is the trustee of a trust that is a devisee under decedent's will. The names and addresses of all persons interested in the trust who are entitled to notice under Probate Code section 13655(b)(2) are listed in Attachment 11.

12. A petition for probate or for administration of the decedent's estate
   a. ☐ is being filed with this petition.
   b. ☐ was filed on *(date):*
   c. ☐ has not been filed and is not being filed with this petition.

13. Number of pages attached: _____

Date:

_____   ▶ _____
(TYPE OR PRINT NAME)   (SIGNATURE OF ATTORNEY)

I declare under penalty of perjury under the laws of the State of California that the foregoing is true and correct.

Date:

_____   ▶ _____
(TYPE OR PRINT NAME)   (SIGNATURE OF PETITIONER)

DE-221 [Rev. January 1, 2005]   **SPOUSAL OR DOMESTIC PARTNER PROPERTY PETITION**   Page 2 of 2
                                                         (Probate—Decedents Estates)

After the court returns the documents, the individuals listed on the petition must receive a notice of the hearing at least 15 days before the hearing date. This notice requirement may vary by state. The notice must be filed with the court after service is completed and before the hearing date.

In order to have all estate property declared community property that passes directly to the surviving spouse, a spousal property order must be prepared for the judge's signature at the hearing. The legal assistant should complete this form and submit it to the court according to local rules. Once the spousal property order is signed, a certified official copy is required for each item of property being transferred to the surviving spouse.

Some states have forms available for the purposes described previously. Other states require typed documents for these transfers. Check your state's court rules to determine the proper procedure for community property transfers and explain the procedures in the following box.

STATE-SPECIFIC INFORMATION

Community property transfers in the state of _____ are accomplished by the following methods:

_____

_____

_____

_____

_____

_____

THE PROBATE PROCESS

The decedent's property must go through a formal probate proceeding if any property remains in addition to the following:

1. property held in joint tenancy
2. property held as community property
3. insurance policies
4. property held in a trust

None of these four items should be included in the formal probate process.

Formal Probate Procedures

In most cases, the client is the executor of the estate and is so named in the decedent's will. If there is no will, if the executor named in the will cannot or will not serve, or if no executor is appointed in the will, the court appoints an administrator to administer the estate.

Before the probate process begins, the legal assistant should check with the individual court in which the case will be filed to identify any special probate rules. Some courts provide a booklet that explains their special requirements.

Petition

Probate begins with the filing of the petition. The original will must be submitted with the petition. Filing is usually done in person. The probate attorneys scrutinize the petition carefully for errors and omissions, and any missing items or discrepancies are documented in the probate notes on file in the clerk's office. Errors must be corrected prior to the hearing, which will be set approximately 30 days after the petition is filed. A sample Petition for Formal Probate of Will and Formal Appointment of Personal Representative for the state of Colorado is shown in Exhibit 9-4.

Notice of Petition to Administer Estate

Some states require that a Notice must be published in a newspaper and mailed to all heirs and beneficiaries at least 15 days before the hearing. It gives notice to all concerned parties of the hearing date.

Generally the notice must be published three times in a newspaper of general circulation in the city in which the decedent lived, commencing approximately 15 days before the hearing. Proof of publication is filed with the court before the hearing. All heirs and beneficiaries under the will must also obtain a copy of the notice.

A Notice of Hearing to Interested Persons for the state of Colorado is shown in Exhibit 9-5.

Check your state's requirements for Notice and complete the following box.

STATE-SPECIFIC INFORMATION

The state of _____ requires the following Notice requirements before the hearing:

_____

_____

_____

_____

_____

_____

Filing Fees

In most states, one filing fee is required for the complete probate action and must accompany the petition. This fee is paid from the assets of

EXHIBIT 9-4   Petition for Formal Probate of Will and Formal Appointment of Personal Representative (Colorado)

From http://www.westlegalstudies.com. Reprinted with permission from Thomson Delmar Learning.

❏ District Court   ❏ Denver Probate Court

_____ County, Colorado

Court Address:

_____

IN THE MATTER OF THE ESTATE OF:

Deceased   ▲ COURT USE ONLY ▲

Attorney or Party Without Attorney (Name and Address):   Case Number:

Phone Number: E-mail:

FAX Number: Atty. Reg. #:   Division   Courtroom

**PETITION FOR FORMAL PROBATE OF WILL
AND FORMAL APPOINTMENT OF PERSONAL REPRESENTATIVE**

---

1. Petitioner, (Name) _____
   as _____, is an interested person. (§15-10-201, C.R.S.)

2. The decedent died on the date of _____, at the age of _____ years, domiciled in the City of
   _____, County of _____, State of _____.

3. Venue for this proceeding is proper in this county because the decedent:

   ❏ was a domiciliary of this county on the date of death.

   ❏ was not a domiciliary of Colorado, but property of the decedent was located in this county on the date of death.

4. ❏ No personal representative has been appointed by a Court in this state or elsewhere.

   ❏ A personal representative of the decedent has been appointed by a Court in this state or elsewhere as shown on the attached explanation.
   (§15-12-301, C.R.S.)

5. Petitioner:

   ❏ has not received a demand for notice and is unaware of any demand for notice of any probate or appointment proceeding concerning the
   decedent that may have been filed in this state or elsewhere.

   ❏ has received, or is aware of, a demand for notice. See attached demand or explanation.

6. The date of decedent's last will is _____. The dates of all codicils are _____
   _____.

   The will and any codicils are referred to as the will. The will:

   ❏ was deposited with this Court before the decedent's death. (§15-11-515, C.R.S.)

   ❏ has been lodged with this Court since the decedent's death. (§15-11-516, C.R.S.)

   ❏ is filed with this petition.

   ❏ has been probated in the State of _____. Authenticated copies of the will and of the statement probating it are filed
   with this petition. (§15-12-402, C.R.S.)

   ❏ is lost, destroyed, or otherwise unavailable. See attached explanation. (§15-12-402, C.R.S.)

7. Except as may be disclosed on an attached explanation and after the exercise of reasonable diligence, petitioner is unaware of any instrument
   revoking the will, is unaware of any prior wills which have not been expressly revoked by a later instrument, and believes that the will is the
   decedent's last will and was validly executed.

8. ❏ No statutory time limitation applies to the commencement of these proceedings. (§15-12-108, C.R.S.)
   ❏ More than 3 years have passed since decedent's death. A statutory time limitation would apply to the commencement of these proceedings
   except for the circumstances described in an attachment to this petition.

9. _____
   Name, address, and telephone number of the nominee for Personal Representative

   _____

   is 21 years of age or older, and has priority for appointment because of:

CPC 9   R7/04   PETITION FOR FORMAL PROBATE OF WILL AND   Page 1 of 2
                FORMAL APPOINTMENT OF PERSONAL REPRESENTATIVE
This form conforms in substance to CPC 9.

continued

Exhibit 9-4 *continued*

❑ nomination by the will.

❑ statutory priority. (§15-12-203, C.R.S.)

❑ reasons stated in the attached explanation.

10. The nominee is to serve:

❑ without bond   ❑ in unsupervised administration

❑ with bond (§15-12-604, C.R.S.)   ❑ in supervised administration

11. The decedent ❑ was ❑ was not   married at time of death.

12. Listed below are the names and addresses of decedent's spouse, children, heirs and devisees, and the names and addresses of guardians or conservators of incapacitated or protected persons. (See instructions below.)

NAME (Include spouse, if any)	ADDRESS (or date of death)	AGE AND DATE OF BIRTH OF MINORS (or nature of disability)	INTEREST AND RELATIONSHIP (See instructions)

PETITIONER REQUESTS that the Court set a time and place of hearing; that notice be given to all interested persons as provided by law; that after notice and hearing, the Court determine the heirs of the decedent and formally admit the decedent's will to probate; that the nominee:

❑ be formally appointed as personal representative   ❑ be formally confirmed as personal representative
❑ without bond   ❑ with bond
❑ in unsupervised administration   ❑ in supervised administration (additional fee required)

and that Letters Testamentary be issued to the personal representative or confirmed. Petitioner also requests:

❑ a setting aside of prior informal findings as to testacy,

❑ a setting aside of prior informal appointment of personal representative,

❑ _____

_____   _____   _____   _____
Signature of Attorney for Petitioner   Date   Signature of Petitioner   Date
(Type or Print name below)   (Type or Print name, address and telephone # below)

_____   _____

                                                         _____

                                                         _____

                                                         _____

INSTRUCTIONS FOR PARAGRAPH 12:

Include any statements of legal disability or other incapacity required by Rule 10, C.R.P.P.

List the names and dates of death of any deceased devisees. (See applicable antilapse statute, §§15-11-601 and 603, C.R.S.)

Where a listed person is an heir, detail the relationship to the decedent which creates heirship. Examples: son, daughter of pre-deceased son. (§§15-11-101 to 114, C.R.S.)

Attach additional sheets if necessary.

CPC 9   R7/04   PETITION FOR FORMAL PROBATE OF WILL AND   Page 2 of 2
                   FORMAL APPOINTMENT OF PERSONAL REPRESENTATIVE
This form conforms in substance to CPC 9.

EXHIBIT 9-5   Notice of Hearing to Interested Persons (Colorado)

From http://www.westlegalstudies.com. Reprinted with permission from Thomson Delmar Learning.

❑ District Court   ❑ Denver Probate Court

_____ County, Colorado

Court Address:

_____

IN THE MATTER OF ❑ THE ESTATE OF:

Respondent   ▲ COURT USE ONLY ▲

Attorney or Party Without Attorney (Name and Address):   Case Number:

Phone Number: E-mail:
FAX Number: Atty. Reg.#:   Division   Courtroom

NOTICE OF HEARING TO INTERESTED PERSONS

TO ALL INTERESTED PERSONS:

A hearing on   ❑ Petition for Appointment of Guardian   ❑ Petition for Appointment of Conservator

❑ _____

a copy of which accompanies this Notice, will be held at the following time and location or at a later date to which the hearing may be continued.

Date and Time: _____

Courtroom or Division: _____

Address: _____

                               _____

The outcome of this proceeding may limit or completely take away the respondent's right to make decisions about the respondent's personal affairs or financial affairs or both. The respondent must appear in person unless excused by the court. The petitioner is required to make reasonable efforts to help the respondent attend the hearing.

The respondent has the right to be represented by an attorney of the respondent's choice at the respondent's expense. If the respondent cannot afford an attorney, one may be appointed for the respondent at State expense. The respondent may request a professional evaluation. The respondent has the right to present evidence and subpoena witnesses and documents; examine witnesses, including any court-appointed physician, psychologist, or other qualified individual providing evaluations, and the court visitor; and otherwise participate in the hearing. The respondent may ask that the hearing be held in a manner that reasonably accommodates the respondent. The respondent has the right to request that the hearing be closed, but the hearing may not be closed over the respondent's objection.

_____
Signature of Attorney for or Person Giving Notice

CPC 2-IP   1/01   NOTICE OF HEARING TO INTERESTED PERSONS   Page 1 of 2
This form conforms in substance to CPC 2-IP.

continued

Exhibit 9-5 *continued*

Certificate of Service

I certify that a copy of the foregoing Notice of Hearing to Interested Persons was served on each of the following:

Name	**Date**	**Address**	**Manner of Service***

_____
Signature of Person Certifying Service

*Insert: hand delivery, first class U.S. mail, certified U.S. mail or registered U.S. mail

INSTRUCTIONS: This Notice of Hearing to Interested Persons must be served on all others listed in the Petition for Appointment of Guardian and Petition for Appointment of Conservator, along with a copy of the petition, at least ten (10) days prior to the hearing pursuant to §15-14-309(2) or §15-14-404(2).

NOTE: This form cannot be used for notice to the respondent. The respondent must be personally served with CPC Form 2-R, along with a copy of the petition, at least ten (10) days prior to the hearing pursuant to §15-14-309(1) or §15-14-404(1).

Do not attach copies of the petition when filing the Notice of Hearing to Interested Persons with the court.

CPC 2-IP 1/01 NOTICE OF HEARING TO INTERESTED PERSONS   Page 2 of 2
This form conforms in substance to CPC 2-IP.

the estate. If the executor or attorney advances the expense, he should be reimbursed after an estate checking account is opened.

STATE-SPECIFIC INFORMATION

The state of _____ charges (one filing fee / separate filing fees) for the probate action.

Proof of Subscribing Witness

If the will is not a **self-proving will,** one witness to the will must sign a proof-of-subscribing-witness form attesting that the decedent signed the will in the witness's presence. However, most wills contain a clause before the witness signature as follows:

> The foregoing document, consisting of four pages including this page, was on this date signed by MARY SMITH and declared to be her will. We are familiar with the testator and know her to be the individual who signed in our presence and in the presence of each of us. We observed the signing of the will by MARY SMITH and by each other witness. Each signature is the signature of the person whose name was signed.
>
> Each of us is now more than eighteen (18) years of age, is a competent witness, and resides at the address signed after her name. We are acquainted with the testator and know she is over the age of eighteen. To our knowledge, she is of sound mind and not acting under duress, menace, fraud, or the undue influence of any person.

_____   Address: _____

_____

_____   Address: _____

_____

Note that some states require three witnesses for a formal will and may have other different requirements as well. If a clause such as the preceding one is included in the will, then the will is considered self-proving and no proof-of-subscribing-witness form is required.

Order for Probate

After the court approves the petition and prior to the hearing, an order for probate must be prepared and submitted to the court for the judge's signature. A sample order is shown in Exhibit 9-6. After the hearing, the judge signs the order appointing the executor. Note that in some states a form may not be available and the legal assistant will be required to prepare the order on legal cap paper with the same or similar information as is included in the form.

self-proving will   a certain clause in a will makes the will self-proving; this clause eliminates the need for the witnesses to sign a proof-of-subscribing-witness form to attest to the authenticity of the decedent's signature

EXHIBIT 9-6 Order for Probate

Reprinted with permission from *California Legal Directory,* Judy Long, 2000: Thomson Delmar Learning.

DE-140

ATTORNEY OR PARTY WITHOUT ATTORNEY *(Name, state bar number, and address):*	TELEPHONE AND FAX NOS.:	FOR COURT USE ONLY

ATTORNEY FOR *(Name):*

SUPERIOR COURT OF CALIFORNIA, COUNTY OF

STREET ADDRESS:

MAILING ADDRESS:

CITY AND ZIP CODE:

BRANCH NAME:

ESTATE OF *(Name):*

DECEDENT

ORDER FOR PROBATE	CASE NUMBER:

ORDER ☐ Executor
APPOINTING ☐ Administrator with Will Annexed
☐ Administrator ☐ Special Administrator
☐ Order Authorizing Independent Administration of Estate
☐ with full authority ☐ with limited authority

WARNING: THIS APPOINTMENT IS NOT EFFECTIVE UNTIL LETTERS HAVE ISSUED.

1. Date of hearing: Time: Dept./Room: Judge:

THE COURT FINDS

2. a. All notices required by law have been given.
   b. Decedent died on *(date):*
      (1) ☐ a resident of the California county named above.
      (2) ☐ a nonresident of California and left an estate in the county named above.
   c. Decedent died
      (1) ☐ intestate
      (2) ☐ testate
      and decedent's will dated: and each codicil dated:
      was admitted to probate by Minute Order on *(date):*

THE COURT ORDERS

3. *(Name):*
   is appointed **personal representative:**
   a. ☐ executor of the decedent's will   d. ☐ special administrator
   b. ☐ administrator with will annexed   (1) ☐ with general powers
   c. ☐ administrator   (2) ☐ with special powers as specified in Attachment 3d(2)
                                                  (3) ☐ without notice of hearing
                                                  (4) ☐ letters will expire on *(date):*
   and letters shall issue on qualification.
4. a. ☐ **Full authority** is granted to administer the estate under the Independent Administration of Estates Act.
   b. ☐ **Limited authority** is granted to administer the estate under the Independent Administration of Estates Act (there is no authority, without court supervision, to (1) sell or exchange real property or (2) grant an option to purchase real property or (3) borrow money with the loan secured by an encumbrance upon real property).
5. a. ☐ Bond is not required.
   b. ☐ Bond is fixed at: $ to be furnished by an authorized surety company or as otherwise provided by law.
   c. ☐ Deposits of: $ are ordered to be placed in a blocked account at *(specify institution and location):*
      and receipts shall be filed. No withdrawals shall be made without a court order. ☐ Additional orders in Attachment 5c.
   d. ☐ The personal representative is not authorized to take possession of money or any other property without a specific court order.
6. ☐ *(Name):*   is appointed probate referee.

Date:

_____
JUDGE OF THE SUPERIOR COURT

7. Number of pages attached: _____   ☐ SIGNATURE FOLLOWS LAST ATTACHMENT

Form Approved by the Judicial Council of California DE-140 [Rev. January 1, 1998] Mandatory Form [1/1/2000]	**ORDER FOR PROBATE**	Probate Code, §§ 8006, 8400 American LegalNet, Inc. www.USCourtForms.com

Letters Testamentary

A sample form for letters testamentary is shown in Exhibit 9-7. Note that this form is from the state of Colorado. If your state does not provide a form for this purpose, then the legal assistant must prepare the letters on legal cap paper. In some states, this form must be accompanied by a document titled "Duties and Liabilities of Personal Representative." Some states provide a form for this purpose; in other states, the document may have to be prepared on legal cap paper with the same information that is included in the form in Exhibit 9-8.

Notice of Proposed Action

If the executor must sell real property of the estate before the closing, a notice of proposed action (Exhibit 9-9) should be completed and filed with the court. All individuals who are beneficiaries of the property must receive a copy of the notice. For example, if the executor must sell a house that was left to the decedent's two children, each child must receive a copy of the notice indicating the executor's intent.

Note that if a form is not available in your state, the legal assistant may be required to prepare this notice on legal cap.

Inventory and Appraisal

An inventory and appraisal of estate assets must be filed with the court within four months of the time the letters are issued. This time may vary in different states. Some states, such as California, have a form for this purpose. Other states require an office-typed document on legal cap with the same information contained therein. The inventory and appraisal must include attachments listing all of the estate's assets with their value. Attachment 1 should include assets that have readily ascertainable values, such as bank accounts, cash on hand, and salary or retirement funds issued after death. Note that some government-administered retirement plans and social security require that the benefits for the month in which the decedent died must be returned. Attachment 2 lists all assets that have been appraised by a probate referee, who is appointed by the court and paid from estate funds. A sample form and attachments are shown in Exhibit 9-10.

Determine the requirements for your state and complete the following box.

STATE-SPECIFIC INFORMATION

In the state of _____, the inventory and appraisal must be filed with the court within _____ months of the time the letters are issued. In this state

_____the blank form may be obtained from _____

_____an office-typed document on legal cap is required.

EXHIBIT 9-7   Sample Form for Letters Testamentary (Colorado)

From http://www.westlegalstudies.com. Reprinted with permission from Thomson Delmar Learning.

❏ District Court   ❏ Denver Probate Court
_____ County, Colorado

Court Address:

_____

IN THE MATTER OF   ❏   THE ESTATE OF:

▲ COURT USE ONLY ▲

Case Number:

❏ **Deceased** ❏ **Protected Person** ❏ **Minor** ❏ **Ward**

Division: Courtroom:

LETTERS

(Name) _____was appointed or qualified by this Court or its Registrar

on _____(date) as:

❏ Personal Representative. The decedent died on _____ (date).
    ❏ These are Letters of Administration. (The decedent did not leave a will.)
    ❏ These are Letters Testamentary. (The decedent left a will.)

❏ Special Administrator in ❏ an informal ❏ a formal   proceeding. These are Letters of Special Administration.

❏ Conservator. These are Letters of Conservatorship.
    ❏ The protected person is a minor whose date of birth is _____.
    ❏ Special Conservator.

❏ Guardian. These are Letters of Guardianship for:

    ❏ an incapacitated person. ❏ a minor whose date of birth is _____.
    ❏ Emergency Guardian
       (Expires on _____(date), not more than 60 days after appointment per §15-14-312, C.R.S.)
       Appointment or qualification is by ❏ court order. ❏ will. ❏ written instrument.
❏ _____
_____

These Letters evidence full authority, except for the following limitations or restrictions, if any:
_____
_____

Dated: _____   _____
                                                (Deputy) Clerk or Registrar of Court

CERTIFICATION

    Certification Stamp   or   Certified to be a true copy of the original in my
                                                custody and to be in full force and effect as of:

Dated: _____   _____
                                                (Deputy) Clerk of Court

CPC 17   R1/03   LETTERS
This forms conforms in substance to CPC 17.

EXHIBIT 9-8   Duties and Liabilities of Personal Representative

DE-147

ATTORNEY OR PARTY WITHOUT ATTORNEY *(Name, state bar number, and address):*	FOR COURT USE ONLY

TELEPHONE NO.:   FAX NO. *(Optional):*
E-MAIL ADDRESS *(Optional):*
ATTORNEY FOR *(Name):*

SUPERIOR COURT OF CALIFORNIA, COUNTY OF
STREET ADDRESS:
MAILING ADDRESS:
CITY AND ZIP CODE:
BRANCH NAME:

ESTATE OF *(Name):*

DECEDENT

DUTIES AND LIABILITIES OF PERSONAL REPRESENTATIVE and Acknowledgment of Receipt	CASE NUMBER:

DUTIES AND LIABILITIES OF PERSONAL REPRESENTATIVE

When the court appoints you as personal representative of an estate, you become an officer of the court and assume certain duties and obligations. An attorney is best qualified to advise you about these matters. You should understand the following:

1. MANAGING THE ESTATE'S ASSETS

a. Prudent investments
You must manage the estate assets with the care of a prudent person dealing with someone else's property. This means that you must be cautious and may not make any speculative investments.

b. Keep estate assets separate
You must keep the money and property in this estate separate from anyone else's, including your own. When you open a bank account for the estate, the account name must indicate that it is an estate account and not your personal account. Never deposit estate funds in your personal account or otherwise mix them with your or anyone else's property. Securities in the estate must also be held in a name that shows they are estate property and not your personal property.

c. Interest-bearing accounts and other investments
Except for checking accounts intended for ordinary administration expenses, estate accounts must earn interest. You may deposit estate funds in insured accounts in financial institutions, but you should consult with an attorney before making other kinds of investments.

d. Other restrictions
There are many other restrictions on your authority to deal with estate property. You should not spend any of the estate's money unless you have received permission from the court or have been advised to do so by an attorney. You may reimburse yourself for official court costs paid by you to the county clerk and for the premium on your bond. Without prior order of the court, you may not pay fees to yourself or to your attorney, if you have one. If you do not obtain the court's permission when it is required, you may be removed as personal representative or you may be required to reimburse the estate from your own personal funds, or both. You should consult with an attorney concerning the legal requirements affecting sales, leases, mortgages, and investments of estate property.

2. INVENTORY OF ESTATE PROPERTY

a. Locate the estate's property
You must attempt to locate and take possession of all the decedent's property to be administered in the estate.

b. Determine the value of the property
You must arrange to have a court-appointed referee determine the value of the property unless the appointment is waived by the court. You, rather than the referee, must determine the value of certain "cash items." An attorney can advise you about how to do this.

c. File an inventory and appraisal
Within four months after Letters are first issued to you as personal representative, you must file with the court an inventory and appraisal of all the assets in the estate.

Page 1 of 2

Form Adopted for Mandatory Use Judicial Council of California DE-147 [Rev. January 1, 2002]	DUTIES AND LIABILITIES OF PERSONAL REPRESENTATIVE (Probate)	Probate Code, § 8404 American LegalNet, Inc. www.USCourtForms.com

continued

Exhibit 9-8 *continued*

ESTATE OF *(Name)*:	CASE NUMBER:
DECEDENT	

d. File a change of ownership

At the time you file the inventory and appraisal, you must also file a change of ownership statement with the county recorder or assessor in each county where the decedent owned real property at the time of death, as provided in section 480 of the California Revenue and Taxation Code.

3. NOTICE TO CREDITORS

You must mail a notice of administration to each known creditor of the decedent within four months after your appointment as personal representative. If the decedent received Medi-Cal assistance, you must notify the State Director of Health Services within 90 days after appointment.

4. INSURANCE

You should determine that there is appropriate and adequate insurance covering the assets and risks of the estate. Maintain the insurance in force during the entire period of the administration.

5. RECORD KEEPING

a. Keep accounts

You must keep complete and accurate records of each financial transaction affecting the estate. You will have to prepare an account of all money and property you have received, what you have spent, and the date of each transaction. You must describe in detail what you have left after the payment of expenses.

b. Court review

Your account will be reviewed by the court. Save your receipts because the court may ask to review them. If you do not file your accounts as required, the court will order you to do so. You may be removed as personal representative if you fail to comply.

6. CONSULTING AN ATTORNEY

If you have an attorney, you should cooperate with the attorney at all times. You and your attorney are responsible for completing the estate administration as promptly as possible. **When in doubt, contact your attorney.**

NOTICE: 1. **This statement of duties and liabilities is a summary and is not a complete statement of the law. Your conduct as a personal representative is governed by the law itself and not by this summary.**
2. **If you fail to perform your duties or to meet the deadlines, the court may reduce your compensation, remove you from office, and impose other sanctions.**

ACKNOWLEDGMENT OF RECEIPT

1. I have petitioned the court to be appointed as a personal representative.

2. My address and telephone number are *(specify)*:

3. I acknowledge that I have received a copy of this statement of the duties and liabilities of the office of personal representative.

Date:

_____ ▶ _____
(TYPE OR PRINT NAME)   (SIGNATURE OF PETITIONER)

Date:

_____ ▶ _____
(TYPE OR PRINT NAME)   (SIGNATURE OF PETITIONER)

CONFIDENTIAL INFORMATION: If required to do so by local court rule, you must provide your date of birth and driver's license number on supplemental Form DE-147S. (Prob. Code, § 8404(b).)

DE-147 [Rev. January 1, 2002] **DUTIES AND LIABILITIES OF PERSONAL REPRESENTATIVE** Page 2 of 2
(Probate)

EXHIBIT 9-9   Notice of Proposed Action

DE-165

ATTORNEY OR PARTY WITHOUT ATTORNEY *(Name, state bar number, and address):*	TELEPHONE AND FAX NOS.:	*FOR COURT USE ONLY*

ATTORNEY FOR *(Name):*

SUPERIOR COURT OF CALIFORNIA, COUNTY OF

STREET ADDRESS:

MAILING ADDRESS:

CITY AND ZIP CODE:

BRANCH NAME:

ESTATE OF *(Name):*

DECEDENT

NOTICE OF PROPOSED ACTION **Independent Administration of Estates Act** ☐ **Objection** ☐ **Consent**	CASE NUMBER:

> **NOTICE: If you do not object in writing or obtain a court order preventing the action proposed below, you will be treated as if you consented to the proposed action and you may not object after the proposed action has been taken. If you object, the personal representative may take the proposed action only under court supervision. An objection form is on the reverse. If you wish to object, you may use the form or prepare your own written objection.**

1.   The personal representative (executor or administrator) of the estate of the deceased is *(names):*

2.   The personal representative has authority to administer the estate without court supervision under the Independent Administration of Estates Act (Prob. Code, § 10400 et seq.)

   a. ☐ with **full authority** under the act.

   b. ☐ with **limited authority** under the act (there is no authority, without court supervision, to (1) sell or exchange real property or (2) grant an option to purchase real property or (3) borrow money with the loan secured by an encumbrance upon real property).

3.   **On or after** *(date):* [＿＿＿＿＿＿] , the personal representative will take the following action without court supervision *(describe in specific terms here or in Attachment 3):*

   ☐ The proposed action is described in an attachment labeled Attachment 3.

4.   ☐ **Real property transaction** *(Check this box and complete item 4b if the proposed action involves a sale or exchange or a grant of an option to purchase real property.)*
   a. The material terms of the transaction are specified in item 3, including any sale price and the amount of or method of calculating any commission or compensation to an agent or broker.
   b. **$**＿＿＿＿＿＿＿   is the value of the subject property in the probate inventory.   ☐ No inventory yet.

> **NOTICE: A sale of real property without court supervision means that the sale will NOT be presented to the court for confirmation at a hearing at which higher bids for the property may be presented and the property sold to the highest bidder.**

(Continued on reverse)

Form Approved by the Judicial Council of California DE-165 [Rev. January 1, 1998] Mandatory Form [1/1/2000]	**NOTICE OF PROPOSED ACTION** **Objection—Consent** **(Probate)**	Probate Code, § 10580 et seq. American LegalNet, Inc. www.USCourtForms.com

continued

Exhibit 9-9 *continued*

ESTATE OF *(Name):*	CASE NUMBER:
DECEDENT	

5. **If you OBJECT to the proposed action**

   a. **Sign** the objection form below and deliver or mail it to the personal representative at the following address *(specify name and address):*

   OR

   b. **Send** your own written objection to the address in item 5a. *(Be sure to identify the proposed action and state that you object to it.)*

   OR

   c. **Apply** to the court for an order preventing the personal representative from taking the proposed action without court supervision.

   d. **NOTE:** Your written objection or the court order must be received by the personal representative before the date in the box in item 3, or before the proposed action is taken, whichever is later. If you object, the personal representative may take the proposed action only under court supervision.

6. **If you APPROVE the proposed action,** you may sign the consent form below and return it to the address in item 5a. If you do not object in writing or obtain a court order, you will be treated as if you consented to the proposed action.

7. **If you need more INFORMATION, call** *(name):*

   (telephone):

Date:

.... ▶ _____

(TYPE OR PRINT NAME)   (SIGNATURE OF PERSONAL REPRESENTATIVE OR ATTORNEY)

OBJECTION TO PROPOSED ACTION

☐ **I OBJECT** to the action proposed in item 3.

> **NOTICE: Sign and return this form (both sides) to the address in item 5a. The form must be received before the date in the box in item 3, or before the proposed action is taken, whichever is later. *(You may want to use certified mail, with return receipt requested. Make a copy of this form for your records.)***

Date:

.... ▶ _____

(TYPE OR PRINT NAME)   (SIGNATURE OF OBJECTOR)

CONSENT TO PROPOSED ACTION

☐ **I CONSENT** to the action proposed in item 3.

> **NOTICE: You may indicate your *consent* by signing and returning this form (both sides) to the address in item 5a. If you do not object in writing or obtain a court order, you will be treated as if you consented to the proposed action.**

Date:

.... ▶ _____

(TYPE OR PRINT NAME)   (SIGNATURE OF CONSENTER)

DE-165 [Rev. January 1, 1998]   **NOTICE OF PROPOSED ACTION**   Page two
Objection—Consent
(Probate)

EXHIBIT 9-10   Inventory and Appraisal Form with Attachment (California)

DE-160/GC-040

ATTORNEY OR PARTY WITHOUT ATTORNEY *(Name, state bar number, and address)*:	FOR COURT USE ONLY

TELEPHONE NO.:   FAX NO. *(Optional)*:

E-MAIL ADDRESS *(Optional)*:

ATTORNEY FOR *(Name)*:

SUPERIOR COURT OF CALIFORNIA, COUNTY OF

STREET ADDRESS:

MAILING ADDRESS:

CITY AND ZIP CODE:

BRANCH NAME:

ESTATE OF *(Name)*:

☐ DECEDENT   ☐ CONSERVATEE   ☐ MINOR

INVENTORY AND APPRAISAL	CASE NUMBER:
☐ **Partial No.:** ☐ **Corrected**	
☐ **Final** ☐ **Reappraisal for Sale**	Date of Death of Decedent or of Appointment
☐ **Supplemental** ☐ **Property Tax Certificate**	of Guardian or Conservator:

APPRAISALS

1. Total appraisal by representative, guardian, or conservator (Attachment 1): $
2. Total appraisal by referee (Attachment 2): $
                                                            TOTAL: $

DECLARATION OF REPRESENTATIVE, GUARDIAN, CONSERVATOR, OR SMALL ESTATE CLAIMANT

3. Attachments 1 and 2 together with all prior inventories filed contain a true statement of
   ☐ all ☐ a portion of the estate that has come to my knowledge or possession, including particularly all money and all
   just claims the estate has against me. I have truly, honestly, and impartially appraised to the best of my ability each item set forth in
   Attachment 1.

4. ☐ No probate referee is required   ☐ by order of the court dated *(specify)*:

5. **Property tax certificate.** I certify that the requirements of Revenue and Taxation Code section 480
   a. ☐ are not applicable because the decedent owned no real property in California at the time of death.
   b. ☐ have been satisfied by the filing of a change of ownership statement with the county recorder or assessor of each county in California in
      which the decedent owned property at the time of death.

I declare under penalty of perjury under the laws of the State of California that the foregoing is true and correct.

Date:

►

_____   _____
(TYPE OR PRINT NAME; INCLUDE TITLE IF CORPORATE OFFICER)   (SIGNATURE)

STATEMENT ABOUT THE BOND

(Complete in all cases. Must be signed by attorney for fiduciary, or by fiduciary without an attorney.)

6. ☐ Bond is waived, or the sole fiduciary is a corporate fiduciary or an exempt government agency.

7. ☐ Bond filed in the amount of: $ ☐ Sufficient   ☐ Insufficient

8. ☐ Receipts for: $ have been filed with the court for deposits in a blocked account at *(specify institution and location)*:

Date:

►

_____   _____
(TYPE OR PRINT NAME)   (SIGNATURE OF ATTORNEY OR PARTY WITHOUT ATTORNEY)

Page 1 of 2

Form Adopted for Mandatory Use	**INVENTORY AND APPRAISAL**	Probate Code, §§ 2610–2616, 8800–8980;
Judicial Council of California		Cal. Rules of Court, rule 7.501
DE-160/GC-040 [Rev. January 1, 2003]		

American LegalNet, Inc.
www.USCourtForms.com

continued

Exhibit 9-10 *continued*

ESTATE OF *(Name):*	CASE NUMBER:
☐ DECEDENT ☐ CONSERVATEE ☐ MINOR	

DECLARATION OF PROBATE REFEREE

9. I have truly, honestly, and impartially appraised to the best of my ability each item set forth in Attachment 2.

10. A true account of my commission and expenses actually and necessarily incurred pursuant to my appointment is:

Statutory commission: $

Expenses *(specify):* $

TOTAL: $

I declare under penalty of perjury under the laws of the State of California that the foregoing is true and correct.

Date:

▶

_____   _____
(TYPE OR PRINT NAME)   (SIGNATURE OF REFEREE)

INSTRUCTIONS
(See Probate Code sections 2610–2616, 8801, 8804, 8852, 8905, 8960, 8961, and 8963 for additional instructions.)

1. See Probate Code section 8850 for items to be included in the inventory.

2. If the minor or conservatee is or has been during the guardianship or conservatorship confined in a state hospital under the jurisdiction of the State Department of Mental Health or the State Department of Developmental Services, mail a copy to the director of the appropriate department in Sacramento. (Prob. Code, § 2611.)

3. The representative, guardian, conservator, or small estate claimant shall list on Attachment 1 and appraise as of the date of death of the decedent or the date of appointment of the guardian or conservator, at fair market value, moneys, currency, cash items, bank accounts and amounts on deposit with each financial institution (as defined in Probate Code section 40), and the proceeds of life and accident insurance policies and retirement plans payable upon death in lump sum amounts to the estate, except items whose fair market value is, in the opinion of the representative, an amount different from the ostensible value or specified amount.

4. The representative, guardian, conservator, or small estate claimant shall list in Attachment 2 all other assets of the estate which shall be appraised by the referee.

5. If joint tenancy and other assets are listed for appraisal purposes only and not as part of the probate estate, they must be separately listed on additional attachments and their value excluded from the total valuation of Attachments 1 and 2.

6. Each attachment should conform to the format approved by the Judicial Council. (See *Inventory and Appraisal Attachment* (form DE-161/GC-041) and Cal. Rules of Court, rule 201.)

continued

Exhibit 9-10   *continued*

DE-161, GC-041

ESTATE OF *(Name):*	CASE NUMBER:

INVENTORY AND APPRAISAL

ATTACHMENT NO.:_____

*(In decedents' estates, attachments must conform to Probate
Code section 8850(c) regarding community and separate property.)*

Page: _____of: _____total pages.
(Add pages as required.)

Item No.	Description	Appraised value
1.		$

Form Approved by the
Judicial Council of California
DE-161, GC-041 [Rev. January 1, 1998]
Mandatory Form [1/1/2000]

INVENTORY AND APPRAISAL ATTACHMENT

Probate Code, §§ 301,
2610-2613, 8800-8920,
10309

Notice to Creditors

The executor must send a notice to all known creditors of the decedent. The notice may be a form or an office-typed document. The creditors are notified where to file a claim against the estate, as well as the time requirements for filing. In most states, the creditors must file a claim against the estate before the later of

1. four months after the date letters were first issued to the executor, or
2. 60 days after the date the notice was mailed or personally delivered to the creditor.

A proof of service must be completed with the name and address of each entity to which notice was mailed. A creditor who does not meet the deadline may be barred from making a late claim. In some states, creditors must submit claims on a creditor's claim form.

Executors are under a fiduciary duty to the estate to preserve estate assets. Therefore, claims should not be paid automatically unless it can be ascertained that they are legitimate debts of the decedent. If the executor rejects the claim, the creditor may petition the court within three months by filing suit against the estate. For each claim the executor receives, an allowance or rejection must be prepared and filed with the court, along with a copy of the claim itself. This document must also be served on the creditor.

All bills paid on behalf of the decedent or the estate must be paid from a separate checking account. The executor must open this account in the name of the decedent's estate by submitting a signed copy of the letters testamentary and the death certificate to the bank with the request. The bank usually does not have to keep the letters, but makes a copy for its records. The account is then set up for "Estate of John Smith" with the executor having signatory powers.

The executor is also required to pay all claims for funeral expenses, last-illness expenses, and wage claims that have been approved, as well as any taxes due. An income tax return must be completed if the decedent had income in the year he died. Medical insurance payments should be checked against all bills received for last-illness expenses to avoid duplicate payment.

Petition for Final Distribution

Once the period for creditors' claims has passed and all estate matters have been concluded, the final petition may be filed. This may not be accomplished until at least four months after the letters are issued. All taxes must also have been paid. The petition must be prepared on pleading paper with the following items included:

1. name of decedent and date of death
2. information about creditor claims and payments
3. indications that all debts have been paid
4. actions taken by the executor in relation to the estate property
5. computation of payment to the executor

6. a list of creditors receiving notice
7. a list of creditor claims and when they were paid
8. a list of property and its value
9. a list of beneficiaries and the proposed distribution to each of them
10. waiver forms signed by all beneficiaries waiving a final accounting
11. verification signed by the executor

A cover letter should be prepared and all of these items should be sent to the court for filing. An original and two extra copies of the petition should be sent, with instructions to return conformed copies. In some states, this number may vary. Some states require a filing fee.

In some states, a notice of hearing is prepared and included in the mailing. When the court returns the notice with the date and time of the hearing noted, a copy should be sent to all beneficiaries at least 15 days before the hearing. Again, the time may vary in different states.

Federal Estate Taxes

As of the writing of this text, federal estate taxes are paid on estates with assets exceeding $1 million. However, each year this figure is increased. Therefore, readers should review the current statutes to determine the current amount.

Order of Final Distribution

In some states, the court prepares an order of final distribution. Other states require the attorney's office to prepare the order. The appropriate procedure may be obtained from the probate clerk's office. Some courts require that the order be submitted to them a few days before the hearing. When the court approves the order, the assets may be distributed to the beneficiaries.

Receipts from Beneficiaries

Each individual receiving any property from the estate must sign a receipt indicating the exact property that was transferred to him. These receipts must be filed with the court to effectuate the final discharge.

Final Discharge

The executor must file an affidavit for final discharge with the court, with the accompanying receipts from the beneficiaries. If real property was distributed to beneficiaries in the order for final distribution, a notation should be made indicating that the order was recorded in the county recorder's office for the county where the property is located.

Some states require that an order approving the final report, releasing the executor, and closing the estate be prepared. A sample closing report from the state of Iowa is shown in Exhibit 9-11.

EXHIBIT 9-11   Closing Report (Iowa)

Reprinted with permission from *A Practical Guide to Estate Planning and Administration* by Michael Gau, Thomson/Delmar, 2005.

THE IOWA DISTRICT COURT
DUBUQUE COUNTY

IN THE ESTATE OF   Probate No. 01311 ESPRO 41569

Michael J. Bond, Deceased

ORDER APPROVING FINAL REPORT, RELEASING EXECUTOR AND CLOSING THE ESTATE

On this _____day of _____, 200_, the final report having been presented to this court and this court having examined the final report and the probate file, the court hereby finds:

1. All interested persons have waived notice of the time and place of hearing on the final report, have consented to its approval and to the closing of this estate.

2. All interested persons have waived an accounting of all property coming into the hands of the executor and a detailed accounting of all cash receipts and disbursements, and such waivers are on file.

3. There are no known or reasonably ascertainable creditors who have not either been paid or notified in writing in accordance with the law and the decedent's heirs, surviving spouse, and devisees under the decedent's will of admission of the decedent's will to probate. All statutory requirements pertaining to taxes have been complied with, all claims have been paid, and no lien exists on any property as security for any claim.

4. More than four months have elapsed since the second publication of the Notice of Appointment of the Executor and no reason exists why an Order should not now be entered as prayed by the executor in his final report.

5. The estate has been fully administered in accordance with the law and the orders of this court. The work of the executor has been completed and the executor should be discharged and the estate settled and closed.

IT IS ORDERED:
1. The final report is hereby approved;
2. Each and action of the executor, Wilson A. Bond, is approved and confirmed; and
3. The executor is released and discharged, and the estate is settled and closed.

_____

Judge, First Judicial District

Estate Close

Once all of the preceding items have been taken care of, the estate is closed and the executor is relieved of all responsibilities regarding the estate.

● KEY TERMS

administrator

executor

probate

self-proving will

● SELF TEST

1. What are the most popular probate avoidance measures?

2. Do all states have the same formal probate procedures?

3. List the types of property that are not probated.

4. How are creditors notified that the decedent has died?

● NOTEBOOK PROJECTS

1. Research the procedures for probating an estate in your state. Copy the pertinent parts and include them in your notebook.

2. Obtain a sample of all forms used in probate in your state.

3. Interview an attorney, paralegal, or legal assistant who specializes in probate in your state. Obtain samples of documents used in the probate process.

4. Complete all State-Specific Information boxes and file them in your notebook.

For additional resources, visit our Web site at **www.paralegal.delmar.cengage.com.**

BANKRUPTCY LAW

CHAPTER OUTCOMES

After studying this chapter, the student will understand

1. the different types of bankruptcies.
2. the circumstances under which each type of bankruptcy is filed.
3. what types of bankruptcies are appropriate in individual cases.
4. how to complete the forms required for an individual bankruptcy.
5. the federal and governing laws in bankruptcy.

DEFINITIONS

Unlike civil litigation, in which the parties are the *plaintiff* and the *defendant,* a bankruptcy proceeding involves a *debtor,* the *creditors,* and the *trustee.* The **debtor** usually institutes the bankruptcy proceeding and is the individual or corporation that is bankrupt and owes the debts. The debts are owed to the **creditors.** The trustee is an independent party appointed by the court to liquidate the assets and distribute funds to the creditors.

CORPORATE BANKRUPTCY

Bankruptcy is a federal court proceeding. Businesses may file either a Chapter 7 or a Chapter 11 bankruptcy. Attorneys who handle these cases must file a *statement of compensation* with the bankruptcy court to report the fees the attorney is to be paid for handling the bankruptcy as well as all fees paid to the attorney by the bankruptcy client during the previous year. The attorney must be a disinterested party in the case except in a Chapter 7 bankruptcy filing, in which a party with an interest in the case may represent the debtor. Therefore, attorneys employed by a corporation may represent it in a Chapter 7 bankruptcy proceeding. The chapter numbers refer to the federal Bankruptcy Code, in which the information and laws are found. The applicable chapters of the code are as follows:

Chapter 1: General Provisions and Introduction

Chapter 3: Case Administration

Chapter 5: Creditors and their Claims, the Debtor, and the Estate

debtor an individual or entity that owes money and initiates a bankruptcy proceeding

creditors individuals or entities to whom the debtor owes money

These sections of the code will be used more often by the attorney than the legal assistant, because they deal with substantive and procedural issues and definitions related to information that should be given to the legal assistant prior to preparation of the bankruptcy documents.

The following chapters in the code indicate the types of bankruptcy proceedings available and the circumstances under which each is used. Those used by corporations are Chapter 7 and Chapter 11.

Chapter 7: Liquidation (of debts)

Chapter 9: Adjustment of Debts of a Municipality (can be used only by a city or local government entity)

Chapter 11: Reorganization

Chapter 12: Adjustment of Debts of a Family Farmer with Regular Annual Income

Chapter 13: Adjustment of Debts of an Individual with Regular Income

BANKRUPTCY ABUSE PREVENTION AND CONSUMER PROTECTION ACT OF 2005

The major changes to the bankruptcy law as a result of this act include the following:

1. All debtors are required to get credit counseling with an agency approved by the United States Trustee's office before they can file for bankruptcy.

2. Some individuals with high incomes will not be allowed to use Chapter 7 but will have to repay some of their debt under Chapter 13.

3. To determine whether a person is eligible to file for Chapter 7, consider her average monthly income for the last six months before filing. Compare this to the median income for a family of that size in the state. If her income is less than or equal to the median, Chapter 7 may be used. If not, then she must pass the means test.

4. The means test requires starting with the average monthly income calculated in item 3. Subtract allowed expenses in amounts set by the IRS; that is, a debtor may not deduct the amount she spent on these items but the amount the IRS determines is the limit for that state. Subtract monthly payments on secured debts (such as mortgage and car payments) and priority debts (such as child support, alimony, tax debts, and wages to employees). If total monthly disposable income is then less than $100, the individual may file for Chapter 7. If the remaining income is between $100 and $166.66, the individual must determine whether what is left over is enough to pay more than 25 percent of other debts (such as credit cards, medical bills, and student loans) over five years. If so, Chapter 7 will not be available to the individual. If not, she may use Chapter 7.

Under this new law, calculations to determine eligibility are more difficult than under the previous law. Therefore, lawyers will find representation of clients filing for bankruptcy to be more time consuming and more complicated, and thus more expensive for the individual. Lawyers must also personally vouch for the accuracy of all information that their clients provide to them.

Although the new laws make it more difficult for an individual to discharge her debts in a bankruptcy proceeding, it is unclear what effect this new legislation will have on corporate bankruptcy filings because the major provisions refer to individual filings.

Reasons for Reform

The Bankruptcy Abuse Prevention and Consumer Protection Act of 2005 signifies the most wide-ranging reform of the bankruptcy system in more than 25 years. Several factors contributed to the passing of this new law.

Consumer bankruptcy filings have been increasing steadily. In 1998, filings reached the 1 million mark for the first time in history. In 2004, filings increased to more than 1.6 million cases. The government reasoned that the increased number of filings meant that bankruptcy relief is too readily available.

The debts that are not collected in bankruptcy filings are passed on to the consumer. Each of us must pay for those losses in larger down payments, higher interest rates, and increased costs of goods and services.

It has been said that increased consumer bankruptcies have an adverse financial effect on our nation's economy. In 1997 alone, more than $44 billion of debt was discharged by debtors who filed bankruptcy, which amounts to a loss of at least $110 million a day for a year.

Our former bankruptcy system had many loopholes that enabled abuse of the system. Debtor misconduct and abuse, problems with bankruptcy petition preparers, and cases in which a debtor's discharge should have been challenged are examples of the problems with the former system.

The new system relies on the debtor's ability to repay part, if not all, of her debts in the bankruptcy proceeding. Although debtors may be able to repay a large amount of their debts, the prior law had no clear directive requiring them to do so. The new law closes this loophole and imposes more stringent requirements for the repayment of debt.

OVERVIEW OF CHAPTER 7 BANKRUPTCY

The most common bankruptcy has been Chapter 7 liquidation. The individual, corporation, or business has its debts discharged in exchange for giving up property, which is sold to pay creditors. Some assets are exempt. The bankruptcy must be filed in the district bankruptcy court where the principal place of the business was located or the principal corporate assets were situated during the past 180 days.

The business or individual must enumerate assets and liabilities, as well as income and expenses, and must list any exempt property. The bankruptcy court appoints a trustee to administer the case. Once the case is completed, the debts that have been discharged in the bankruptcy need not be paid. However, the business must cease operation.

A recent development that makes significant changes in the Chapter 7 filing is the Bankruptcy Abuse Prevention and Consumer Protection Act of 2005, a major reform of the bankruptcy system that took effect on October 17, 2005. Because this text is being completed shortly after the new law becomes effective, it is unknown what the overall effect will be on business bankruptcy filings under Chapter 7. The new law makes it more difficult to file Chapter 7 bankruptcies but encourages filings under Chapter 11. However, at present, no changes have been made to the requirements for business filings.

CHAPTER 7 PROCEDURES

●

Note that a debtor must meet the described qualifications before being allowed to file a Chapter 7 bankruptcy based on the new law. The new forms are available from the federal bankruptcy court at

http://www.uscourts.gov/bankruptcycourts.html

or at the local bankruptcy court.

Filing Statement of Compensation

The attorneys and other professionals rendering services must file a *statement of compensation* with the court to have their employment and fees approved. Notice must be given to all creditors.

Filing Petition

The petition must be filed by the debtor corporation with the appropriate bankruptcy court. Exhibit 10-1 shows a sample petition, which must be accompanied by a cover sheet indicating the various schedules attached to it (see Exhibit 10-2).

Schedules must be prepared indicating all creditors holding secured and unsecured claims against the corporation. If the corporation has outstanding **executory contracts** and/or unexpired leases, the Schedule G—Executory Contracts and Unexpired Leases form (see Exhibit 10-3) must also be prepared and submitted.

In addition to these general bankruptcy forms, each individual court may have its own local forms and rules that must be followed. The legal assistant should contact the court that has jurisdiction over the matter to determine whether any additional materials are required. Other schedules may also be required, as noted in the page 195. Note that these forms may have been changed and/or updated after

executory contract   a contract whose terms have not yet been carried out and that may depend on a future event

EXHIBIT 10-1 Voluntary Bankruptcy Petition

From http://www.uscourts.gov.

(Official Form 1) (10/05)

United States Bankruptcy Court _____ District of _____	Voluntary Petition

Name of Debtor (if individual, enter Last, First, Middle):	Name of Joint Debtor (Spouse) (Last, First, Middle):
All Other Names used by the Debtor in the last 8 years (include married, maiden, and trade names):	All Other Names used by the Joint Debtor in the last 8 years (include married, maiden, and trade names):
Last four digits of Soc. Sec./Complete EIN or other Tax I.D. No. (if more than one, state all):	Last four digits of Soc. Sec./Complete EIN or other Tax I.D. No. (if more than one, state all):
Street Address of Debtor (No. & Street, City, and State): ZIPCODE	Street Address of Joint Debtor (No. & Street, City, and State): ZIPCODE
County of Residence or of the Principal Place of Business:	County of Residence or of the Principal Place of Business:
Mailing Address of Debtor (if different from street address): ZIPCODE	Mailing Address of Joint Debtor (if different from street address): ZIPCODE
Location of Principal Assets of Business Debtor (if different from street address above): ZIPCODE	

Type of Debtor (Form of Organization)
(Check **one** box.)

☐ Individual (includes Joint Debtors)
☐ Corporation (includes LLC and LLP)
☐ Partnership
☐ Other (If debtor is not one of the above entities, check this box and provide the information requested below.)

State type of entity: _____
_____

Nature of Business
(Check **all** applicable boxes.)

☐ Health Care Business
☐ Single Asset Real Estate as defined in 11 U.S.C. § 101 (51B)
☐ Railroad
☐ Stockbroker
☐ Commodity Broker
☐ Clearing Bank
☐ Nonprofit Organization qualified under 15 U.S.C. § 501(c)(3)

Chapter of Bankruptcy Code Under Which the Petition is Filed (Check one box)

☐ Chapter 7   ☐ Chapter 11   ☐ Chapter 15 Petition for Recognition of a Foreign Main Proceeding
☐ Chapter 9   ☐ Chapter 12   ☐ Chapter 15 Petition for Recognition of a Foreign Nonmain Proceeding
          ☐ Chapter 13

Nature of Debts (Check one box)

☐ Consumer/Non-Business   ☐ Business

Chapter 11 Debtors

Check one box:
☐ Debtor is a small business debtor as defined in 11 U.S.C. § 101(51D).
☐ Debtor is not a small business debtor as defined in 11 U.S.C. § 101(51D).
– –
Check if:
☐ Debtor's aggregate noncontingent liquidated debts owed to non-insiders or affiliates are less than $2 million.

Filing Fee (Check one box)

☐ Full Filing Fee attached
☐ Filing Fee to be paid in installments (Applicable to individuals only) Must attach signed application for the court's consideration certifying that the debtor is unable to pay fee except in installments. Rule 1006(b). See Official Form 3A.
☐ Filing Fee waiver requested (Applicable to chapter 7 individuals only). Must attach signed application for the court's consideration. See Official Form 3B.

Statistical/Administrative Information

☐ Debtor estimates that funds will be available for distribution to unsecured creditors.
☐ Debtor estimates that, after any exempt property is excluded and administrative expenses paid, there will be no funds available for distribution to unsecured creditors.

THIS SPACE IS FOR COURT USE ONLY

Estimated Number of Creditors

1-49	50-99	100-199	200-999	1,000-5,000	5,001-10,000	10,001-25,000	25,001-50,000	50,001-100,000	OVER 100,000
☐	☐	☐	☐	☐	☐	☐	☐	☐	☐

Estimated Assets

$0 to $50,000	$50,001 to $100,000	$100,001 to $500,000	$500,001 to $1 million	$1,000,001 to $10 million	$10,000,001 to $50 million	$50,000,001 to $100 million	More than $100 million
☐	☐	☐	☐	☐	☐	☐	☐

Estimated Debts

$0 to $50,000	$50,001 to $100,000	$100,001 to $500,000	$500,001 to $1 million	$1,000,001 to $10 million	$10,000,001 to $50 million	$50,000,001 to $100 million	More than $100 million
☐	☐	☐	☐	☐	☐	☐	☐

continued

Exhibit 10-1 *continued*

(Official Form 1) (10/05)	FORM B1, Page 2

Voluntary Petition *(This page must be completed and filed in every case)*	Name of Debtor(s):

Prior Bankruptcy Case Filed Within Last 8 Years (If more than one, attach additional sheet)

Location Where Filed:	Case Number:	Date Filed:

Pending Bankruptcy Case Filed by any Spouse, Partner or Affiliate of this Debtor (If more than **one**, attach additional sheet)

Name of Debtor:	Case Number:	Date Filed:
District:	Relationship:	Judge:

<table>
<tr>
<td>

Exhibit A

(To be completed if debtor is required to file periodic reports (e.g., forms 10K and 10Q) with the Securities and Exchange Commission pursuant to Section 13 or 15(d) of the Securities Exchange Act of 1934 and is requesting relief under chapter 11.)

☐ Exhibit A is attached and made a part of this petition.

</td>
<td>

Exhibit B

(To be completed if debtor is an individual
whose debts are primarily consumer debts.)

I, the attorney for the petitioner named in the foregoing petition, declare that I have informed the petitioner that [he or she] may proceed under chapter 7, 11, 12, or 13 of title 11, United States Code, and have explained the relief available under each such chapter.
I further certify that I delivered to the debtor the notice required by § 342(b) of the Bankruptcy Code.

X _____

Signature of Attorney for Debtor(s)   Date

</td>
</tr>
<tr>
<td>

Exhibit C

Does the debtor own or have possession of any property that poses or is alleged to pose a threat of imminent and identifiable harm to public health or safety?

☐ Yes, and Exhibit C is attached and made a part of this petition.

☐ No

</td>
<td>

Certification Concerning Debt Counseling by Individual/Joint Debtor(s)

☐ I/we have received approved budget and credit counseling during the 180-day period preceding the filing of this petition.

☐ I/we request a waiver of the requirement to obtain budget and credit counseling prior to filing based on exigent circumstances. (Must attach certification describing.)

</td>
</tr>
</table>

Information Regarding the Debtor (Check the Applicable Boxes)

Venue (Check any applicable box)

☐ Debtor has been domiciled or has had a residence, principal place of business, or principal assets in this District for 180 days immediately preceding the date of this petition or for a longer part of such 180 days than in any other District.

☐ There is a bankruptcy case concerning debtor's affiliate, general partner, or partnership pending in this District.

☐ Debtor is a debtor in a foreign proceeding and has its principal place of business or principal assets in the United States in this District, or has no principal place of business or assets in the United States but is a defendant in an action or proceeding [in a federal or state court] in this District, or the interests of the parties will be served in regard to the relief sought in this District.

Statement by a Debtor Who Resides as a Tenant of Residential Property

Check all applicable boxes.

☐ Landlord has a judgment against the debtor for possession of debtor's residence. (If box checked, complete the following.)

_____

(Name of landlord that obtained judgment)

_____

(Address of landlord)

☐ Debtor claims that under applicable nonbankruptcy law, there are circumstances under which the debtor would be permitted to cure the entire monetary default that gave rise to the judgment for possession, after the judgment for possession was entered, and

☐ Debtor has included in this petition the deposit with the court of any rent that would become due during the 30-day period after the filing of the petition.

continued

Exhibit 10-1   *continued*

(Official Form 1) (10/05)	FORM B1, Page 3

Voluntary Petition *(This page must be completed and filed in every case)*	Name of Debtor(s):

Signatures

Signature(s) of Debtor(s) (Individual/Joint)

I declare under penalty of perjury that the information provided in this petition is true and correct.

[If petitioner is an individual whose debts are primarily consumer debts and has chosen to file under chapter 7] I am aware that I may proceed under chapter 7, 11, 12 or 13 of title 11, United States Code, understand the relief available under each such chapter, and choose to proceed under chapter 7.

[If no attorney represents me and no bankruptcy petition preparer signs the petition] I have obtained and read the notice required by § 342(b) of the Bankruptcy Code.

I request relief in accordance with the chapter of title 11, United States Code, specified in this petition.

X_____
Signature of Debtor

X_____
Signature of Joint Debtor

_____
Telephone Number (If not represented by attorney)

_____
Date

Signature of a Foreign Representative

I declare under penalty of perjury that the information provided in this petition is true and correct, that I am the foreign representative of a debtor in a foreign proceeding, and that I am authorized to file this petition.

(Check only one box.)

☐   I request relief in accordance with chapter 15 of title 11, United States Code. Certified copies of the documents required by § 1515 of title 11 are attached.

☐   Pursuant to § 1511 of title 11, United States Code, I request relief in accordance with the chapter of title 11 specified in this petition. A certified copy of the order granting recognition of the foreign main proceeding is attached.

X_____
(Signature of Foreign Representative)

_____
(Printed Name of Foreign Representative)

_____
Date

Signature of Attorney

X_____
Signature of Attorney for Debtor(s)

_____
Printed Name of Attorney for Debtor(s)

_____
Firm Name

_____
Address

_____

_____
Telephone Number

_____
Date

Signature of Non-Attorney Bankruptcy Petition Preparer

I declare under penalty of perjury that: (1) I am a bankruptcy petition preparer as defined in 11 U.S.C. § 110; (2) I prepared this document for compensation and have provided the debtor with a copy of this document and the notices and information required under 11 U.S.C. §§ 110(b), 110(h), and 342(b); and, (3) if rules or guidelines have been promulgated pursuant to 11 U.S.C. § 110(h) setting a maximum fee for services chargeable by bankruptcy petition preparers, I have given the debtor notice of the maximum amount before preparing any document for filing for a debtor or accepting any fee from the debtor, as required in that section. Official Form 19B is attached.

_____
Printed Name and title, if any, of Bankruptcy Petition Preparer

_____
Social Security number (If the bankruptcy petition preparer is not an individual, state the Social Security number of the officer, principal, responsible person or partner of the bankruptcy petition preparer.) (Required by 11 U.S.C. § 110.)

_____
Address

_____

X_____

_____
Date

Signature of Bankruptcy Petition Preparer or officer, principal, responsible person, or partner whose social security number is provided above.

Names and Social Security numbers of all other individuals who prepared or assisted in preparing this document unless the bankruptcy petition preparer is not an individual:

If more than one person prepared this document, attach additional sheets conforming to the appropriate official form for each person.

A bankruptcy petition preparer's failure to comply with the provisions of title 11 and the Federal Rules of Bankruptcy Procedure may result in fines or imprisonment or both 11 U.S.C. §110; 18 U.S.C. §156.

Signature of Debtor (Corporation/Partnership)

I declare under penalty of perjury that the information provided in this petition is true and correct, and that I have been authorized to file this petition on behalf of the debtor.

The debtor requests relief in accordance with the chapter of title 11, United States Code, specified in this petition.

X_____
Signature of Authorized Individual

_____
Printed Name of Authorized Individual

_____
Title of Authorized Individual

_____
Date

EXHIBIT 10-2   Summary of Schedules

From http://www.uscourts.gov.

FORM B6-Cont.
(6/90)

UNITED STATES BANKRUPTCY COURT

_____District of _____

In re _____ ,   Case No. _____
              Debtor   **(If known)**

SUMMARY OF SCHEDULES

Indicate as to each schedule whether that schedule is attached and state the number of pages in each. Report the totals from Schedules A, B, D, E, F, I, and J in the boxes provided. Add the amounts from Schedules A and B to determine the total amount of the debtor's assets. Add the amounts from Schedules D, E, and F to determine the total amount of the debtor's liabilities.

AMOUNTS SCHEDULED

NAME OF SCHEDULE	ATTACHED (YES/NO)	NO. OF SHEETS	ASSETS	LIABILITIES	OTHER
A - Real Property			$		
B - Personal Property			$		
C - Property Claimed as Exempt					
D - Creditors Holding Secured Claims				$	
E - Creditors Holding Unsecured Priority Claims				$	
F - Creditors Holding Unsecured Nonpriority Claims				$	
G - Executory Contracts and Unexpired Leases					
H - Codebtors					
I - Current Income of Individual Debtor(s)					$
J - Current Expenditures of Individual Debtor(s)					$
Total Number of Sheets of ALL Schedules ➤					
Total Assets ➤			$		
Total Liabilities ➤				$	

EXHIBIT 10-3 Schedule G—Executory Contracts and Unexpired Leases

From http://www.uscourts.gov.

Form B6G
(10/05)

In re _____,   Case No. _____
              Debtor   **(if known)**

SCHEDULE G - EXECUTORY CONTRACTS AND UNEXPIRED LEASES

Describe all executory contracts of any nature and all unexpired leases of real or personal property. Include any timeshare interests. State nature of debtor's interest in contract, i.e., "Purchaser," "Agent," etc. State whether debtor is the lessor or lessee of a lease. Provide the names and complete mailing addresses of all other parties to each lease or contract described. If a minor child is a party to one of the leases or contracts, indicate that by stating "a minor child" and do not disclose the child's name. See 11 U.S.C. § 112; Fed.R. Bankr. P. 1007(m).

☐ Check this box if debtor has no executory contracts or unexpired leases.

NAME AND MAILING ADDRESS, INCLUDING ZIP CODE, OF OTHER PARTIES TO LEASE OR CONTRACT.	DESCRIPTION OF CONTRACT OR LEASE AND NATURE OF DEBTOR'S INTEREST. STATE WHETHER LEASE IS FOR NONRESIDENTIAL REAL PROPERTY. STATE CONTRACT NUMBER OF ANY GOVERNMENT CONTRACT.

the publication of this textbook to comply with the new law that was effective October 17, 2005.

    A. Form 6
        1. A—real property
        2. B—personal property
        3. C—exempt property
        4. D—creditors holding secured claims
        5. E—creditors holding unsecured priority claims
        6. F—creditors holding unsecured nonpriority claims
        7. G—executory contracts and unexpired leases
        8. H—co-debtors
        9. I—current income
      10. J—current expenditures
      11. Summary schedules

    B. Statement of Financial Affairs—Form 7

One may obtain all required forms from the local bankruptcy court or from the federal court's Web page. Information to include in the forms is self-explanatory. Be sure to have the forms signed by an appropriate officer of the corporation prior to filing.

Trustee Appointment

The United States Trustee has the power to make an interim appointment of a **trustee** to serve in this capacity until the meeting of creditors. This individual will be chosen from a panel of private individuals who assume such responsibility on a regular basis.

Notice to Creditors

Approximately five to seven days after the petition is filed, notice will be sent to the debtor and creditors advising them of the filing of an *order for relief* and the appointment of the interim trustee, who will also receive the notice.

Notice of Creditors' Meeting

Notice will be given by the United States Trustee to all creditors, advising them of the *creditors' meeting,* including time, date, and place. The meeting must occur not less than 20 nor more than 40 days after the order for relief has been entered. The debtor and a representative of the United States Trustee's office must also appear at the meeting. Both the representative and the creditors may pose questions to the debtor, primarily to verify whether the previously submitted statements and schedules accurately reflect the assets owned by the debtor. The creditors will appoint a permanent trustee.

trustee an independent party appointed by the court in a bankruptcy proceeding for the purpose of liquidating the assets and distributing funds to creditors

Discharge

If no objections are filed relating to the bankruptcy proceedings, a discharge will automatically be issued by the bankruptcy court. Most debts will be discharged at this point. Secured debts, however, are not dischargeable.

OVERVIEW OF CHAPTER 11 BANKRUPTCY

Corporations that file under Chapter 11 intend to reorganize the company rather than liquidate it. In recent years, many large corporations have used this method. The major advantage is that the corporation may continue to operate even though it has serious financial problems. During this period, the business reorganizes to a more economically sound structure. The company must adhere to stringent rules, and its affairs become public knowledge in that the creditors and the trustee may scrutinize its activities. In general, corporations that file for Chapter 11 bankruptcy have enough income to pay off a portion of their debts over a period of time.

Although a Chapter 11 bankruptcy is more expensive and time consuming than a Chapter 7 bankruptcy, it is the best alternative for a business that wishes to remain in operation during the reorganization process. Strict deadlines exist for the filing of documents with the bankruptcy court. Note that the new law did not address Chapter 11 bankruptcies.

CHAPTER 11 PROCEEDING

If the corporation wishes to remain in business, it may file a Chapter 11 reorganization proceeding and must follow these procedures:

1. *Initial filing:* Items to include at the initial filing are the petition, the filing fee, a corporate resolution authorizing the bankruptcy, all creditors' names and addresses, and the 20 largest creditors' claims.

2. *Up to 15 days after initial filing:* Additional items that must be filed include a statement of financial affairs, a list of all equity security holders, schedules of assets and liabilities, and a statement of executory contracts.

3. *Within 30 days of initial filing:* The debtor must file an inventory of assets if the trustee so orders. All operating reports must be filed. Applications to hire attorneys or other professionals must be filed. Alternatively an application may be filed within 30 days of retaining the professional.

4. *Within 60 days of initial filing:* A debtor in possession of property must assume any lease, or it is considered rejected. The debtor must also deposit all funds in an approved bank. Old bank accounts must be canceled and new ones established, called *general, tax,* and *payroll* accounts. The corporation's checkbook must

state that it is a *debtor-in-possession.* These accounts operate as an attorney's trust account. All funds received are deposited into the general account; disbursements are made into the payroll account as payroll must be paid. Regular reports must be filed with the court on income and disbursements.

5. *Filing of a plan of reorganization and disclosure statement:* The debtor must file its own reorganization plan, along with disclosures about the plan telling the creditors information that might affect their vote for or against the plan.

6. *Notice to creditors 25 days before hearing:* A hearing will be held in the bankruptcy court to approve the disclosure statement; notice must be sent to creditors at least 25 days before this hearing. Accompanying the notice to creditors are the following: a copy of the reorganization plan, a copy of the disclosure statement, a copy of the approval of the disclosure statement, and a ballot to vote on the plan. These documents are known as the *confirmation packet.*

7. *Confirmation hearing:* The court either confirms or denies confirmation of the corporation's plan for reorganization. Typically the confirmation process takes approximately four or five months.

The only method for a corporation to use to discharge its debts, if it wishes to stay in business, is the Chapter 11 bankruptcy process. Confirmation of the Chapter 11 plan results in a discharge of obligations pursuant to Section 1141 of the Bankruptcy Code. See 11 U.S.C. Sec. 1129 et seq.

Only a brief overview of the corporate bankruptcy process has been given here. The legal assistant should consult a recent text on bankruptcy to obtain further information. Forms used in the bankruptcy process may be downloaded from the federal courts Web site at

http://www.uscourts.gov.

The new forms that were issued in October 2005 by the Northern Illinois bankruptcy courts may be found at

http://www.ilnb.uscourts.gov/Bankruptcy_Forms.html.

Copies of these forms are also available in the Web Companion that accompanies this text. The forms may be adapted for use in other courts. Determine whether your state's bankruptcy courts have a Web site with downloadable forms and complete the following box.

STATE-SPECIFIC INFORMATION

The new bankruptcy forms for the state of _____ may be found at this Web site:

_____

● KEY TERMS

creditors

debtor

executory contract

trustee

● SELF TEST

1. Explain the different types of bankruptcies.

2. Under what circumstances is each type of bankruptcy used?

3. Explain the new law that took effect in October 2005.

4. What types of bankruptcy are affected by the new law?

● NOTEBOOK PROJECTS

1. Obtain a packet of the new forms for bankruptcy.

2. Interview an attorney who specializes in bankruptcy and ask her to explain the advantages and disadvantages of working in this type of practice.

3. Call the local bankruptcy court in your state to determine the filing requirements and fees. Prepare a report for your instructor.

 For additional resources, visit our Web site at **www.paralegal.delmar.cengage.com.**

PROPERTY LAW

CHAPTER OUTCOMES

After studying this chapter, the student will understand

1. the difference between real and personal property.
2. the forms of ownership of real property.
3. the difference between the condominium and cooperative forms of ownership.
4. the basis of a nuisance suit.
5. issues involved in landlord/tenant disputes.

INTRODUCTION

Real property includes land and things permanently attached to the land. Homes, garages and other buildings, in-ground swimming pools, minerals in the ground, trees, and fixtures are examples of real property. A *fixture* is an item of **personal property** that is affixed to the land or to a building in such a way that it becomes part of the real property. For example, a light fixture purchased at a store is personal property. Once the light fixture is permanently attached to the ceiling of your home, however, it becomes real property. Other examples of fixtures that become real property are furnaces, built-in bookcases, and wall-to-wall carpeting.

Fixtures can also become personal property. For instance, a growing tree is considered real property because it is attached to the land. Once the tree is cut down, it becomes personal property.

real property land or items affixed thereto or growing thereon

personal property all property that is not real property; movable property

tenancy in common ownership of property by two or more individuals, with each owning a proportion of the property

PROPERTY OWNERSHIP

Tenancy in Common

When two or more individuals own a piece of property together, with each having a certain proportion, the property is owned as a **tenancy in common.** For example, if three sisters own a farm in tenancy in common, each has a one-third interest in the property. Each individual may sell her share of the property or leave it to her heirs.

Joint Tenancy

Joint tenancy is a form of ownership in which two or more people have an undivided ownership interest in the property, with a right of survivorship. Although joint tenancy ownership is not reserved for spouses, many married couples hold their real property in joint tenancy. The primary advantage of this type of ownership is the right of survivorship; that is, upon the death of one joint tenant, the property passes automatically to the other joint tenant(s) without having to be mentioned in the decedent's will or without having to go through the probate process. A simple document is required to transfer full title to the survivor(s) upon the death of the joint tenant.

Community Property

Community property, property acquired after marriage that is not a gift or inheritance, is valid only if a married couple lives in a state that recognizes it. Many states are now community property states. Check your state's laws to determine whether the state recognizes community property (see the State-Specific Information box in Chapter 7).

Community property includes any property acquired during the marriage that is not a separate gift or inheritance. The property must have been acquired during a valid marriage and before a divorce was initiated or the couple permanently separated. Married couples may hold property as community property. The deed would state, for example:

NICHOLAS WILLIAM LANGFORD AND BARBARA ANN LANGFORD, a married couple, as community property. . . .

Each spouse would then own a one-half interest in the property.

CONDOMINIUMS

In the **condominium** type of ownership, different people own individual units within a multiple-unit complex. Each unit is owned by a single person or a number of individuals in any of the forms of ownership described previously. The interior of the unit within the building is the bounds of what each owner owns. The owner of a unit may use a portion of the property not within the bounds of the unit, such as a garage or storage area. Other areas of the complex are common areas, owned by all owners of the condominiums as tenants in common. Owners may not transfer ownership of the common areas unless they transfer their individual units.

Everyday management of the complex is handled by a property management company that takes care of building maintenance, financial affairs, and landscaping and upkeep of the common areas. Each owner may obtain a loan on his individual unit; a master loan may be made on the complex itself and may be paid from the monthly fees assessed to each individual owner.

joint tenancy ownership of property by two or more persons each of whom has an undivided ownership interest in the property, with a right of survivorship

condominium a property ownership interest in which individuals own units within a multiple-unit complex

The master deed for the complex should be recorded in the county recorder's office. Each owner has a deed to his unit that should also be recorded. The owners elect a board of directors to establish rules and regulations for the complex. This board may also handle the maintenance and financial affairs of the condominium organization.

COOPERATIVES

A **cooperative** unit is similar to a condominium, except that ownership is in a share of stock that is represented by a unit in the complex. Ownership is more restrictive than the condominium form.

The complex is governed by a board of directors, who are elected by the owners. An owner may not sell his share without permission from the board. The board must generally approve prospective purchasers.

A primary disadvantage of cooperative ownership is the difficulty of obtaining financing on the units. In some cases, the seller must provide a personal loan for the buyer. A client who is considering purchasing a cooperative unit should be advised of the additional restrictions involved as well as the difficulties inherent in the sale.

In recent years, financial institutions have begun to issue loans on these units. With protections against discrimination, it has become increasingly difficult for a board to disapprove prospective purchasers. Therefore, cooperative ownership is becoming more like the condominium form of ownership. The primary difference is that the cooperative owner owns a share of stock that is represented by a unit, while the condominium owner owns the unit outright.

REAL ESTATE SALES

Real estate sales may be handled by agents or by attorneys, depending on the state in which the sale takes place. Real estate agents are paid a percentage of the selling price. Legal assistants employed in real estate offices may help draft real estate contracts of sale.

Different states transfer legal title to property at a closing in an attorney's office or at an escrow office. Legal assistants employed by **escrow** companies or closing attorneys may prepare documents and gather data for the transfer of the property.

A title insurance company checks title to the property prior to the close of escrow or the closing to determine whether the property is free of liens, encumbrances, easements, and other items affecting title. Legal assistants employed by title companies may be required to trace title to property using records in the county recorder's office. They must trace all transfers of title to that piece of property, as well as any liens or encumbrances on it. The buyer receives an *abstract of title* from the title company indicating the results of the title search. If the property is free of encumbrances, the title company issues a *title insurance policy*, insuring that the buyer has received clear title.

Legal assistants employed by title companies may also be required to prepare title documents for the buyer of the property. The paralegal must conduct a thorough title search of the property because a title

cooperative a form of ownership similar to that of a condominium, except that ownership is in a share of stock that is represented by a unit in the complex; ownership is more restrictive than the condominium form

escrow a process by which legal title to property is transferred

insurance policy assures the buyer that there are no outstanding encumbrances on the property. The title insurance company may be held liable if one is found later.

MORTGAGES AND DEEDS OF TRUST

Purchasers of property generally obtain loans to pay for the property. In some states, the loans are known as **mortgages;** in others, they are called **deeds of trust.** The primary difference between a mortgage and a deed of trust is that with a deed of trust, the lender retains title to the property until the loan is paid. Legal assistants who work for banks, lending institutions, or mortgage brokers may help prepare deeds of trust and other loan documents. Those employed by mortgage brokers may search banks to determine which is offering the lowest interest rate at any given time, investigate the terms of the loan requested by the client, and review the client's credit history.

EASEMENTS

An **easement** creates a right to use the property of another for a specific purpose. For example, utility companies are granted easements to install electricity, gas, and telephone lines either under ground or above the ground over one's property. If an individual cannot access a public street from his land, an access easement would give him permission to use the land of another for access purposes. Sometimes certain lots adjacent to golf courses have easements for access to the course.

Adjacent property owners may agree to create an easement across part of each of their properties for building and using a driveway for their vehicles. In some large cities where property is at a premium, lots may not be wide enough for a driveway for each property.

When property is being transferred, the easement must be indicated as a part of the transaction. Although the easement is considered an encumbrance on the property, it often benefits both parties, such as in the preceding cases.

LICENSES

A **license** may be granted on one's land allowing another to perform a particular act on that land without actually being in possession of the property. For instance, if I have a lake on my property and allow you to enter my property to swim in that lake, a license to use my property may be created. Unlike an easement, no property interest to my land results from a license. A license is merely permission to perform an act.

NUISANCE

Nuisance is an area of property law that also involves civil litigation. A nuisance is an invasion of a person's interest in the use and enjoyment of his property. A *private nuisance* affects only one's close neighbors,

mortgage a loan on real property in which the buyer acquires title to the property

deed of trust a loan on property; the lender retains title to the property until the debt is paid

easement the right to use the land of another for a particular and restricted purpose

license permission to enter another's land to perform a particular act; no property possession is granted

nuisance invasion of one's interest in the use and enjoyment of property

whereas a *public nuisance* affects the general public. Often a case of private nuisance can be settled with a simple letter or telephone call. For instance, if a neighbor plays loud music at night so that the client cannot sleep, the legal assistant or attorney may be able to settle the problem with a telephone call to the neighbor or a letter from the law firm. Most cities have ordinances prohibiting loud noises after a certain hour at night, so if confronting the neighbor is not successful, a call to the local police department may solve the problem.

Public nuisance, however, often involves complex litigation. If a chemical plant emits noxious pollutants into the air and a number of people who live nearby become ill, a case for public nuisance may be appropriate. The legal assistant would use two specialty areas of law in dealing with this problem. First, he would have to research real property law to determine whether a cause of action in public nuisance is appropriate. Second, he would have to adhere to the laws of civil procedure and civil law for filing a lawsuit. In some instances, a class-action suit against the chemical company would be appropriate if many close landowners were suffering from the same illness and had similar damages.

LANDLORD-TENANT ISSUES

A **lease** is a contract for the use of land or buildings. The *lessor* (or landlord/owner) and *lessee* (or tenant) enter into an agreement under which the tenant will occupy the landlord's premises for a fee.

The Statute of Frauds provides that all interests in land for one year or more must be in writing. Therefore, all leases or rental agreements for a year or more must be written and signed by the landlord and the tenant. Many landlords also require shorter-term leases to be in writing to protect the parties' interests. The more specifically the rights and obligations of the parties are spelled out in the lease, the less likely it is that there will be misunderstandings about the terms. Typical clauses that should be included in the lease are listed here, along with samples:

1. Names of landlord and all tenants occupying the property
2. Lease term and effective dates

THIS LEASE AGREEMENT is effective for one year commencing October 1, 2006, between WILLIAM OWNER, hereinafter referred to as "Landlord," and JOHN TENNENT, MICHAEL BROOKS, and DANIEL MORROW, hereinafter referred to as "Tenants." The lease term will continue from year to year unless either party notifies the other within one month of the expiration of the lease term that the lease should be terminated. All Tenants must sign the agreement. If one or two Tenants wish to terminate their portion of the lease, then the remaining Tenant or Tenants shall be responsible for the continuing of rights and obligations under the lease.

3. Location of property

Property leased to Tenants is the home located at 4455 Sunset Drive in the City of Palm Springs, State of California, and includes a three-car garage adjacent to the leased property.

lease   a contract for the use of land or buildings

4. Amount of rent and when and where due

Tenants shall pay Landlord the total annual lease payment of $24,000 payable in advance, in monthly installments of $2,000 due on the first day of each month, payable to Landlord at the following location: 62003 East Palm Canyon Drive, Cathedral City, California. Tenants must also pay a refundable deposit of $3,000 to cover unusual repairs or damage to property, not including ordinary wear and tear. Late fees shall accrue for all rent not paid by the first of each month at the rate of 15% per day. Tenants will be charged a $35 fee for all checks returned for insufficient funds.

5. Responsibilities of parties

Tenants shall be responsible for the payment of all utilities on the property. Water fees will be paid by Landlord. Landlord shall be responsible for providing a gardener to maintain the shrubbery and lawn on the premises on a weekly basis. Tenants shall be responsible for all minor repairs on the premises.

Landlord and Tenants shall be responsible for maintaining appropriate insurance for their respective interests in the property and any property located on the premises.

6. Sublease of property

Each Tenant may sublease his share of the leased premises provided that the sublessee is first approved by the Landlord.

7. Who may occupy the premises

Only those Tenants whose names are on the lease or sublease may occupy the premises. No visitor may occupy the premises for longer than a one-month period without the prior written permission of the Landlord.

Various other clauses may be included in the lease, depending on the preferences of the parties. Landlords will wish to have clauses in the lease that protect their interests in the property. Tenants will wish to have clauses in the lease that protect their rights to the quiet enjoyment of their property without interference from the landlord. Either party may wish to have an arbitration clause placed in the lease to settle disputes. A sample real estate lease is shown in Exhibit 11-1. These clauses may be modified to fit individual needs.

Unlawful Detainer/Eviction Actions

eviction a legal action in which a landlord removes a tenant from the property

Different states vary as to their method of **eviction.** Many states employ the *unlawful detainer action* or a similar action. In general, the unlawful detainer action is filed in the lower trial court. These actions are usually entitled to preference in the court and may proceed more rapidly than normal civil actions. An uncontested action typically takes between three and four weeks. If the tenant files an answer, the action may take a few months from the date of filing to complete. The latter case requires a trial at which evidence is presented by both sides.

EXHIBIT 11-1   Sample Real Estate Lease

Reprinted with permission from *California Legal Directory*, Judy Long, 2000: Thomson Delmar Learning.

LEASE

THIS LEASE, made this _____ day of _____, between _____, hereinafter called Owner, and _____, hereinafter called the Tenant:

WITNESSETH: Owner does hereby lease and rent unto Tenant, and Tenant does hereby take as tenant under the Owner the following property: _____ _____, to be used by Tenant during the term only of ____ months, beginning _____, and ending _____, inclusive.

IN CONSIDERATION WHEREOF, and of the covenants hereinafter expressed, it is covenanted and agreed as follows:

1. Tenant agrees to pay to Owner as rent for said premises, the sum of $_____ per _____, payable in advance.

2. Tenant shall not permit any unlawful or immoral practice to be committed on the premises, or to so occupy the premises as to constitute a nuisance.

3. Tenant shall not have the right or power to sublet the premises or any part thereof, or to transfer or assign this lease without the written consent of Owner.

4. Tenant has examined the premises, is satisfied with the physical condition and his taking possession is conclusive evidence of receipt of them in good order and repair, and Tenant agrees that no representation as to condition of repair has been made.

5. If the leased premises shall be abandoned or become vacant during the term of this lease, then in such case Owner shall have the right at his option, to take possession of the leased premises, re-enter the leased premises and annul and terminate this lease.

6. During the period of his tenancy Tenant agrees to maintain this property in as good state as he finds it, reasonable wear and tear excepted; and will have repaired, at his expense, any damage done to the water, gas, and electrical fixtures; replace all broken glass and burned out grates, keep sinks, lavatories, commodes, and sewer lines open; repair any plumbing or heating equipment that may be damaged by his negligence; replace all lost or broken keys.

7. In the event the leased premises are rendered untenantable by fire, rain, wind, or other cause beyond the control of Tenant, or are condemned and ordered torn down by the properly constituted authorities of the State, County or City, then in either of these events the lease shall cease and terminate as of the date of such destruction.

8. Owner shall not be held liable for any injury or damage whatsoever which may arise on account of any defect in the building or premises, or for rain, wind or other clause, all claims for such injury or damage being hereby expressly waived by Tenant.

9. Owner in person or by agent shall have the right at all reasonable times to enter the leased premises and inspect the same and to show the same to prospective tenants or purchasers. Owner may make such repairs and alterations as may be deemed by Owner necessary to the preservation of the leased premises or the buildings, but Owner is not required to do any repairing upon the premises leased unless so agreed in writing in this lease.

10. Tenant shall deposit the sum of $_____ as a security deposit, which deposit will be refunded to Tenant upon tenant vacating the property at the expiration of the Lease. Owner shall not refund the security deposit in the event Tenant vacates prior to the expiration of the Lease. Owner shall deduct from the security deposit any amount necessary to clean or repair the property. Owner may also retain the security deposit and apply it to any unpaid rent.

continued

Exhibit 11-1   *continued*

11. Other conditions: _____
_____
_____
_____
_____

12. Should Tenant fail to pay the rent or any part thereof, as the same becomes due, or violates any other term or condition of this lease, Owner shall then have the right, at his option, to re-enter the leased premises and terminate the lease; such re-entry shall not bar the right of recovery of rent or damages for breach of covenants, nor shall the receipt of rent after conditions broken or be deemed a waiver of forfeiture. And in order to entitle Owner to re-enter it shall not be necessary to give notice of rent being due and unpaid or of other conditions broken to make demands for rent, the execution of this lease being signed by the parties hereto being sufficient notice of the rent being due and demand for the same.

IN WITNESS WHEREOF, the parties hereto have hereunto set their signatures and seals, the day and year first above written.

_____ _____   _____ _____
Tenant   (date signed)   Owner   (date signed)

_____ _____   _____ _____
Tenant   (date signed)   Owner   (date signed)

An unlawful detainer action is commenced by serving a *three-day notice to pay rent or quit* on the tenant. A sample is shown in Exhibit 11-2. If the tenant does not respond within three days of personal service, then the landlord's attorney prepares a *complaint for unlawful detainer,* which is served on the tenant and filed with the court along with a *summons for unlawful detainer.* The legal assistant must calendar the due date for the response to the three-day notice as well as for the answer to the complaint.

The complaint may be a form in some states or an office-typed pleading in others. It must be verified by the landlord; that is, the complaint must contain a verification clause after the attorney's signature in which the landlord attests to the truth of the allegations in the complaint. All individuals occupying the premises must be served. Damages requested in the complaint will consist of possession of the premises, past due rent, and attorney fees. If the landlord can prove malicious willfulness on the part of the tenant, treble damages may be requested.

A response to the complaint must be received by the landlord within five days of personal service on the tenant(s). Note that this due date is considerably shorter than for the ordinary civil complaint.

If the tenant fails to respond, the landlord may enter a default judgment. If the tenant responds by filing an answer within the five-day period, a court hearing is held in which each party presents its side. The court issues a ruling.

In the event of a default judgment, or if the landlord prevails in court, the court issues

1. a judgment for the amount of rent due.
2. a writ of possession in favor of the landlord.

EXHIBIT 11-2   Sample Three-Day Notice to Pay Rent or Quit
Reprinted with permission from *California Legal Directory*, Judy Long, 2000: Thomson Delmar Learning.

3-DAY NOTICE

To Pay Rent or Quit

To _____

TENANT(S) IN POSSESSION OF THE PREMISES AT

_____
(Street Address)

City of _____, County of _____, California

YOU ARE HEREBY NOTIFIED that the rent on the above-described premises occupied by you, in the amount of $_____, for the period from _____ to _____, is now due and payable.

YOU ARE HEREBY REQUIRED to pay the said rent within THREE (3) days from the date of service on you of this notice or to vacate and surrender possession of the premises. In the event you fail to do so, legal proceedings will be instituted against you to recover possession of the premises, declare the forfeiture of the rental agreement or lease under which you occupy the premises, and recover rents, damages and costs of suit.

DATE: _____   _____
                                              OWNER/MANAGER

The sheriff or law enforcement officer serves the tenant with a *writ of execution for possession of real estate*. If the tenant does not vacate the premises within five days, the sheriff may physically remove the tenant and his possessions from the premises. Tenants remaining unlawfully on the premises are called *tenants at sufferance*. Exhibit 11-3 illustrates the steps in the eviction process.

Responses by the Tenant

Habitability Defense.   Most states require that leases and rental agreements include an implied warranty of habitability. This concept creates a vehicle for the courts to define a minimum standard for rental property. Some items that would be required for habitability in most states include the following:

1. effective waterproofing and weather protection of exterior walls, including unbroken windows and doors
2. plumbing or gas facilities that conform to applicable law and are maintained in continuous good working order
3. a water supply approved under applicable law that produces hot and cold running water

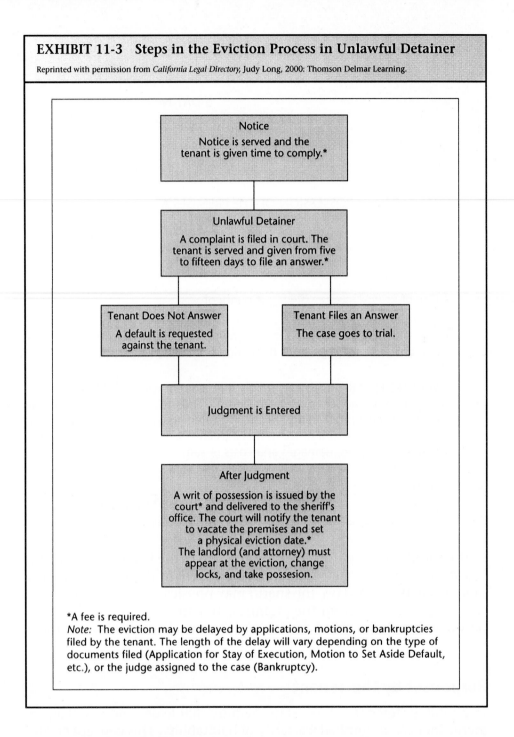

EXHIBIT 11-3   Steps in the Eviction Process in Unlawful Detainer

Reprinted with permission from *California Legal Directory,* Judy Long, 2000: Thomson Delmar Learning.

Notice

Notice is served and the tenant is given time to comply.*

Unlawful Detainer

A complaint is filed in court. The tenant is served and given from five to fifteen days to file an answer.*

Tenant Does Not Answer

A default is requested against the tenant.

Tenant Files an Answer

The case goes to trial.

Judgment is Entered

After Judgment

A writ of possession is issued by the court* and delivered to the sheriff's office. The court will notify the tenant to vacate the premises and set a physical eviction date.* The landlord (and attorney) must appear at the eviction, change locks, and take possesion.

*A fee is required.
Note: The eviction may be delayed by applications, motions, or bankruptcies filed by the tenant. The length of the delay will vary depending on the type of documents filed (Application for Stay of Execution, Motion to Set Aside Default, etc.), or the judge assigned to the case (Bankruptcy).

4. heating facilities that conform to applicable law and are maintained in good working order

5. electrical lighting, wiring, and equipment that conform to the law and are maintained in good working order

6. grounds and appurtenances that are clean, sanitary, and free from all accumulations of debris, filth, rubbish, garbage, rodents, and vermin at the time of commencement of the rental agreement

7. an adequate number of trash receptacles in good condition

8. floors, stairways, and railings in good repair

The court generally requires that the breach of habitability be material to occupancy of the premises. The materiality of the breach may be different in different parts of the state or country. However, it must directly relate to the conditions affecting the health and safety of the occupants. The courts determine the materiality of the breach by its seriousness as well as the length of time it persists. In most cases, problems with plumbing, rodents, or heating that have persisted for a period of time will be considered a material breach.

In most cases, the landlord cannot use the defense that the tenant did not notify him of the defect because the courts usually hold that the landlord had constructive knowledge. That is, the landlord should have known, whether he actually did or not. If the tenants or their guests caused the defect, the landlord may not be held liable. However, the court usually finds that an infestation of cockroaches is the landlord's responsibility. The tenant may also blame an unknown person for defects such as broken windows.

Liability of Landlord for Breach of Implied Warranty of Habitability. Tenants may exercise their rights against the landlord by withholding rent or pursuing an action against the landlord for damages. If the tenant withholds rent because the premises are not habitable, the landlord usually files an unlawful detainer action. To prevail, the tenant must then prove that the landlord breached the warranty. The burden of proof is on the landlord to prove that there was no breach. If the landlord cannot prove that the premises were habitable, the court *abates* the tenant's rent for the period of nonpayment. That is, the court determines the reasonable rent for the period of nonpayment and allows the tenant to remain in possession of the premises upon payment of this abated rental amount. However, if the tenant refuses to pay the abated rent, the landlord may retake possession of the premises. The court may also award attorney's fees and court costs to the tenant.

Affirmative Suit by Tenant for Damages

If the landlord has breached the implied warranty of habitability, the tenant may file an *affirmative suit for damages* and can seek general and punitive damages, attorney's fees, and costs. The tenant may also seek an injunction against the landlord, requiring repairs to be made to make the premises habitable. Note, however, that this is not a defense for nonpayment of rent; it is a suit by the tenant against the landlord while the tenant is still paying rent and remaining in the premises. In this case, the tenant would have to prove the damages.

The tenant may also choose to report the landlord to the proper authorities for the lack of habitability of the premises. In this case, the landlord may not invoke a retaliatory eviction and evict the tenant because the tenant has chosen to report him.

Representing the Landlord

Trial Preparation.   If the tenant does not answer the complaint, the procedures discussed earlier may be followed without the necessity of a trial. If, however, the tenant answers the complaint, the following defenses are usually raised:

1. *Inability to pay rent.* The tenant may allege that he is unable to pay rent. The court will not recognize this as a valid defense and will order the tenant's eviction.

2. *Unwillingness to pay rent.* This defense is raised along with breach of the implied warranty of habitability discussed previously. The tenant must show that there are defects that make the premises uninhabitable. Unless the tenant can prove that the defects substantially affect the habitability of the premises, the court may deny judgment to the tenant and allow the landlord to evict.

Inspections and Repairs. If the landlord is the client and has filed an unlawful detainer against a tenant who claims a habitability defense, the legal assistant should arrange for inspection of the premises. The nature of the defects should be noted and photographs taken. Pictures should include the alleged defects, the interior and exterior of the premises, the surrounding neighborhood, and any other proof that would show the tenant in an unfavorable light. The landlord's attorney will want to prove that the tenant is not caring for the premises properly.

If defects exist on the premises, the attorney should notify the landlord to have them fixed before the trial. The legal assistant may have to arrange for workers to make the needed repairs. Arrangements must be made with the tenant as to time and date of repairs. If the tenant will not cooperate, instruct the worker to contact the tenant and document the attempts to contact by noting them on the bill submitted to the landlord. Repairs do not necessarily have to be made to the tenant's specifications but must bring the premises up to habitable status. Once repairs have been made, the legal assistant should go back to the premises and photograph the repaired items. Courts look favorably on attempts to make needed repairs.

In some cases, the tenant may prevent the owner from getting access to the premises to make needed repairs. The legal assistant should document all attempts to contact the tenant for the purpose of arranging repairs or inspecting the premises. If possible, get a signed note from the tenants stating their refusal to allow access to the premises.

Preparing for Trial. Prior to the trial, the legal assistant or attorney should discuss the matter with the landlord and let him know what materials to bring to court. All bills for repairs and before-and-after pictures of repairs should be taken to court for the trial. Any other favorable evidence for the landlord should be taken. Any documents that the attorney thinks would help the case should be brought to court as well.

In some cases, the legal assistant prepares the landlord to testify at trial. The landlord should be advised to dress in professional business attire. A dark business suit with matching accessories is ideal. If the landlord has never testified in court, advise him to listen to all questions carefully, pause a second before answering, and answer only questions posed to him. The landlord should never offer any additional information not required by the question, particularly during cross-examination by the tenant or his attorney.

If witnesses are required, subpoenas must be issued. Witnesses are paid fees in an amount set by the court for appearing and testifying. The legal assistant may also arrange transportation for the witnesses. On the day of the trial, the legal assistant should be sure that the client and all witnesses are present and ready to testify.

Resolution by Stipulation.   Often the owner's primary objective is to regain possession of the premises so that he can obtain another tenant. Tenants may be willing to vacate the premises by an agreed-upon time. The attorney may negotiate with the tenants or their attorney to determine the amount of money the tenants will pay and the date they will agree to vacate. The legal assistant may draft the stipulation, which is signed by the parties and presented to the court. The court asks both parties if they understand and agree to be bound by the agreement set forth in the stipulation. In this way, a trial may be avoided.

Default Proceedings.   If the tenant/defendant does not appear, the landlord must appear in court with the attorney to testify briefly. The landlord must testify that he owns or manages the property, that a rental agreement is in force, that the tenant was served with a three-day notice and/or complaint, and that the tenant neither vacated nor paid the amount due.

The attorney asks the court for an order for possession of the premises, forfeiture of the rental agreement, and the amount of rent due plus attorney fees and court costs. The court generally grants the motion, after which the attorney presents all documents required to the court. The legal assistant should have completed all of the required paperwork and given it to the attorney before the default hearing.

● KEY TERMS

condominium	lease
cooperative	license
deed of trust	mortgage
easement	nuisance
escrow	personal property
eviction	real property
joint tenancy	tenancy in common

● SELF TEST

1. Describe what makes a home habitable.

2. What are the advantages and disadvantages of the condominium versus the cooperative form of ownership?

3. What is the difference between a mortgage and a deed of trust?

● NOTEBOOK PROJECTS

1. Obtain a real estate sales contract from your state.
2. Describe the escrow or closing procedures in your state in a memorandum to your instructor.
3. Obtain a packet of the forms used in your state for eviction or unlawful detainer.

For additional resources, visit our Web site at **www.paralegal.delmar.cengage.com.**

LEGAL RESEARCH

CHAPTER OUTCOMES

After studying this chapter, the student will understand

1. the difference between primary and secondary sources.
2. how to do legal research on the Internet.
3. how to determine what volumes are available in the law library.
4. how to establish procedures to keep the law library up to date.

INTRODUCTION

The process of legal research requires many skills that a well-trained legal assistant should possess. Legal assistants should have good organizational skills to enable them to organize, catalog, and prioritize information found as a result of a legal research project. Not only must the legal assistant know how to find the information required for a given research assignment, but she must be able to write a clear and easily understood analysis of the project so that the attorney who reads the research report is clear on the outcome. A major complaint of attorneys is that although their assistants can perform excellent legal research, they often lack sufficient writing ability to report the findings in a suitable format that is understandable and easy to read.

Legal assistants may be asked to find statutes, cases, constitutional sections, administrative regulations, and other materials, as well as to prepare a written report to the attorney on their findings. They may also be required to use a computerized legal research system to locate these materials.

PRIMARY SOURCES

Primary sources consist of statutes, constitutions, and cases in the same jurisdiction as the instant case. These sources are considered law in a given jurisdiction and represent the sources the court must use when rendering a decision in a particular case. For example, suppose you are doing research for a case in New York and find an applicable statute from California. The California statute would not be considered law in New York, and therefore the court would not have to use that statute in rendering a decision in the New York case.

primary sources statutes, constitutions, and cases in the same jurisdiction as the instant case

When there is a conflict between the **statutes** and the case law in a given jurisdiction, the statutory law takes precedence. Constitutional law takes precedence over all other statutes. However, remember that the constitution of New York will not apply in a California case.

Legal assistants are not often asked to analyze a statute. Generally a typical legal research project involves finding a particular statute that applies in a certain case.

In most states, the statutes are separated by subject into **codes**. Each code has its own index, and there is an index to all *sections* of the codes. If you are researching a certain topic and there is a code section on this topic, you would find the particular volume covering that topic and use the index to find the particular item related to your case. The codes are arranged alphabetically, with those included in each volume shown on the spine of the book.

The state codes are generally arranged by topic. The federal codes (called the **United States Code**) are arranged by *titles*. Some statutes have sections that state what specific topics are covered in that code, usually at the beginning of the code itself. If the legal assistant needs to complete a comprehensive analysis of a particular code section, she should use the *annotated codes*. Annotated codes are particularly helpful for finding the history of that code, cross-references to other sources and statutes, references to other items that have been written about that code section (such as law review articles), and summaries of the major court decisions that have referred to this particular statute. Remember that when you are dealing with a federal case, you should use the federal codes. When you are dealing with a state problem, you should use only the state codes for that particular state.

Finding Federal Statutes

The United States Constitution may be found in the *United States Code Annotated (USCA)*. Separate volumes exist for the Constitution. The remainder of the federal laws are found in the 50 titles to the code. These titles constitute the subject matter of the code itself. A list of the fifty applicable codes is shown in Exhibit 12-1.

Each year *pocket parts* are published for each volume to reflect changes in that particular law in that year. Every six years a new edition is published. Be sure to look in the pocket parts for each subsequent year since the statute was enacted to determine whether any changes have been made to that particular statute.

Statutory supplements are published every three to four months following the publication of the pocket part. These supplements include any changes to the statute. Each supplement covers a particular time period and must be checked to update research.

Therefore, when you are updating your research, you should perform the following tasks:

1. Check the hardback code volume.
2. Check all editions of the pocket parts after the date of the hardback volume.
3. Check all statutory supplements published after the last pocket part.

statutes   laws passed by the legislature

codes   the subject divisions into which statutes are separated

United States Code   the federal statutes, organized by title and subject

EXHIBIT 12-1   Titles of the *United States Code* and the *United States Code Annotated*

West, a Thomson business, *United States Code Annotated, List of Titles of United States Code and United States Code Annotated* (2000), Title 18, p. II. Reprinted with permission from West, a Thomson business.

1.	General Provisions	27.	Intoxicating Liquors
2.	The Congress	28.	Judiciary and Judicial Procedure
3.	The President	29.	Labor
4.	Flag and Seal, Seat of Government, and the States	30.	Mineral Lands and Mining
5.	Government Organization and Employees	31.	Money and Finance
6.	Surety Bonds (*See Title 31, Money and Finance*)	32.	National Guard
7.	Agriculture	33.	Navigation and Navigable waters
8.	Aliens and Nationality	34.	Navy (*See Title 10, Armed Forces*)
9.	Arbitration	35.	Patents
10.	Armed Forces	36.	Patriotic Societies and National Observances, Ceremonies, and Organizations
11.	Bankruptcy	37.	Pay and Allowances of the Uniformed Services
12.	Banks and Banking		
13.	Census	38.	Veterans' Benefits
14.	Coast Guard	39.	Postal service
15.	Commerce and Trade	40.	Public Buildings, Property, and Works
16.	Conservation	41.	Public contracts
17.	Copyrights	42.	The Public Health and Welfare
18.	Crimes and Criminal Procedure	43.	Public Lands
19.	Customs Duties	44.	Public Printing and Documents
20.	Education	45.	Railroads
21.	Food and Drugs	46.	Shipping
22.	Foreign Relations and Intercourse	47.	Telegraphs, Telephones, and Radiotelegraphs
23.	Highways	48.	Territories and Insular Possessions
24.	Hospitals and Asylums	49.	Transportation
25.	Indians	50.	War and National Defense
26.	Internal Revenue Code		

It is advisable to jot down each volume in which you look to be sure that you have checked all volumes that are appropriate. Make a checklist using the three preceding steps and listing each volume after you review it.

The *General Index to the United States Code Annotated* contains an alphabetic listing of descriptive words or phrases with headings and subheadings. If you do not know the appropriate code section, you may find it by using the words that describe the statute. A sample is shown in Exhibit 12-2.

EXHIBIT 12-2 *USCA General Index* Excerpt

West, a Thomson business, *United States Code Annotated, General Index* (2000), p. 787. Reprinted with permission from West, a Thomson business.

KEROSENE

Reference to Title 7 Section 515 and the Sections that follow

KEROSENE—Cont'd
Summer Fill and Fuel Budgeting Programs, 42 § 6283

KERR-MILLS ACT
Medical Assistance, generally, this index

KERR-SMITH TOBACOO CONTROL ACT
Generally, 7 § 515 et seq.

—KETOBEMIDONE
Controlled Substance, generally, this index

KETTLE RIVER
Wild and scenic rivers, 16 § 1276

KETTLEHOLES
Ice Age National Scientific Reserve, generally, this index

KEWEENAW NATIONAL HISTORICAL PARK
Generally, 16 § 410yy et seq.

KEY LARGO CORAL REEF PRESERVE
Generally, 16 § 461, nt, PN 3339

KEY LARGO NATIONAL MARINE SANCTUARY
Designation, 16 § 1433 nt

Reference to Title and Section

KEYS
Defense Department, Security, theft, forgery, fines, penalties and forfeitures, 18 § 1386
Internal Revenue Service, proprietors of distilled spirits plants to furnish to Secretary, 26 § 5203

KHMER REPUBLIC
Kampuchea, generally, this index

KIAVAH WILDERNESS
Generally, 16 § 1132 nt

KICK-BACK RACKET ACT
Generally, 40 § 276c
Public Building, Property, and Works, generally, this index

KICK-BACKS
Anti-Kickback, generally, this index Health insurance for aged and disabled, 42 § 1320a-7b
Income tax, deductions, 26 § 162
Medical assistance programs, grants to States for, criminal penalty, 42 § 1320a-7b
Presidential Election Campaign Fund, 26 § 9012
Presidential primary matching payment account, 26 § 9042
Public works, 18 § 874
Real Estate Settlement Procedures, this index
Sentence and punishment, 18 USSG §2B4.1

KICKAPOO INDIANS
Indians, this index

KIDNAPPING
Generally, 18 § 1201 et seq.
Aircraft, jurisdiction, 18 § 1201
Attempts, 18 § 1201
Attorney General, this index

KIDNAPPING—Cont'd
Banks and banking, robbery, 18 § 2113
Cabinet departments, heads and deputies,
Interception of wire, oral, or electronic communications, 18 § 2516
Kidnapping, attempts, conspiracy, penalties and forfeitures, 18 § 351
Chief Justice of Supreme Court, kidnapping, attempts, conspiracy, fines, penalties and forfeitures, 18 § 351
Children and Minors, this index
CIA, director, deputy director, fines penalties and forfeitures, 18 § 351
Congress, this index
Conspiracy.
Against right of inhabitants, fines, penalties and forfeitures, 18 § 241
Fines, penalties and forfeitures, 18 § 1201
Foreign countries, 18 § 956
Deprivation of rights under color of law, fines, penalties and forfeitures, 18 § 242
Domestic violence, parental kidnapping, reports, 28 § 1738A nt
Employee Retirement Income Security Program, protection of employee benefit rights, fiduciary responsibility, 29 § 1111
Evidence, congress, cabinet department heads, knowledge, 18 § 351
Fair housing, sale or rental, intimidation, interference, penalties, 42 § 3631
FBI database, crimes against children, registration, 42 §14072
Federal officials, fines, penalties and forfeitures, 18 § 1201
Federally protected activities, intimidation, interference, fines, penalties and forfeitures, 18 §245
Fines, penalties and forfeitures, 18 § 1201
Indian lands and reservations, 18 § 1153
Ransom money, 18 § 1202
Transportation, interstate commerce, 18 § 1201
Foreign countries
Children and minors, 42 § 11608a
Conspiracy, 18 § 956
U.S. citizens, 22 § 2715a
Foreign Diplomatic and Consular Officers, this index
Forfeitures. Fines, penalties and forfeitures, generally, ante
Indians, this index
Interception of wire, oral, or electronic communications, President, congress, 18 § 2516
International Child Abduction Remedies, generally, this index
Interstate and Foreign Commerce, this index
Involuntary servitude, intent to sell, 18 § 1583
Jurisdiction,
Indian lands and reservations, 18 § 3242
Internationally protected persons, victims, 18 § 1201

The last volume of the *General Index* contains a Popular Name Table, which lists statutes by their popular names, such as the Americans with Disabilities Act. If you know the popular name of a statute but do not have its citation, use this table to locate the statute.

A similar series of volumes is called the *United States Code Service (USCS)*, which is published by Lexis-Nexis. This series shows the federal codes in a manner similar to that of the *United States Code Annotated (USCA)*. Differences include the following:

1. The *USCS* supplements are cumulative, so only the latest supplement must be checked for updates.
2. The *USCA* has more court decisions in its annotations.

State Statutes

Each state has its own series of statutes arranged by codes, similar to the United States Code. The annotated state codes contain similar supplemental material, but on the state level. Some states have two series of statutes, one official and the other unofficial. When you are citing from a code section, you must use the official citation. Many states have only one series. The state constitutions are included with the state codes. The state codes are updated annually with pocket parts inserted in the volume itself or separate paper volumes.

STATE-SPECIFIC INFORMATION

The official state codes for the state of _____ are called

_____

The unofficial version is called

_____

Court Rules

Each court has its own set of rules to which the attorneys must adhere. They include the format of court documents, the use of court forms, and the procedures followed in each particular court. Some states have a *looseleaf series* with inserts for each county. The major portion of the series describes the court rules for the state in general. The county inserts describe the specific differences between the rules and procedures for each county.

Case Law

The second primary source of law is the body of law created by court opinions that create precedents for later cases. This type of law is known as *common law* and is found in the written court opinions. Although statutory law takes precedence over **case law**, considerably more volumes of case law are available.

case law a primary source of law created by court opinions that create precedents for later cases

Case law has a standardized format. The first item in the case is the name of the case and the **case citation.** After the name and citation, you will find the following:

1. the facts of the case
2. the history of the case in the lower courts
3. the issues addressed in the case, shown as *headnotes*
4. the court opinion itself

Only the court opinion itself consists of the law and may be quoted in subsequent proceedings. The opinion is written by an appellate or supreme court justice and describes the rule of law that governs the case and the manner in which the court applied this law to reach its decision. The final item gives the actual decision of the court.

Citations

Each statute and case decision has its own identifying citation to enable the researcher to find it. The citation includes the name of the case or statute and the volume number, name of the reporter, page number, and year of the case. For example, to find the case

Smith v. Jones, 45 U.S. 322 (1975)

you would look in volume 45 of the *United States Reports* on page 322. The decision was rendered in 1975.

Citations to statutes should include the title number (federal), name of the code, section number, and year. For example,

44 U.S.C. § 1989 (1998)

would be the citation for volume 44 of the United States Code, section 1989, passed in 1998.

Delmar, Cengage Learning/Paralegal Studies publishes a brief supplemental *Citation at a Glance,* which provides a brief description of the most common citations. The official method for writing citations may be found in *The Bluebook: A Uniform System of Citation.* Some states have requirements for styles other than the Bluebook. For example, the California Supreme Court requires the *California Style Manual.* Determine the requirements in your state and complete the following box.

case or **statute citation**
name of the case or statute
and the volume number,
name of the reporter, page
number, and year of the
case or statute

STATE-SPECIFIC INFORMATION

The proper style manual for the courts of the state of _____ is

_____

Specific courts with different requirements are as follows:

_____

_____

_____

Case Briefs

A **case brief** is a summary of the opinion in a case and may be written in the following manner:

1. the name of the case and citation
2. a brief statement of the facts
3. the main issue in the case
4. the rule of law that applied in the case
5. how this particular rule was applied in this case
6. the court decision

Although many attorneys prepare their own case briefs, sometimes a paralegal or legal assistant is asked to prepare a case brief.

SECONDARY SOURCES

Secondary sources consist of other sources for legal research that are not the law itself. They include legal encyclopedias, digests, treatises and texts, Shepard's citations, and Internet sources. Each of these authorities will be described next.

Legal Encyclopedias

Legal encyclopedias are used to find general information about a given area of law. They are arranged similarly to a regular encyclopedia, alphabetically by subject. Within each topic one may find references to cases and statutes. The two major national legal encyclopedias are *Corpus Juris Secundum (C.J.S.)* and *American Jurisprudence 2d (Am. Jur. 2d)*. They present a general overview of both federal and some state law. Some states have their own encyclopedia series for their state's laws. For example, California's state encyclopedia is called *California Jurisprudence.*

STATE-SPECIFIC INFORMATION

The state encyclopedia for the state of _____ is called

_____

Subjects are arranged alphabetically, and each individual topic has its own index. Each set also has a general index. Pocket parts are used to update each volume as changes are made.

Digests

Digests are arranged in the following manner:

1. topic title
2. subtopics covered and not covered

case brief a summary of the opinion in a case

secondary sources sources for legal research that are not primary authority, such as legal encyclopedias, digests, treatises, and textbooks

3. table of contents
4. summaries of cases

Each digest also includes the following:

1. list of topics included
2. descriptive word index
3. plaintiff/defendant table
4. table of cases
5. updates (pocket parts and supplementary pamphlets)

The *American Digest System* includes summaries of all cases on the state and federal level. Each set covers a specific time period, which makes it more cumbersome to find all cases on a given topic. The *United States Supreme Court Digest* provides summaries of all opinions of the United States Supreme Court. The *West Federal Practice Digest* covers opinions from the federal courts and the Supreme Court. State digests are published for most states, not including Delaware, Nevada, and Utah. However, regional digests include those states. Delaware is included in the *Atlantic Digest,* and Nevada and Utah may be found in the *Pacific Digest.* State court decisions and federal court decisions from each state are included in the state digests.

Treatises and Texts

A *treatise* provides a comprehensive analysis of one area of the law, such as wills or probate. *Texts* also provide detailed analyses of given legal topics. If one is unfamiliar with a specific area of law, the text or treatise will provide a detailed explanation of the various subtopics within that specific legal specialty.

Shepard's Citations

Shepard's citations provide a method of updating statute and case law. Each volume of Shepard's covers a different series of volumes. For example, *Shepard's California Citations* includes references to all cases in California. You must find the appropriate volume of Shepard's, which has the volumes listed on the spine of the book. Suppose you were looking for a case in the *California Reporter* series. Once you found the *California Reporter* listed on the spine, you would look in that volume to find the volume within the *California Reporter,* then look further to find the page number. References in Shepard's show the name of the series at the top of each page, with the volume number and page numbers on the page itself. The case citation in Shepard's lists subsequent cases that have used that case in the opinion. A series of reference letters may be found in the front of the volume. Most critical is the letter *o,* which means that particular case overruled the case for which you are searching. Supplementary paper volumes of Shepard's should also be checked as mentioned previously. You may have to check the bound volume, several paperback volumes, and small supplementary sheets to update the case completely. Jot down the periods covered in each supplement so that you are sure that all time periods after the case decision are covered. This updating is known as **Sheparding.**

COMPUTERIZED LEGAL RESEARCH

The two most comprehensive sources for computerized legal research are WESTLAW and Lexis, which are available on the Internet via their respective Web sites. You must subscribe to the service in order to use these systems. You must enter a password to gain access to the database; your time using the database is computed automatically. These sites are available at

http://www.westlaw.com
http://www.lexis.com

Additional sources are also available on these Web sites. For instance, *Delmar's Legal Directory of Attorneys* may be accessed from the WESTLAW Web site.

Legal Research on the Internet

Several specialized search mechanisms are available for the legal profession. The Library of Congress maintains a Web site that provides a catalog of all available publications. You can search for any book that has been published and has an ISBN number. Searches may be undertaken by title, keywords, or author. The site for the Library of Congress is located at

http://lcweb.loc.gov

One of the more comprehensive Web sites for finding information about different areas of law is available at

http://www.amicus.ca

This site provides information on specific practice areas along with background information on law-related topics. It is particularly useful for finding resources in a practice area with which you are unfamiliar or when more information is required than can be found under the federal or state links. The site includes the following practice areas of law:

1. bankruptcy
2. business law
3. civil litigation
4. commercial law
5. constitutional law and civil rights
6. corporate safety
7. criminal law

Shepardize to update a case by using Shepard's citations to determine whether it is still good law

8. employment law

9. family law

10. health and disability law

11. insurance law

12. labor law

13. environmental law

14. probate law

15. real property law

16. personal injury

This site provides resources on the growing body of law governing Internet use, as well as additional links connected to the subject. General links are provided to hardware and software information along with leads for doing searches.

Links to Law Sites

FindLaw has been touted as being the best site to find other legal resources. The FindLaw Web site is available at

http://www.findlaw.com

Some links on the FindLaw site provide information on the following:

1. consumer law

2. United States Supreme Court cases

3. state cases and laws

4. law schools

5. legal subject indexes

6. state law resources

7. foreign and international resources

8. law firms

9. legal organizations

10. government directories

11. legal practice materials

If you are looking for a site on a law subject and do not know the Web site address, it is often easier to find the site on FindLaw than to do a search on your own. FindLaw is especially valuable if you are not sure exactly under which topic to conduct your keyword search. Exhibit 12-3 shows the FindLaw home page.

The American Bar Association maintains a "Lawlink" legal research Web page that has links to all branches of government as well as the courts, Judicial Council, court home pages, law school libraries, and a number of other legal reference sources. It is located at

http://www.abanet.org

EXHIBIT 12-3   FindLaw Web Site

Reprinted with permission of FindLaw.com, a Thomson business.

For the Public   For Legal Professionals

Find a lawyer. Find answers.

Legal Professionals ▶▶
go here

Search for a Local Lawyer   **Search FindLaw**

Legal Issue (e.g. bankruptcy)   **Location** (e.g. Palo Alto, CA or 94306)

[   ]   [   ]   Find Lawyers!   Search by Name
Advanced Search

OR: Get help now — free, confidential, service matches you with lawyers in your area. Try LegalConnection.

Browse Legal Information   **View all topics**

 Accidents & Injuries
Personal Injury, Medical
Malpractice, More...

 Dangerous Products
Asbestos, Benzene,
Dangerous Drugs, More...

 Immigration
Citizenship, Green Cards,
Visas, More...

 Bankruptcy & Debt
New Bankruptcy Law, Debt
Relief, More...

 Divorce & Family Law
Adoption, Child Custody,
Child Support, Divorce

 Real Estate
For Homeowners, Tenants,
Landlords, Mold, More...

 Car Accidents
Truck Accidents,
Motorcycle Accidents,
More...

 DUI / DWI
State DUI Laws, DUI
Resources, More...

 Small Business
Incorporation, Forms &
Contracts, Employment, More...

 Civil Rights
Employment, Housing,
Laws, More...

 Employee Rights
Losing a Job, Wages,
Harassment, More...

 Traffic Violations
Tickets A to Z, State Traffic Law,
DMVs, More...

 Criminal Law
Crimes A to Z, Your
Rights, More...

 Estate Planning
Wills, Trusts, Living Wills,
Probate, More...

 **Don't see what you're
looking for?**
More Topics...

Did You Know?

Constitutional Amendments
The U.S. Constitution has been amended
27 times. Learn more...

1900s ▬▬▬▬▬▬▬▬▬ 12
1800s ▬▬▬ 4
1700s ▬▬▬▬▬▬▬▬ 11
Number of Amendments, by century

Today's Legal Headlines
● 'Bad Santa' Charged With Kidnapping
● Mich. Couple's Parental Rights Revoked

More Legal News | Commentary | Blog

Tips & Tools

Forms & Contracts
Business Forms, Living Wills, More...

State Laws
Business, Child Custody, Criminal,
Divorce, DUI, Property, More...

State Courts
Bankruptcy, Family, Probate, Small
Claims, More...

● Guide to Hiring a Lawyer
● Legal Dictionary
● December Spotlight: Travel Tips

**Start your business
with the law on your side.**

● Name your business
● Choose a corporate structure
● Obtain licenses and permits

FindLaw Small Business Center
Find Help Now

FindLaw
Find a lawyer. Find answers.

 2005 Webby
Award Winner

 Time.com: 50 Coolest
Websites 2005

Attorneys: Market Your Law Firm: Website development, Advertising opportunities, and more marketing tools!
Local Lawyers: Atlanta Lawyers, Chicago Lawyers, Houston Lawyers, Los Angeles Lawyers, New York City Lawyers, More...

Advertise With Us - Link to FindLaw - Comments - @Justice.com Email
Help - Disclaimer - Privacy - Jobs - About Us
Copyright @1994-2006 FindLaw, a Thomson business

Federal and State Sources on the Internet

Contacting government agencies by telephone or postal mail is often difficult and time consuming. Spending the necessary time to reach the correct department or person is an arduous task. Most government agencies and departments now have Web sites, most of which give accurate and timely information. The federal courts, codes, and many cases are also available online.

Government Agencies

Aviation. Two government agencies are primarily responsible for information regarding airline accidents and incident reports. The National Transportation Safety Board (NTSB) Web site, located at

http://www.ntsb.gov

gives information helpful for aviation litigation, specifically information about airline crashes and incidents related to certain aircraft. Much of this information is available because of the Freedom of Information Act; however, if you request it using postal mail, several weeks may pass before it arrives. Much of the same information is available on the Web site.

The Federal Aviation Administration (FAA), whose Web site is located at

http://www.faa.gov

is responsible for the safety of civil aviation. As a component of the Department of Transportation, its functions include the following:

1. regulating civil aviation to promote safety
2. encouraging the development of air commerce and civil aeronautics
3. developing and operating air traffic control and navigation systems for both civil and military aircraft
4. developing and executing programs to control aircraft noise and other environmental effects of civil aviation
5. regulating commercial space transportation

The following additional information is available on the FAA Web site:

1. agency policies
2. regulations
3. air traffic and safety information
4. regional offices and site maps
5. commercial space transportation regulations
6. civil aviation security policies

These sites are particularly helpful for law offices engaged in aviation litigation, particularly accident/incident reports and incidents involving certain types of aircraft and/or certain airlines.

Transportation Security Administration (TSA). The TSA was created as a response to the terrorist attacks of September 11, 2001. It was moved from the Department of Transportation to the Department of Homeland Security in 2003. Its purpose is to protect our nation's transportation systems by ensuring freedom of movement for individuals as well as for commerce. In 2002, the TSA assumed responsibility for security at our nation's airports. It employs a federal security workforce for screening all passengers and baggage at airports. The TSA Web site may be found at

http://www.tsa.gov

The TSA home page is shown in Exhibit 12-4.

Department of Transportation (DOT). The DOT governs transportation agencies of the government, including the FAA. The DOT Web site is located at

http://www.dot.gov

and includes links to other divisions within the department, including the FAA, the Federal Highway Administration, the Federal Railroad Administration, the Federal Transit Administration, the Maritime Administration, the National Highway Traffic Safety Administration, and the United States Coast Guard. If the law office has a case that involves safety considerations on a federal highway or waterway, this site would be helpful.

State Department. The secretary of state is appointed by the president and is the chief foreign affairs adviser. She oversees the State Department, which is the senior executive department of the United States government. Activities of the department include the following:

1. advising on foreign policy
2. negotiating in foreign affairs
3. negotiating, interpreting, and terminating treaties
4. granting and issuing passports
5. protecting American citizens in foreign countries
6. supervising immigration laws abroad
7. providing information about travel conditions in foreign countries

The State Department Web site is located at

http://www.state.gov

This department also maintains a special page of travel advisories for individuals traveling to foreign countries, including areas of political unrest or recent uprisings. The main page is available at

http://travel.state.gov and then to
http://travel.state.gov/travel/warnings.html/

EXHIBIT 12-4 Transportation Security Administration Home Page

From http://www.tsa.gov.

Home | Contact Us | Frequently Asked Questions

Transportation
Security
Administration

Search [Enter Search Term] [Go]

Advanced Search

Who We Are | Our Travelers | What We Do | Join Us | Our Approach | Media Room | Research Center

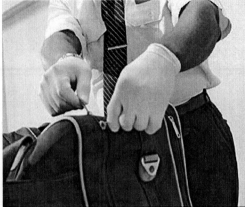

Get The 3-1-1 for Carry-ons
CLICK HERE

Permitted and Prohibited Items

Learn How To Be Prepared For Enhanced Security This Holiday Season »

‖ ▶ 1 2 3 4

In The News

» Read Homeland Security Secretary Michael Chertoff's Remarks on Protecting the Homeland: Meeting Challenges and Looking Forward

» DHS Targets High Risk Hazardous Materials in Transit to Protect High Threat Urban Areas

» TSA Names Three Area Directors to Oversee Transportation Security Nationwide

» TSA Sets Fee for Registered Traveler Program

3 1 1 for Carry-ons
Prepare for Take-off →

Know Before You Go

Liquids, gels and aerosols must be in three-ounce or smaller containers and in a one-quart, zip-top bag.

» Get the 3-1-1 for Carry-ons and make the most of your trip

» Our 3-1-1 Holiday Travel Tips

» What can I bring? Some do's and don'ts of packing

RSS Feeds

🔊RSS **Click Here** for TSA's RSS Feeds.

Resource Center

» **Permitted & Prohibited Items**

» **Need Something Specific?**

» **Traveling With Children?**

» **Duty Free Goods Info**

» **Check Your Claim Status**

Problems Getting On The Plane?

TSA's Traveler Identity Verification Program can help.
Learn more »

International Travelers

For passengers traveling to and from the United States.
Learn more »

Explosives Detection Canine Teams

Canine teams are an effective tool in air cargo screening.
Learn more »

Who We Are

Aviation Security Inspector Colby Matte and Transportation Security Officer Arlene Albino »

Home   Contact Us   Privacy Policy   Website Policies   No FEAR   Accessibility   FOIA   FirstGov

Transportation Security Administration | U.S. Department of Homeland Security

and is particularly useful for attorneys who travel to foreign countries on a regular basis. An e-mail subscription to travel advisories may also be obtained on the Web site so that whenever a travel advisory is given for a country, you will receive an e-mail stating the name of the country and the circumstances of the advisory.

United States Census Bureau.   Statistical information gathered from the census is available at

http://www.census.gov

and includes census data, financial data for government, economic and population studies, and links to other related sites.

Government Printing Office.   Documents available from this office may be obtained from its Web site at

http://www.access.gpo.gov

Information is available about the intelligence community, Congress, the Office of the Special Counsel, the General Accounting Office, the Department of the Interior, the Executive Office of the President, and various other departments.

The White House.   The White House Web site is located at

http://www.whitehouse.gov

Information available at this site includes data about the President and Vice President; the history of the White House and tour information; a library of press releases, radio addresses, and related Web pages; summaries of today's press releases; the Constitution; and a considerable amount of material on current events. Cabinet offices and executive branch agencies are listed with addresses and telephone numbers at

http://www.whitehouse.gov

Central Intelligence Agency (CIA).   The director of the CIA heads the agencies that constitute the intelligence community of the United States. They conduct investigations, surveillance, research, and other activities. The CIA Web site is located at

http://www.cia.gov

and describes the functions of the agency as well as providing links to readings about the intelligence community.

Federal Bureau of Investigation (FBI).   The FBI Web site may be useful for those who work in law offices that specialize in criminal law. It is located at

http://www.fbi.gov

and includes information about the bureau's history, programs, speeches, press releases, chief investigations, and Most Wanted List.

Library of the House of Representatives. An extensive law library, particularly valuable for federal sources, is available at the House of Representatives Web site at

http://www.house.gov

The site also contains the text of pending legislation as well as congressional testimony.

Citizenship and Immigration Services (CIS). CIS (formerly the Immigration and Naturalization Service, or INS) is an agency of the Department of Homeland Security and is responsible for the admission, naturalization, stopping of illegal entry, and deportation of foreign nationals. Its Appeals Board hears appeals to deportation orders.

Immigration laws change rapidly. Anyone employed in the area of immigration law should consult the CIS Web site to obtain the latest rules and regulations. The Web site also contains forms used in an immigration law practice. It is located at

http://www.uscis.gov

Department of Justice (DOJ). The DOJ manages the legal business of the United States. All federal law enforcement agencies are within the DOJ. It represents the United States in civil and criminal cases; runs the federal prison system; and oversees the Antitrust Division, the Civil Rights Division, the FBI, the Drug Enforcement Administration (DEA), and other agencies. It is headed by the attorney general of the United States. The DOJ Web site is located at

http://www.usdoj.gov

and includes information on the various agencies in the department, recent case decisions involving the Justice Department, and other information related to the United States legal community.

Department of Commerce/Patent and Trademark Office. Patent attorneys and paralegals find this site particularly valuable for obtaining information about trademarks and patents. It provides forms to register and maintain trademarks and patents, as well as links to related sites. The site may be found at

http://www.uspto.gov

Internal Revenue Service (IRS). A considerable amount of tax information is provided at the IRS Web site at

http://www.irs.ustreas.gov

Tax forms may be downloaded from the site. Publications on IRS regulations are also available for downloading.

Department of Labor. The Department of Labor regulates working conditions, workforce development, and labor-management relations. Its Web site contains information on wages, hours, workplace issues, running small businesses, and federal labor regulations, and is located at

http://www.dol.gov

Securities and Exchange Commission (SEC). The SEC administers the federal and state laws that regulate the sale of securities. Its Web site includes the Securities Act of 1933, which requires the registration of securities to be sold to the public and the disclosure of complete information to possible buyers; the Securities and Exchange Act of 1934, which regulates both stock exchanges and sales of stock over the counter; and a number of other laws related to the purchase and sale of securities that the SEC enforces. The site is particularly useful for law offices specializing in corporate law and is located at

http://www.sec.gov

The Web site provides a method for filing online, information on other corporate filings, a database to search for information on filings, information for small businesses, and current rules and regulations.

Social Security Administration (SSA). The SSA Web site provides the ability to access one's own personal earnings and future benefits estimates. Information is provided about Social Security benefits and Medicare. Explanations are provided for the system's regulations. The SSA Web site is located at

http://www.ssa.gov

Library of Congress. Many additional departments and agencies exist in the federal government that are not listed here. The best place to find listings of federal, state, and local governments and agencies is on the Library of Congress Web site, which provides links to other government departments. The site may be found at

http://lcweb.loc.gov

FEDERAL COURTS

The federal courts are divided into the following general areas:

1. United States Supreme Court
2. Circuit Courts of Appeals
3. federal district courts

United States Supreme Court

The *Supreme Court of the United States* is the highest court in our country. It is located in Washington, D.C., and sits from the first Monday in October until June. Nine justices sit on the court, one of whom is the *chief justice,* who presides over the court. All decisions of the federal Circuit Courts of Appeal may be appealed to the Supreme Court. It may also hear cases in which the highest state court has issued a decision that challenges the validity of a federal law. Generally the court hears only cases that raise significant issues and declines to hear most cases appealed. The Supreme Court Web site may be found at

http://www.supremecourtus.gov

or as a link from the United States Courts Web site:

http://www.uscourts.gov

The home page of the Supreme Court of the United States is shown in Exhibit 12-5. The "About the Supreme Court" link shows the page in Exhibit 12-6. Any of the information listed on this page may be found by clicking on the link provided.

Circuit Courts of Appeal

The intermediary federal courts for appeals are the *Circuit Courts of Appeal,* which hear cases appealed from the United States District Courts. The 13 circuits each represent several states and the federal system.

Twelve regional circuits represent intermediate courts of appeal. They hear appeals from the following United States District Courts in each state: bankruptcy courts, tax courts, and administrative agency tribunals.

The United States Court of Appeals for the Federal Circuit represents federal appeals from the Court of Federal Claims, the Court of International Trade, the Court of Appeals for Veterans Claims, the patents and trademarks appeals boards, and other courts with special jurisdiction. The number of judges in each circuit varies with the size of the court and the number of cases being heard.

The United States Courts Web site provides a link to the United States Courts of Appeals, as well as to the federal district courts and the bankruptcy courts. The United States Courts home page is shown in Exhibit 12-7 and is located at

http://www.uscourts.gov

The "Court Links" page provides a map with links to all of the various circuit courts as well as the ability to search for district courts, bankruptcy courts, probation offices, and pretrial services offices, by city and state, zip code, county and state, or area code. See Exhibit 12-8.

EXHIBIT 12-5   Supreme Court of the United States Home Page

From http://www.supremecourtus.gov.

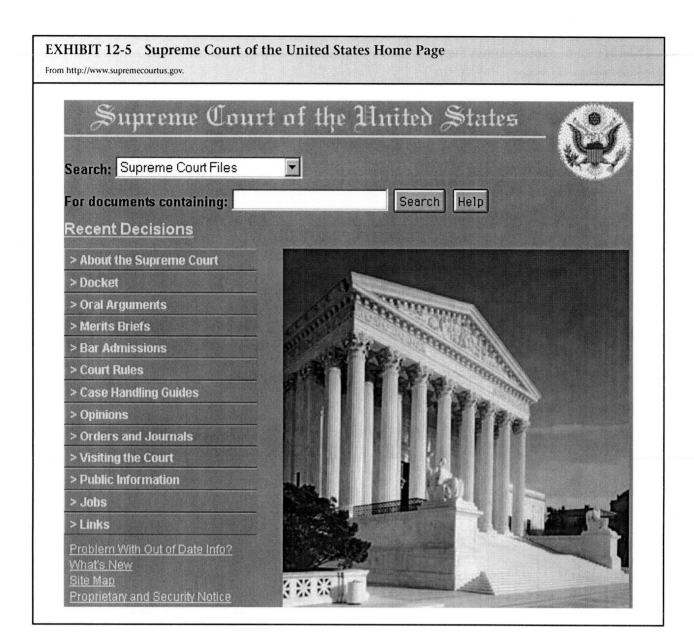

Federal District Courts

The *United States District Courts* are the trial courts on the federal level. There are 94 federal judicial districts, with at least one in each state. Larger and heavily populated states have several districts. Most cases heard in these courts involve questions of federal law, such as statutes, treaties, the Constitution, or federal crimes. Cases against the United States government, cases involving diversity of citizenship (in which the plaintiff and defendant reside in different states and the amount in controversy is more than a certain amount), and cases in specialized areas such as customs and admiralty also come under the original jurisdiction of these courts.

The federal district courts are accessible from the United States Courts Web site. See Exhibit 12-7.

EXHIBIT 12-6   United States Supreme Court—"About the Supreme Court" Page

From http://www.supremecourtus.gov.

ABOUT THE SUPREME COURT

- Constitution of the United States of America

- A Brief Overview of the Supreme Court (PDF)

- The Court and Constitutional Interpretation (PDF)

- The Court as an Institution (PDF)

- The Court and Its Traditions (PDF)

- The Court and Its Procedures (PDF)

- The Justices' Caseload (PDF)

- Biographies of Current Members of the Supreme Court (PDF)

- Members of the Supreme Court (1789 to Present) (PDF)

- The Supreme Court Building (PDF)

- Circuit Assignments of Justices (PDF)

- Problem With Out of Date Information?

Search Tip: Use the binocular icons to search within PDF documents.

HOME | ABOUT THE COURT | DOCKET | ORAL ARGUMENTS | MERITS BRIEFS | BAR ADMISSIONS | COURT RULES
CASE HANDLING GUIDES | OPINIONS | ORDERS | VISITING THE COURT | PUBLIC INFORMATION | JOBS | LINKS

EXHIBIT 12-7   United States Courts Home Page

From http://www.uscourts.gov.

STATE SOURCES

Each state generally has its own Web site that includes links to state government offices. Find your state's Web site and indicate its address in the following box.

> STATE-SPECIFIC INFORMATION
>
> The address for the Web site of the state of _____ is
>
> _____

Each state's Web site provides links to state statutes, cases, courts, court rules, and other state government agencies. One particularly

EXHIBIT 12-8 United States Courts—"Court Links" Page

From http://www.uscourts.gov.

helpful link for state information may be found on the FindLaw Web site at

http://www.findlaw.com

This source also provides links for federal government sources, legal news, law reviews, statutes, law schools, cases, professional legal organizations, experts in various specialty fields, and international legal sources.

LAW FIRMS

Many private attorneys and law firms have their own Web site. The best way to find a specific law firm's Web site is to do a search using the name of the firm in quotation marks. If you are not certain of the firm's full name, enter the name as you think it is without the quotation marks.

The *Paralegal Directory* represents biographical listings of more than 800,000 lawyers. Searches are possible by subject, practice area, attributes of the attorney, and location. For example, it would be possible to search for "a Spanish-speaking immigration attorney in Los Angeles." It is possible to search the following subjects in the *Paralegal Directory,* accessible at

http://lawyers.findlaw.com

1. search by name
2. United States lawyers
3. international counsel
4. corporate lawyers
5. government lawyers
6. United States courts
7. law students
8. lawyer services guides
9. areas of law
10. state law information
11. overview of the courts
12. law dictionary
13. articles from law firms
14. how to hire a lawyer

In addition, each day certain articles from law firms are featured by provided links.

Most people who have worked in law offices are familiar with the *Martindale-Hubbell Legal Directory of Attorneys and Law Firms,* which is provided online at

http://www.martindale.com

It includes more than 900,000 listings of law firms and attorneys in the United States and other countries. Searches are possible by name, city, state, country, language, and province. It is also possible to search here for government attorneys and corporate law departments. Individual listings for attorneys include their name, address, telephone number, areas of practice, educational background, professional affiliations, and sometimes representative clients.

PROFESSIONAL ORGANIZATIONS

The Web sites of some professional organizations are listed here:

American Bar Association	**http://www.abanet.org**
National Association of Legal Assistants	**http://www.nala.org**
National Federation of Paralegal Associations	**http://www.paralegals.org**
Association of Legal Administrators	**http://www.alanet.org**
National Notary Association	**http://www.nationalnotary.org**
NALS, . . . the association for legal professionals (formerly the National Association of Legal Secretaries)	**http://www.nals.org**

SPECIALIZED TOPICS

Some Web sites for different legal specialties are listed in this section. The FindLaw Web site is an excellent source with which to begin your search; it includes several specialty-area links and may be found at

http://www.findlaw.com

The Law round the Net Web site also provides links to different specialty areas and is located at

http://www.law.net

The following sites are listed under the specialty areas they represent:

Bankruptcy	**http://www.uscourts.gov**
	http://bankrupt.com
Civil Rights	**http://www.aclu.org**
	http://www1.umn.edu/humanrts
Consumer Law	**http://www.fraud.org**
Copyright	**http://www.copyright.com**
Corporate Law	**http://www.law.uc.edu/CCL**
	http://www.sec.gov

Criminal Law	**http://www.findlaw.com**
	http://www.ilj.org
	http://www.payles.com/law/criminal.html
Elder Law	**http://www.seniorlaw.com**
	http://www.catalaw.com
Environmental Law	**http://www.law.indiana.edu**
	http://www.epa.gov
	http://www.usgs.gov
	http://www.wetlands.com
Estate Planning	**http://www.law.cornell.edu/wex/index.php/Estate_Planning**
Family Law	**http://www.divorcenet.com**
Immigration Law	**http://www.uscis.gov**
	http://www.us-immigration.com
	http://www.wave.net/upg/immigration/resource.html
Litigation/Personal Injury Law	**http://www.hoovers.com**
	http://www.nhtsa.dot.gov
	http://www.cpsc.gov
	http://www.medhelp.org
	http://www.expertlaw.com
	http://www.kbb.com
Real Property Law	**http://www.datatrac.com**
	http://www.realtor.com
	http://www.ccim.com
Tax Law	**http://www.irs.ustreas.gov**
	http://www.el.com/elinks/taxes

Note that Web sites change quite often; some of these may have changed or been deleted by the time this book is published. They are given as a list of sites available and not necessarily as a recommendation by the author as a site to use when dealing with the particular specialty area of law listed.

THE LAW LIBRARY

Every law office has a law library that is kept up to date by a law librarian, legal professional, legal assistant, or paralegal. Although this may seem a tedious and boring task, dire consequences might result if the attorney is using a book that has not been updated. For instance, suppose the attorney is relying on a particular statute to argue a case. A new pocket part has been issued that states that the statute has been changed, but the law librarian has neglected to place the new pocket part in the code book. The attorney could end up losing the case based on that one oversight.

The author attended a state supreme court hearing in which an attorney was arguing a major issue in his case based on a prior precedent-setting case on the same subject. One of the justices asked if the attorney had Shepardized the case, to which he did not respond immediately. The justice went on to say that had the attorney Shepardized the case he would have found that same court had overruled that case. Perhaps the latest pocket part or insert had not been filed in a timely fashion. Or perhaps the attorney had given the responsibility for Shepardizing to a subordinate who had failed to do so properly. In any event, this attorney may have lost the case based on a simple error.

All law books in the library must be kept up to date. A legal professional who has been given this responsibility should endeavor to leave some time at the end of each day to insert new sections and take out old sections of the library books.

● KEY TERMS

case brief

case law

case or statute citation

codes

primary sources

Shepardize

statutes

United States Code

● SELF TEST

1. Describe the difference between primary and secondary sources.

2. Give two examples of primary sources and two examples of secondary sources.

3. For what purpose is a digest used?

● NOTEBOOK PROJECTS

1. Visit a law office or invite an attorney to speak to the class about writing a legal research report. Put examples of the reports in your notebook.

2. Find Web sites for your state's laws, courts, and court rules. List the Web sites in your notebook.

For additional resources, visit our Web site at **www.paralegal.delmar.cengage.com**.

PATENT LAW

CHAPTER OUTCOMES

After studying this chapter, the student will understand

1. the basic organization of patent law.
2. how to conduct patent searches.
3. the process of patent applications.
4. the process of patent infringement lawsuits.

INTRODUCTION

The law of **intellectual property** is a broad category that includes patent law, trademarks, trade secrets, and the law of copyrights. This chapter describes the procedures required to obtain a patent application as well as the process of patent infringement lawsuits.

PATENT LAW

A **patent** is issued by the federal government to an individual who makes an application, granting this person the exclusive authority to make, use, and sell the invention for a specified period of time. *Utility patents* are granted for useful items or processes for 20 years. *Plant patents* are issued for distinctive items for 20 years. *Design patents* are issued for ornamental items for 14 years.

The individual seeking a patent must apply to the Patent and Trademark Office (PTO), which is part of the Department of Commerce. This agency examines the application and determines whether the same patent has been previously issued to another individual. If not, the agency issues a patent to the individual granting the exclusive authority to make, use, and sell the invention.

The United States Constitution, Article 1, Section 8, Clause 8, specifically grants Congress the power to pass patent and copyright laws to protect inventors' rights to their own creations. Inventors must, however, obtain a patent to protect and put in force their rights to their inventions. For example, one may not sue another for patent infringement unless he has a registered patent for that particular item.

intellectual property a broad category of law that includes patent law, trademarks, trade secrets, and the law of copyrights

patent a right given by the federal government to an individual, for a specified number of years, to make, use, and sell his invention

PATENT AND TRADEMARK OFFICE WEB SITE

The Patent and Trademark Office maintains a Web site to obtain information about obtaining patents. It provides downloadable forms, fee requirements, and other general information. The Patent and Trademark Office's publication titled *Manual of Patent Examining Procedure (MPEP)* may also be downloaded from the Web site. This manual includes the regulations for examining and issuing patents. Most patent law offices use this manual for any specific questions or problems. The site is located at

http://www.uspto.gov

The PTO home page is shown in Exhibit 13-1.

EXHIBIT 13-1   Patent and Trademark Office Home Page

From http://www.uspto.gov.

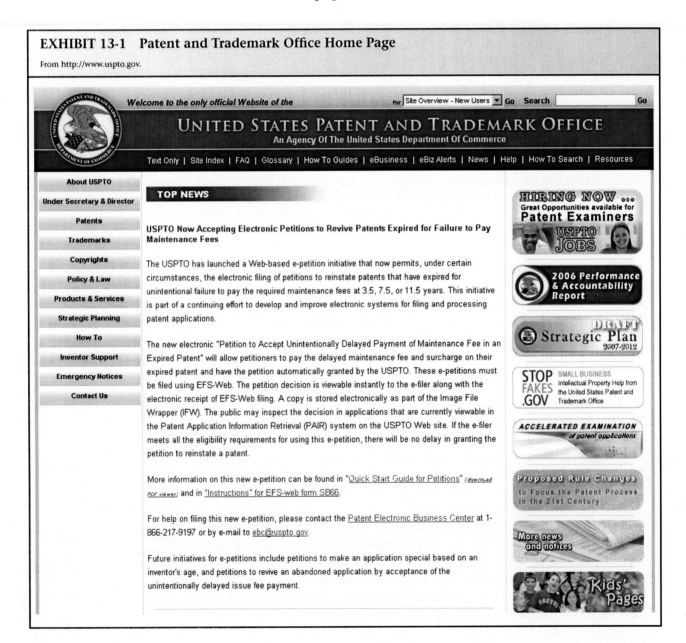

STEPS TO OBTAINING A PATENT

The process of applying for a patent and following through on the application until the patent is granted is known as **prosecution**. Either a patent attorney representing the inventor, a registered patent agent, or the inventor himself must file the application. The process follows:

1. The inventor files the application.
2. The Patent and Trademark Office assigns the application to a patent examiner with experience in the technical area of the patent.
3. If the examiner makes any objections to the application, the inventor or his representative must respond by telephone or in writing.
4. The examiner either accepts the response or rejects the application.
5. If the application is rejected, the rejection may be appealed to the Board of Patent Appeals and Interferences.
6. If the examiner accepts the response, a Notice of Allowance is forwarded to the inventor or representative, who must then pay an issue fee for issuance of the patent.

The patent application process can be lengthy and costly. Typically the application takes about two years to be issued, and the costs average approximately $12,000. Unless the invention is economically feasible, it may not be worth the lengthy and costly process to obtain the patent. The attorney should advise the client accordingly in those cases.

Patent attorneys are required to have not only a knowledge of patent law, but technical knowledge in the appropriate field. Many patent attorneys possess advanced degrees in such areas as physics, biotechnology, chemistry, engineering, or computers. Most patent law firms hire attorneys skilled in a variety of these subject areas. In addition to passing the state bar in the state in which the attorney is licensed, the attorney must also pass the Patent Bar, which requires knowledge in science and/or engineering in the specific topics of inventions that are mechanical, electrical, or chemical.

Registered patent agents are either engineers or scientists who have passed the examination specifically for patent agents. They must have a bachelor's degree and knowledge in the given subject area.

Attorneys may become registered patent agents, but nonattorneys who are patent agents may not engage in the unauthorized practice of law, such as giving legal advice to applicants or representing individuals in patent infringement or other types of lawsuits.

Registered Attorneys and Patent Agents

The PTO maintains a page listing all attorneys and agents who are licensed to practice before it. This page is located at

http://www.uspto.gov/ and then to OEDCI.

prosecution   the process of preparing the application for a patent and following through to its being granted

Alternatively the Government Printing Office also maintains a list of licensed agents and attorneys.

Patent Application Preparation

Exhibit 13-2 shows the 2006 fee schedule for patent application filing fees. It also includes fees for patent searches, post allowances, maintenance, post issuance, extensions of time, appeals and interferences, foreign and international patents, services, patent enrollment, computer records, trademark processing, and other general fees.

The Patent Electronic Business Center offers links to assist in searches for issued patents and published applications for patents. Searches may be conducted by name or number. Databases show the patent images, status, and event history. The published applications also show their status and event history. Exhibit 13-3 shows this page, located at

http://www.uspto.gov

A number of forms are downloadable for use in the patent and trademark application process. They may be found at

http://www.uspto.gov

A list of the available forms as shown on the Web site may be found in Exhibit 13-4.

EXHIBIT 13-2   United States Patent and Trademark Office 2006 Fee Schedule

From http://www.uspto.gov.

Fee Code	37 CFR	Description	Fee	Small Entity Fee (if applicable)
Patent Application Filing Fees				
1011/2011	1.16(a)(1)	Basic filing fee - Utility *filed on or after December 8, 2004*	300.00	150.00
4011[†]	1.16(a)(1)	Basic filing fee - Utility (electronic filing for small entities) *filed on or after December 8, 2004*	n/a	75.00
1001/2001	1.16(a)(2)	Basic filing fee - Utility *filed before December 8, 2004*	790.00	395.00
1201/2201	1.16(h)	Independent claims in excess of three	200.00	100.00
1202/2202	1.16(i)	Claims in excess of twenty	50.00	25.00
1203/2203	1.16(j)	Multiple dependent claim	360.00	180.00
1051/2051	1.16(f)	Surcharge - Late filing fee, search fee, examination fee or oath or declaration	130.00	65.00
1081/2081	1.16(s)	Utility Application Size Fee - for each additional 50 sheets that exceeds 100 sheets	250.00	125.00
1012/2012	1.16(b)(1)	Basic filing fee - Design *filed on or after December 8, 2004*	200.00	100.00
1002/2002	1.16(b)(2)	Basic filing fee - Design *filed before December 8, 2004*	350.00	175.00

continued

Exhibit 13-2 *continued*

1017/2017	1.16(b)(1)	Basic filing fee - Design (CPA) *filed on or after December 8, 2004*	200.00	100.00
1007/2007	1.16(b)(2)	Basic filing fee - Design (CPA) *filed before December 8, 2004*	350.00	175.00
1082/2082	1.16(s)	Design Application Size Fee - for each additional 50 sheets that exceeds 100 sheets	250.00	125.00
1013/2013	1.16(c)(1)	Basic filing fee - Plant *filed on or after December 8, 2004*	200.00	100.00
1003/2003	1.16(c)(2)	Basic filing fee - Plant *filed before December 8, 2004*	550.00	275.00
1083/2083	1.16(s)	Plant Application Size Fee - for each additional 50 sheets that exceeds 100 sheets	250.00	125.00
1014/2014	1.16(e)(1)	Basic filing fee - Reissue *filed on or after December 8, 2004*	300.00	150.00
1004/2004	1.16(e)(2)	Basic filing fee - Reissue *filed before December 8, 2004*	790.00	395.00
1019/2019	1.16(e)(1)	Basic filing fee - Design Reissue (CPA) *filed on or after December 8, 2004*	300.00	150.00
1009/2009	1.16(e)(2)	Basic filing fee - Design Reissue (CPA) *filed before December 8, 2004*	790.00	395.00
1204/2204	1.16(h)	Reissue independent claims in excess of three	200.00	100.00
1205/2205	1.16(i)	Reissue claims in excess of twenty	50.00	25.00
1084/2084	1.16(s)	Reissue Application Size Fee - for each additional 50 sheets that exceeds 100 sheets	250.00	125.00
1005/2005	1.16(d)	Provisional application filing fee	200.00	100.00
1085/2085	1.16(s)	Provisional Application Size Fee - for each additional 50 sheets that exceeds 100 sheets	250.00	125.00
1052/2052	1.16(g)	Surcharge - Late provisional filing fee or cover sheet	50.00	25.00
1053	1.17(i)	Non-English specification	130.00	
† The 4000 series fee code may be used via EFS at http://www.uspto.gov/ebc/efs/index.html				
Patent Search Fees				
1111/2111	1.16(k)	Utility Search Fee	500.00	250.00
1112/2112	1.16(l)	Design Search Fee	100.00	50.00
1113/2113	1.16(m)	Plant Search Fee	300.00	150.00
1114/2114	1.16(n)	Reissue Search Fee	500.00	250.00
Patent Examination Fees				
1311/2311	1.16(o)	Utility Examination Fee	200.00	100.00
1312/2312	1.16(p)	Design Examination Fee	130.00	65.00
1313/2313	1.16(q)	Plant Examination Fee	160.00	80.00
1314/2314	1.16(r)	Reissue Examination Fee	600.00	300.00
Patent Post-Allowance Fees				
1501/2501	1.18(a)	Utility issue fee	1,400.00	700.00
1502/2502	1.18(b)	Design issue fee	800.00	400.00
1503/2503	1.18(c)	Plant issue fee	1,100.00	550.00
1511/2511	1.18(a)	Reissue issue fee	1,400.00	700.00
1504	1.18(d)	Publication fee for early, voluntary, or normal publication	300.00	
1505	1.18(d)	Publication fee for republication	300.00	
Patent Maintenance Fees				
1551/2551	1.20(e)	Due at 3.5 years	900.00	450.00
1552/2552	1.20(f)	Due at 7.5 years	2,300.00	1,150.00

continued

Exhibit 13-2 *continued*

1553/2553	1.20(g)	Due at 11.5 years	3,800.00	1,900.00
1554/2554	1.20(h)	Surcharge - 3.5 year - Late payment within 6 months	130.00	65.00
1555/2555	1.20(h)	Surcharge - 7.5 year - Late payment within 6 months	130.00	65.00
1556/2556	1.20(h)	Surcharge - 11.5 year - Late payment within 6 months	130.00	65.00
1557	1.20(i)(1)	Surcharge after expiration - Late payment is unavoidable	700.00	
1558	1.20(i)(2)	Surcharge after expiration - Late payment is unintentional	1,640.00	
Miscellaneous Patent Fees				
1801/2801	1.17(e)	Request for continued examination (RCE) (see 37 CFR 1.114)	790.00	395.00
1808	1.17(i)	Processing fee, except in provisional applications	130.00	
1803	1.17(i)	Request for voluntary publication or republication	130.00	
1802	1.17(k)	Request for expedited examination of a design application	900.00	
1804	1.17(n)	Request for publication of SIR - Prior to examiner's action	920.00*	
1805	1.17(o)	Request for publication of SIR - After examiner's action	1,840.00*	
1806	1.17(p)	Submission of an Information Disclosure Statement	180.00	
1807	1.17(q)	Processing fee for provisional applications	50.00	
1809/2809	1.17(r)	Filing a submission after final rejection (see 37 CFR 1.129(a))	790.00	395.00
1810/2810	1.17(s)	For each additional invention to be examined (see 37 CFR 1.129(b))	790.00	395.00
*Reduced by basic filing fee paid.				
Post Issuance Fees				
1811	1.20(a)	Certificate of correction	100.00	
1812	1.20(c)(1)	Request for ex parte reexamination	2,520.00	
1813	1.20(c)(2)	Request for inter partes reexamination	8,800.00	
1821/2821	1.20(c)(3)	Reexamination independent claims in excess of three and also in excess of the number of such claims in the patent under reexamination	200.00	100.00
1822/2822	1.20(c)(4)	Reexamination claims in excess of twenty and also in excess of the number of claims in the patent under reexamination	50.00	25.00
1814/2814	1.20(d)	Statutory disclaimer	130.00	65.00
Patent Extension of Time Fees				
1251/2251	1.17(a)(1)	Extension for response within first month	120.00	60.00
1252/2252	1.17(a)(2)	Extension for response within second month	450.00	225.00
1253/2253	1.17(a)(3)	Extension for response within third month	1,020.00	510.00
1254/2254	1.17(a)(4)	Extension for response within fourth month	1,590.00	795.00
1255/2255	1.17(a)(5)	Extension for response within fifth month	2,160.00	1,080.00
Patent Appeals/Interference Fees				
1401/2401	41.20(b)(1)	Notice of appeal	500.00	250.00
1402/2402	41.20(b)(2)	Filing a brief in support of an appeal	500.00	250.00
1403/2403	41.20(b)(3)	Request for oral hearing	1,000.00	500.00
Patent Petition Fees				
1462	1.17(f)	Petitions requiring the petition fee set forth in 37 CFR 1.17(f) (Group I)	400.00	
1463	1.17(g)	Petitions requiring the petition fee set forth in 37 CFR 1.17(g) (Group II)	200.00	
1464	1.17(h)	Petitions requiring the petition fee set forth in 37 CFR 1.17(h) (Group III)	130.00	
1451	1.17(j)	Petition to institute a public use proceeding	1,510.00	

continued

Exhibit 13-2 *continued*

1452/2452	1.17(l)	Petition to revive unavoidably abandoned application	500.00	250.00
1453/2453	1.17(m)	Petition to revive unintentionally abandoned application	1,500.00	750.00
1454	1.17(t)	Acceptance of an unintentionally delayed claim for priority	1,370.00	
1455	1.18(e)	Filing an application for patent term adjustment	200.00	
1456	1.18(f)	Request for reinstatement of term reduced	400.00	
1457	1.20(j)(1)	Extension of term of patent	1,120.00	
1458	1.20(j)(2)	Initial application for interim extension (see 37 CFR 1.790)	420.00	
1459	1.20(j)(3)	Subsequent application for interim extension (see 37 CFR 1.790)	220.00	
PCT Fees - National Stage				
1631/2631	1.492(a)	Basic National Stage Fee	300.00	150.00
1640/2640	1.492(b)(1)	National Stage Search Fee - U.S. was ISA or IPEA and all claims satisfy PCT Article 33(1)-(4)	0.00	0.00
1641/2641	1.492(b)(2)	National Stage Search Fee - U.S. was the ISA	100.00	50.00
1642/2642	1.492(b)(3)	National Stage Search Fee - search report prepared and provided to USPTO	400.00	200.00
1632/2632	1.492(b)(4)	National Stage Search Fee - all other situations	500.00	250.00
1643/2643	1.492(c)(1)	National Stage Examination Fee - U.S. was ISA or IPEA and, all claims satisfy PCT Article 33(1)-(4)	0.00	0.00
1633/2633	1.492(c)(2)	National Stage Examination Fee - all other situations	200.00	100.00
1614/2614	1.492(d)	Claims - extra independent (over three)	200.00	100.00
1615/2615	1.492(e)	Claims - extra total (over twenty)	50.00	25.00
1616/2616	1.492(f)	Claims - multiple dependent	360.00	180.00
1681/2681	1.492(j)	National Stage Application Size Fee - for each additional 50 sheets that exceeds 100 sheet	250.00	125.00
1617/2617	1.492(h)	Search fee, examination fee or oath or declaration after thirty months from priority date	130.00	65.00
1618	1.492(i)	English translation after thirty months from priority date	130.00	
PCT Fees - International Stage				
1601	1.445(a)(1)	Transmittal fee	300.00	
1602	1.445(a)(2)	PCT search fee - no prior U.S. application filed under 35 USC 111(a)	1,000.00	
1603	1.445(a)(2)	PCT search - prior U.S. application filed under 35 USC 111(a) with basic filing fee under 37CFR 1.16(a) paid, identified at time of filing international application	300.00	
1604	1.445(a)(3)	Supplemental search fee per additional invention	1,000.00	
1605	1.482(a)(1)	Preliminary examination fee - U.S. was the ISA	600.00	
1606	1.482(a)(1)	Preliminary examination fee - U.S. was not the ISA	750.00	
1607	1.482(a)(2)	Supplemental examination fee per additional invention	600.00	
1619		Late payment fee	variable	
1621		Transmitting application to Intl. Bureau to act as receiving office	300.00	
** Fee only applies to international applications filed prior to January 1, 2004.				
PCT Fees to Foreign Offices***				
1701		International filing fee (first thirty pages) - PCT Easy	1,008.00	
1702		International filing fee (first thirty pages)	1,086.00	
1703		Supplemental international filing fee (for each page over thirty)	12.00	
1704		International search (EPO)	1,925.00	

continued

Exhibit 13-2 *continued*

1709		International search (KIPO)	232.00	
1705		Handling fee	155.00	
1706		Handling Fee - 75% reduction. if applicant, or 2 or more applicants each meet criteria specified at: http://www.wipo.int/pct/en/fees/fee_reduction.pdf	38.75	
1708		International CD applications	4,800.00	

*** PCT Fees to Foreign Offices subject to periodic change due to fluctuations in exchange rate. Refer to the Official Gazette of the United States Patent and Trademark Office for current amounts.

Patent Service Fees

8001	1.19(a)(1)	Printed copy of patent w/o color, delivery by USPS, USPTO Box, or electronic means	3.00	
8003	1.19(a)(2)	Printed copy of plant patent in color	15.00	
8004	1.19(a)(3)	Color copy of patent (other than plant patent) or SIR containing a color drawing	25.00	
8005	1.19(a)(1)	Patent Application Publication (PAP)	3.00	
8007	1.19(b)(1)(i)(A)	Copy of patent application as filed	20.00	
8008	1.19(b)(1)(i)(B)	Copy of patent-related file wrapper and contents of 400 or fewer pages, if provided on paper	200.00	
8009	1.19(b)(1)(i)(C)	Additional fee for each additional 100 pages of patent-related file wrapper and (paper) contents, or portion thereof	40.00	
8010	1.19(b)(1)(i)(D)	Individual application documents, other than application as filed, per document	25.00	
8011	1.19(b)(1)(ii)(B)	Copy of patent-related file wrapper and contents if provided electronically or on a physical electronic medium as specified in 1.19(b)(1)(ii)	55.00	
8012	1.19(b)(1)(ii)(C)	Additional fee for each continuing physical electronic medium in single order of 1.19(b)(1)(ii)(B)	15.00	
8041	1.19(b)(2)(i)(A)	Copy of patent-related file wrapper contents that were submitted and are stored on compact disk or other electronic form (e.g., compact disks stored in Artifact folder), other than as available in 1.19(b)(1); first physical electronic medium in a single order	55.00	
8042	1.19(b)(2)(i)(B)	Additional fee for each continuing copy of patent-related file wrapper contents as specified in 1.19(b)(2)(i)(A)	15.00	
8043	1.19(b)(2)(ii)	Copy of patent-related file wrapper contents that were submitted and are stored on compact disk, or other electronic form, other than as available in 1.19(b)(1); if provided electronically other than on a physical electronic medium, per order	55.00	
8013	1.19(b)(3)	Copy of office records, except copies of applications as filed	25.00	
8014	1.19(b)(4)	For assignment records, abstract of title and certification, per patent	25.00	
8904	1.19(c)	Library service	50.00	
8015	1.19(d)	List of U.S. patents and SIRs in subclass	3.00	
8016	1.19(e)	Uncertified statement re status of maintenance fee payments	10.00	
8017	1.19(f)	Copy of non-U.S. document	25.00	
8050	1.19(g)	Petitions for documents in form other than that provided by this part, or in form other than that generally provided by Director, to be decided in accordance with merits	AT COST	
8018	1.21(c)	Disclosure document filing fee	10.00	

continued

Exhibit 13-2   *continued*

8019	1.21(d)	Local delivery box rental, annually	50.00	
8020	1.21(e)	International type search report	40.00	
8902	1.21(g)	Self-service copy charge, per page	0.25	
8021	1.21(h)	Recording each patent assignment, agreement or other paper, per property	40.00	
8022	1.21(i)	Publication in Official Gazette	25.00	
8023	1.21(j)	Labor charges for services, per hour or fraction thereof	40.00	
8024	1.21(k)	Unspecified other services, excluding labor	AT COST	
8025	1.21(l)	Retaining abandoned application	130.00	
8026	1.21(n)	Handling fee for incomplete or improper application	130.00	
8027	1.296	Handling fee for withdrawal of SIR	130.00	
Patent Enrollment Fees				
9001	1.21(a)(1)(i)	Application fee (non-refundable)	40.00	
9003	1.21(a)(2)	Registration to practice or grant of limited recognition under §11.9(b) or (c)	100.00	
9004	1.21(a)(3)	Reinstatement to practice	40.00	
9005	1.21(a)(4)	Certificate of good standing as an attorney or agent	10.00	
9006	1.21(a)(4)	Certificate of good standing as an attorney or agent, suitable for framing	20.00	
9010	1.21(a)(1)(ii)(A)	For test administration by commercial entity	200.00	
9011	1.21(a)(1)(ii)(B)	For test administration by the USPTO	450.00	
9012	1.21(a)(5)(i)	Review of decision by the Director of Enrollment and Discipline under §11.2(c)	130.00	
9013	1.21(a)(5)(ii)	Review of decision of the Director of Enrollment and Discipline under §11.2(d)	130.00	
9014	1.21(a)(10)	Application fee for person disciplined, convicted of a felony or certain misdemeanors under §11.7(h)	1,600.00	
GENERAL FEES				
Finance Service Fees				
9201	1.21(b)(1) or 2.6(b)(13)(i)	Establish deposit account	10.00	
9202	1.21(b)(2) or 2.6(b)(13)(ii)	Service charge for below minimum balance	25.00	
9202	1.21(b)(3)	Service charge for below minimum balance restricted subscription deposit account	25.00	
9101	1.21(m) or 2.6(b)(12)	Processing each payment refused or charged back	50.00	
Computer Service Fees				
8031/8531		Computer records	AT COST	
Trademark Processing Fees ****				
6001	2.6(a)(1)(i)	Application for registration, per international class (paper filing)	375.00	
7001	2.6(a)(1)(ii)	Application for registration, per international class (electronic filing, TEAS application)	325.00	
7007	2.6(a)(1)(iii)	Application for registration, per international class (electronic filing, TEAS Plus application)	275.00	
6002/7002	2.6(a)(2)	Filing an Amendment to Allege Use under §1(c), per class	100.00	
6003/7003	2.6(a)(3)	Filing a Statement of Use under §1(d)(1), per class	100.00	
6004/7004	2.6(a)(4)	Filing a Request for a Six-month Extension of Time for Filing a Statement of Use under §1(d)(1), per class	150.00	

continued

Exhibit 13-2 *continued*

6005/7005	2.6(a)(15)	Petitions to the Director	100.00	
6006	2.6(a)(19)	Dividing an application, per new application (file wrapper) created	100.00	
6008/7008	2.6(a)(1)(iv)	Additional fee for application that doesn't meet TEAS Plus filing requirements, per class	50.00	
6201/7201	2.6(a)(5)	Application for renewal, per class	400.00	
6203/7203	2.6(a)(6)	Additional fee for filing renewal application during grace period, per class	100.00	
6204	2.6(a)(21)	Correcting a deficiency in a renewal application	100.00	
6205/7205	2.6(a)(12)	Filing §8 affidavit, per class	100.00	
6206/7206	2.6(a)(14)	Additional fee for filing §8 affidavit during grace period, per class	100.00	
6207	2.6(a)(20)	Correcting a deficiency in a §8 affidavit	100.00	
6208/7208	2.6(a)(13)	Filing §15 affidavit, per class	200.00	
6210	2.6(a)(7)	Publication of mark under §12(c), per class	100.00	
6211	2.6(a)(8)	Issuing new certificate of registration	100.00	
6212	2.6(a)(9)	Certificate of correction, registrant's error	100.00	
6213	2.6(a)(10)	Filing disclaimer to registration	100.00	
6214	2.6(a)(11)	Filing amendment to registration	100.00	
6401/7401	2.6(a)(16)	Petition for cancellation, per class	300.00	
6402/7402	2.6(a)(17)	Notice of opposition, per class	300.00	
6403/7403	2.6(a)(18)	Ex parte appeal, per class	100.00	
Trademark Madrid Protocol Fees****				
6901/7901	7.6(a)(1)	Certifying an International application based on single application or registration, per class	100.00	
6902/7902	7.6(a)(2)	Certifying an International application based on more than one basic application or registration, per class	150.00	
6903/7903	7.6(a)(3)	Transmitting a Request to Record an Assignment or restriction under 7.23 or 7.24	100.00	
6904/7904	7.6(a)(4)	Filing a Notice of Replacement, per class	100.00	
6905/7905	7.6(a)(5)	Filing an affidavit under 71 of the Act, per class	100.00	
6906/7906	7.6(a)(6)	Surcharge for filing affidavit under 71 of the Act during grace period, per class	100.00	
6907/7907	7.6(a)(7)	Transmitting a subsequent designation	100.00	
Trademark International Application Fees****				
7951	7.7(1)	International application fee	Reference CFR 7.7 for payment of fees to International Bureau (IB) and IB calculator at: http://www.wipo.int/madrid/en.	
7952	7.14(c)	Correcting irregularities in an International application		
7953	7.21	Subsequent designation fee		
7954	7.23	Recording of an assignment of an international registration under 7.23		
****The 7000 series fee code (e.g., 7001, 7002, etc.) is used for electronic filing via TEAS, which is available at www.uspto.gov/teas/. In addition, the 6000 series fee codes under the Trademark Madrid Protocol Fees are being offered for use as a paper-based filing alternative.				
Trademark Service Fees				
8501	2.6(b)(1)	Printed copy of registered mark, delivery by USPS, USPTO Box, or electronic means	3.00	
8503	2.6(b)(4)(i)	Certified copy of registered mark, with title and/or status, regular service	15.00	
8504	2.6(b)(4)(ii)	Certified copy of registered mark, with title and/or status, expedited local service	30.00	

continued

Exhibit 13-2 *continued*

8507	2.6(b)(2)	Certified copy of trademark application as filed	15.00	
8508	2.6(b)(3)	Certified or uncertified copy of trademark-related file wrapper and contents	50.00	
8513	2.6(b)(5)	Certified or uncertified copy of trademark document, unless otherwise provided	25.00	
8514	2.6(b)(7)	For assignment records, abstracts of title and certification per registration	25.00	
8902	2.6(b)(9)	Self-service copy charge, per page	0.25	
8521	2.6(b)(6)	Recording trademark assignment, agreement or other paper, first mark per document	40.00	
8522	2.6(b)(6)	For second and subsequent marks in the same document	25.00	
8523	2.6(b)(10)	Labor charges for services, per hour or fraction thereof	40.00	
8524	2.6(b)(11)	Unspecified other services, excluding labor	AT COST	
Fastener Quality Act Fees				
6991	2.7(a)	Recordal application fee	20.00	
6992	2.7(b)	Renewal application fee	20.00	
6993	2.7(c)	Late fee for renewal application	20.00	

EXHIBIT 13-3 Patent Full-Text and Full-Page Image Databases

From http://www.uspto.gov.

United States Patent and Trademark Office   PATENTS

Home | Site Index | Search | FAQ | Glossary | Guides | Contacts | eBusiness | eBiz alerts | News | Help

Patent Electronic Business Center > Patent Full-Text and Full-Page Image Databases

Issued Patents (PatFT)
(full-text since 1976, full-page images since 1790)

● Quick Search
● Advanced Search
● Patent Number Search

● View Patent Full-Page Images
   How to View Patent Images

● Status & Event History
● Database Contents
● Help Files

Published Applications (AppFT)
(published since 15 March 2001)

● Quick Search
● Advanced Search
● Publication Number Search

● View Publication Full-Page Images
   How to View Published Application Images

● Status & Event History
● Help Files

Information Applicable to Both Databases

Important Notices and Policies -- *Please read!*
How to Access and View Full-Page Images
Problems Using the Databases?
Report Errors in Data Content

Related USPTO Services

Tools to Help in Searching by Patent Classification

Patent Application Information Retrieval (PAIR)
Patent Assignment Database
Downloadable Published Sequence Listings

KEY: ✑=online business system $ =fees ▤=forms ✍ =help ▤=laws/regulations ▨=definition (glossary)

The Inventors Assistance Center is available to help you on patent matters. Send questions about USPTO programs and services to the USPTO Contact Center (UCC). You can suggest USPTO webpages or material you would like featured on this section by E-mail to the webmaster@uspto.gov. While we cannot promise to accommodate all requests, your suggestions will be considered and may lead to other improvements on the website.

| HOME | SITE INDEX | SEARCH | eBUSINESS | HELP | PRIVACY POLICY

Last Modified: 07/07/2006 18:21:41

EXHIBIT 13-4 USPTO Forms

From http://www.uspto.gov.

Form Number	Fillable PDF	Last Updated	Form Title
General Business Transactions			
PTO-2038	**PTO-2038** (last updated 2006/02)	2006/02	Credit Card Payment Form and Instructions
Patent Related Forms			
PTO-2042			Certificate Action Form
PTOL-85B	PTOL-85B (last updated 2006/07)	2006/07	Fee Transmittal (Part B) of the Notice of Allowance and Fee(s) Due form
PTO/SB/01	SB01 (last updated 2006/07)	2006/07	Declaration for Utility or Design Patent Application [2 pages]. To appoint an attorney or agent, use form PTO/SB/81
PTO/SB/01A	SB01A (last updated 2006/07)	2006/07	Declaration (37 CFR 1.63) for Utility or Design Application Using An Application Data Sheet (37 CFR 1.76). To appoint an attorney or agent, use form PTO/SB/81
PTO/SB/02	SB02 (last updated 2006/07)	2006/07	Declaration (Additional Inventors) and Supplemental Priority Data Sheet [2 pages].
PTO/SB/02LR		2006/07	Declaration (Supplemental sheets for Legal Representatives)
PTO/SB/03		2006/07	Plant Patent Application (35 USC 161) Declaration (37 CFR 1.63) [2 pages]. To appoint an attorney or agent, use form PTO/SB/81
PTO/SB/03a		2006/07	Declaration (37 CFR 1.63) for Plant Application Using An Application Data Sheet (37 CFR 1.76). To appoint an attorney or agent, use form PTO/SB/81
PTO/SB/04		2006/07	Supplemental Declaration for Utility or Design Patent Application (37 CFR 1.67) [2 pages]. To appoint an attorney or agent, use form PTO/SB/81
PTO/SB/05	SB05 (last updated 2006/07)	2006/07	Utility Patent Application Transmittal
PTO/SB/06 (same as PTO-875)		2006/07	Patent Application Fee Determination Record
PTO/SB/07 (same as PTO-1360)		2006/07	Multiple Dependent Claim Fee Calculation Sheet
PTO/SB/08a (pg 1) PTO/SB/08b (pg 2) (same as PTO-1449)	SB08A (pg 1) SB08B (pg 2) (last updated 2006/07)	2006/07	Information Disclosure Statement by Applicant [2 pages]. *Click Here* for a listing of kind codes used on U.S. patent documents
PTO/SB/14	**SB14** (EFS-Web)	2005/08	Application Data Sheet 37 CFR 1.76
Former PTO/SB/15		2003/08	Sample Form for an Assignment of Application (Deleted as of 10/2005)
PTO/SB/16	SB16 (last updated 2006/07)	2006/07	Provisional Application for Patent Cover Sheet
PTO/SB/17		2006/07	Fee Transmittal (for more information, *click here*)
PTO/SB/17i (Effective 22NOV2004!)		2006/07	Processing Fee Under 37 CFR 17(i) Transmittal
PTO/SB/17p (Effective 22NOV2004!)		2006/07	Petition Fee Under 37 CFR 17(f), (g) & (h) Transmittal
PTO/SB/18	SB18 (last updated 2006/07)	2006/07	Design Patent Application Transmittal
PTO/SB/19		2006/07	Plant Patent Application Transmittal

continued

Exhibit 13-4   *continued*

PTO/SB/20		2006/05	Request for Patent Prosecution Highway (PPH) Pilot Program Between the JPO and the USPTO
PTO/SB/21	*SB21* (last updated 2004/09)	2006/07	Transmittal Form
PTO/SB/22		2006/07	Petition for Extension of Time under 37 CFR 1.136(a)
PTO/SB/23 (Effective 22NOV2004!)		2006/07	Petition for Extension of Time under 37 CFR 1.136(b)
PTO/SB/24		2006/07	Express Abandonment Under 37 CFR 1.138
PTO/SB/24a		2006/07	Petition for Express Abandonment to Avoid Publication under 37 CFR 1.138(c)
PTO/SB/24b		2006/07	Petition for Express Abandonment to Obtain a Refund
PTO/SB/25	*SB25* (last updated 2006/07)	2006/07	Terminal Disclaimer to Obviate a Provisional Double Patenting Rejection over a Pending Second Application
PTO/SB/26	*SB26* (last updated 2006/07)	2006/07	Terminal Disclaimer to Obviate a Double Patenting Rejection over a Prior Patent
PTO/SB/27		2006/07	Request for Expedited Examination of a Design Application (37 CFR 1.155)
PTO/SB/28	**SB28** (*only* for use through EFS-Web on or after 8/25/06)	2006/08	Petition to Make Special Under Accelerated Examination Program Adobe Reader version 7.0.8 or greater required.
PTO/SB/29		2006/07	For Design Applications Only: Continued Prosecution Application (CPA) Request Transmittal [2 pages]
PTO/SB/29a		2006/07	For Design Applications Only: Receipt For Facsimile Transmitted CPA
PTO/SB/30	*SB30* (last updated 2006/07)	2006/07	Request for Continued Examination (RCE) Transmittal
PTO/SB/31		2006/07	Notice of Appeal from the Examiner to the Board of Patent Appeals and Interferences
PTO/SB/32	*SB32* (last updated 2006/07)	2006/07	Request for Oral Hearing before the Board of Patent Appeals and Interferences
PTO/SB/33		2005/07	Pre-Appeal Brief Request for Review (For more information, *click here*)
PTO/SB/35		2006/07	Nonpublication Request under 35 U.S.C. 122(b) (2)(B)(i)
PTO/SB/36		2006/07	Rescission of Previous Nonpublication Request (35 U.S.C. 122(b)(2)(B)(ii)) and, if applicable, Notice of Foreign Filing (35 U.S.C. 122(b)(2)(B)(iii))
PTO/SB/37		2006/07	Request for Deferral of Examination 37 CFR 1.103(d)
Former PTO/SB/41		2001/05	Sample Form for an Assignment of Patent (Deleted as of 10/2005)
PTO/SB/42		2006/07	37 CFR 1.501 Information Disclosure Citation in a Patent
PTO/SB/43		2006/07	Disclaimer in Patent under 37 CFR 1.321(a)
PTO/SB/44 (*same as* PTO-1050)	*SB44* (last updated 2005/04)	2005/04	Certificate of Correction
PTO/SB/45	*SB45* (last updated 2004/12)	2004/12	Maintenance Fee Transmittal Form. *Click Here* for an explanation on how to assert a change in small entity status when filing this form
PTO/SB/47	*SB47* (last updated 2005/04)	2005/04	"Fee Address" Indication Form
PTO/SB/50	*SB50* (last updated 2005/04)	2005/04	Reissue Patent Application Transmittal

continued

Exhibit 13-4 *continued*

PTO/SB/51		2005/10	Reissue Application Declaration by the Inventor [2 pages]
PTO/SB/51S		2005/10	Supplemental Declaration for Reissue Patent Application to Correct "Errors" Statement (37 CFR 1.175)
PTO/SB/52		2005/10	Reissue Application Declaration by the Assignee [2 pages]
PTO/SB/53		2004/04	Reissue Application: Consent of Assignee; Statement of Non-Assignment
PTO/SB/55		2003/05	Reissue Patent Application Statement as to Loss of Original Patent >> See changes to 37 CFR 1.178. >> *Read more [PDF]*
PTO/SB/56	SB56 (last updated 2005/02)	2005/02	Reissue Application Fee Transmittal Form
PTO/SB/57		2005/04	Request for *Ex Parte* Reexamination Transmittal Form
PTO/SB/58		2005/04	Request for *Inter Partes* Reexamination Transmittal Form
PTO/SB/61		2006/07	Petition for Revival of an Application for Patent Abandoned Unavoidably under 37 CFR 1.137(a) [3 pages]
PTO/SB/62	SB62 (last updated 2006/07)	2006/07	Terminal Disclaimer to Accompany Petition (Period Specified)
PTO/SB/63	SB63 (last updated 2006/07)	2006/07	Terminal Disclaimer to Accompany Petition (Period of Disclaimer to be Completed by Petitions Examiner)
PTO/SB/64	SB64 (last updated 2006/07)	2006/07	Petition for Revival of an Application for Patent Abandoned Unintentionally Under 37 CFR 1.137(b) [2 pages]
PTO/SB/64a	SB64a (last updated 2006/07)	2006/07	Petition for Revival of an Application for Patent Abandoned for Failure to Notify the Office of a Foreign or International Filing (37 CFR 1.137(f))
PTO/SB/65		2005/10	Petition to Accept Unavoidably Delayed Payment of Maintenance Fee in an Expired Patent (37 CFR 1.378(b)) [4 pages]
PTO/SB/66	SB66 (last updated 2005/10)	2005/10	Petition to Accept Unintentionally Delayed Payment of Maintenance Fee in an Expired Patent (37 CFR 1.378(c)) [3 pages]
PTO/SB/67		2004/11	Power to Inspect/Copy
PTO/SB/68		2004/11	Request for Access to an Abandoned Application under 37 CFR 1.14
PTO/SB/80		2006/01	Power of Attorney to Prosecute Applications Before the USPTO (for more information *click here*)
PTO/SB/81	SB81 (last updated 2006/01)	2006/01	Power of Attorney and Correspondence Address Indication Form.
PTO/SB/82	SB82 (last updated 2006/01)	2006/01	Revocation of Power of Attorney with New Power of Attorney and Change of Correspondence Address.
PTO/SB/83	SB83 (last updated 2006/01)	2006/01	Request for Withdrawal As Attorney or Agent and Change of Correspondence Address
PTO/SB/84		2006/01	Authorization to Act in a Representative Capacity (for more information *click here*)
PTO/SB/91		2004/09	Deposit Account Order Form
PTO/SB/92		2004/09	Certification of Mailing under 37 CFR 1.8
PTO/SB/94		2004/11	Request for Statutory Invention Registration [2 pages]
PTO/SB/95		2005/07	Disclosure Document Deposit Request
PTO/SB/96	SB96 (last updated 2005/12)	2005/12	Statement Under 37 CFR 3.73(b)
PTO/SB/97		2004/09	Certificate of Transmission under 37 CFR 1.8

continued

Exhibit 13-4   *continued*

PTO/SB/101		1995/05	Declaration and Power of Attorney for Patent Application (Chinese Language Declaration) [3 pages]
PTO/SB/102		1995/06	(Dutch Language Declaration) [5 pages]
PTO/SB/103		1996/08	(German Language Declaration) [3 pages]
PTO/SB/104		1996/08	(Italian Language Declaration) [3 pages]
PTO/SB/105		1996/08	(French Language Declaration) [3 pages]
PTO/SB/106		2000/06	(Japanese Language Declaration) [3 pages]
PTO/SB/107		1996/05	(Russian Language Declaration) [3 pages]
PTO/SB/108		1996/08	(Swedish Language Declaration) [3 pages]
PTO/SB/109		1996/08	(Spanish Language Declaration) [3 pages]
PTO/SB/110		1995/05	(Korean Language Declaration) [3 pages]
PTO/SB/121			Deleted as of 7/03. Please use forms PTO/SB/122 or PTO/SB/123, or the batch update practice (contact the *Electronic Business Center* for further information).
PTO/SB/122	*SB122* (last updated 2006/01)	2006/01	Change of Correspondence Address, Application
PTO/SB/123	*SB123* (last updated 2006/01)	2006/01	Change of Correspondence Address, Patent
PTO/SB/124	*SB124* (last updated 2006/01)	2006/01	Request for Customer Number Data Change
PTO/SB/125	*SB125* (last updated 2006/01)	2006/01	Request for Customer Number
PTO/SB/158		2005/11	Application for Registration to Practice Before the USPTO
PTO/SB/275		2004/06	Undertaking under 37 CFR 10.10(b)
PTOL-413A		2004/09	Applicant Initiated Interview Request Form. This form is to implement a policy change regarding interview summaries. See MPEP 713.04 *Link to MPEP.*
PTO-875			See PTO/SB/06
PTO-1050			See PTO/SB/44
PTO/SB/1209		2000/02	Oath or Affirmation
PTO-1360			See PTO/SB/07
PTO-1449			See PTO/SB/08
PTO-1595	*PT01595* (last updated 2005/07)	2005/08	Recordation Form Cover Sheet
PTO-1619 (8–96)			This form has been *replaced* by **PTO-1595**.
PTO/SB/2048	*PTO/SB/2048* (last updated 2003/12)	2003/12	Complaint Regarding Invention Promoter
Patent Cooperation Treaty Related Forms			
PTO/SB/13pct		2006/07	Request for Filing a Continuation or Division of an International Application [2 pages]
PTO/SB/61pct		2005/10	Petition for Revival of an International Application for Patent Designating the US Abandoned Unavoidably under 37 CFR 1.137(a) [3 pages]
PTO/SB/64pct		2005/10	Petition for Revival of an International Application for Patent Designating the US Abandoned Unintentionally under 37 CFR 1.137(b) [2 pages]
PTO-1390		2005/07	Transmittal Letter for 371 filing
Trademark Related Forms Please check TEAS for online alternatives to most trademark forms.			
The Forms below are best viewed with the Latest Version of *Adobe's free Acrobat reader.*			
PTO/TM/1478		2000/02	Trademark/Servicemark Application, Principal Register

continued

Exhibit 13-4 *continued*

PTO/TM/1553		2000/02	Statement of Use/Amendment to Allege Use for Intent-to-Use Application
PTO/TM/1581		2000/02	Request for Extension of Time to File a Statement of Use
PTO/TM/1583		2000/02	Declaration of Use of a Mark under Section 8
PTO/TM/4.16		2000/02	Declaration of Incontestability of a Mark under Section 15
PTO Form 1963		2000/02	Combined declaration of use in commerce/application for renewal of registration of mark under Sections 8 & 9
PTO Form 1583		2000/02	Combined declaration of use & incontestability under Sections 8 & 15
PTO/TM/4.8		2000/02	Collective Membership Mark Application, Principal Register
PTO/TM/4.9		2000/02	Certification Mark Application, Principal Register
PTO/TM/1478(a)		2000/02	Collective Trademark/Service Mark Application, Principal Register
PTO/TM/oppositionformat		2001/07	Opposition to the Registration of a Mark
PTO-1594	**PTO-1594** (last updated 2005/07)	2005/07	Recordation Form Cover Sheet
PTO/TM/1618		This form has been *replaced* by **PTO-1594**	
PTO/TM/cancellationformat		2001/07	Cancellation of a Registered mark

PATENT TERMS

In 1995, the terms for utility and plant patents were changed from 17 years from issuance to 20 years from the date the patent application was filed. The term for design patents is 14 years from the date the patent is issued. Extensions of patents may be issued for the following:

1. patent applications that have been the subject of an interference action
2. applications that must be reviewed by other agencies
3. patent applications that have been successfully reviewed via the appellate process
4. a **secrecy order**

OWNERSHIP OF PATENTS

Initially most patents are owned by the inventor. However, because ownership of a patent is a property right, that right may be transferred to another individual or entity. Some employers require that any inventions made by their employees become the property of the employer.

The Official Gazette publishes lists of patents that are offered for sale or license. Legal assistants may be required to review the publication to determine whether clients might wish to be informed of the patents that are being sold.

secrecy order an order made by the government to protect inventions that relate to national security

PATENT INFRINGEMENT

Lawsuits in the patents area often result from **patent infringement.** If an individual sells a part of a patented invention, the seller may be held liable if he knows that the item may be used for patent infringement. In order for the inventor to prevail in a suit for patent infringement, he must have first been issued a patent by the Patent and Trademark Office.

Lawsuits for patent infringement may be instituted for direct infringement or for inducing another individual to infringe the patent. For instance, if a third party persuades an individual to infringe the patent of another, that third party may also be held liable for patent infringement.

If the plaintiff wins the lawsuit for patent infringement, the plaintiff may receive the following:

1. *Injunction*—the defendant must stop infringing the patent
2. **Compensatory damages**—reasonable damages to compensate the plaintiff
3. **Punitive damages**—if willfulness or bad faith is proven, the plaintiff may receive treble damages. In this case, the plaintiff may also receive reasonable attorney fees.

patent infringement the unauthorized manufacture, use, sale, or distribution of a patented invention

compensatory damages reasonable damages that compensate the plaintiff for the defendant's wrongful act

punitive damages punishment damages assessed against the defendant if willfulness or bad faith is proven; damages will be three times the compensatory damages

● KEY TERMS

compensatory damages

intellectual property

patent

patent infringement

prosecution

punitive damages

secrecy order

● SELF TEST

1. What specific areas of law are included in the term *intellectual property?*
2. Describe the process required for prosecution.
3. What qualifications are required for an attorney who represents an inventor in the patent application process?

● NOTEBOOK PROJECTS

1. Research recent cases in patent infringement from your local court.
2. Prepare an interoffice memorandum to your instructor with a summary of the case in question 1.

 For additional resources, visit our Web site at **www.paralegal.delmar.cengage.com.**

GLOSSARY

A

administrator an individual appointed by the court to administer the deceased's estate when there is no will or when no executor is appointed in the will to take care of the distribution of assets.

adoption a legal proceeding whereby an individual or a couple become parents to a child who was not born to them.

agency a relationship in which one party acts for another by the latter party's authority.

agent for process an individual chosen by the corporation to act on its behalf; an agent must be chosen for each state in which the corporation operates.

alimony support of the other spouse upon divorce or dissolution.

annulment the act of making a marriage void; nullity.

anticipatory breach (anticipatory repudiation) breaching a contract by refusing to fulfill one's obligations once the contract has been entered into but before the time for performance.

arraignment a hearing in which the defendant is brought before a judge to hear the charges against her and to enter a plea.

arson intentional burning of another's home, structure, or building.

articles of incorporation the first document prepared for corporate formation; it includes corporate name, purpose, agent, stock structure, duration, and names of incorporators and members of the board of directors. The articles must be filed with the secretary of state's office in the state of formation. A name is reserved with that same office.

assault an attempted battery.

B

bailee the person who gets custody of the property in a bailment.

bailment a temporary delivery of property by the owner into another person's custody (keeping).

bailor the person who possesses the personal property and turns it over to the other party.

battery harmful or offensive touching of another without consent.

beneficiary one who receives property under a will.

bilateral contract a contract formed by mutual promises.

burglary unlawful entry of a building of another with the intent to commit a felony therein.

bylaws rules and regulations adopted by a corporation.

C

case brief a summary of the opinion in a case.

case law a primary source of law created by court opinions that create precedents for later cases.

case law judicial opinions of appellate and supreme courts that establish precedents for future cases.

case or statute citation name of the case or statute and the volume number, name of the reporter, page number, and year of the case or statute.

cause of action facts or legal theory on which the case is based.

charitable trust a trust made for the benefit of a charity.

chattel an item of personal property.

civil law laws protecting individuals and entities; used to redress wrongs and enforce rights.

close corporation a corporation owned by a few individuals who run the corporation and control business operations.

codes the subject divisions into which statutes are separated.

codicil a formal document making changes to a will.

cohabitation living together without a marriage contract.

commercial paper negotiable instruments relating to business.

common-law marriage the condition that exists when a man and a woman agree to enter a marital relationship and live together as if married but without a formal marriage ceremony.

community property property acquired during the marriage that is not separate property; the concept is used in community property states.

compensatory damages damages awarded for the actual loss of the plaintiff.

compensatory damages reasonable damages that compensate the plaintiff for the defendant's wrongful act.

complaint the first pleading filed to commence a lawsuit.

condominium a property ownership interest in which individuals own units within a multiple-unit complex.

consent a defense to assault, battery, and/or false imprisonment; if the plaintiff consents to the touching or the imprisonment, then the defense is valid.

consideration something of value given in a contract.

consolidation the formation of a new corporation from two or more dissolved corporations.

contract a legally binding agreement among two or more parties; requires an offer, acceptance, and consideration.

cooperative a form of ownership similar to that of a condominium, except that ownership is in a share of stock that is represented by a unit in the complex; ownership is more restrictive than the condominium form.

corporation a business entity that exists separate and apart from its owners, who are called shareholders.

creditors individuals or entities to whom the debtor owes money.

criminal law law that protects society from wrongful conduct.

cross-complaint a complaint by the defendant against the plaintiff or a complaint by one defendant against another defendant.

D

debtor an individual or entity that owes money and initiates a bankruptcy proceeding.

decedent an individual who dies.

deed of trust a loan on property; the lender retains title to the property until the debt is paid.

default judgment a judgment taken when the defendant fails to respond to the complaint.

demand for inspection one party's demand on the other party to inspect records or documents relevant to the case.

demurrer a document stating that the other side does not have a legitimate legal argument in the case and that the propounding party should prevail.

deponent an individual whose deposition is taken.

deposition a pretrial in-person examination of a party or a witness to a lawsuit.

derivative suit a lawsuit filed by shareholders against the corporation if a director or officer of the corporation commits an *ultra vires* act, which includes actions outside the scope of the powers or activities permitted by the Articles of Incorporation.

discovery a formal exchange of information by both parties.

dissolution no-fault divorce; no grounds are required, and either party may file a petition.

dissolution the dissolving of a corporation; may be voluntary or involuntary (by the state).

divorce an adversary proceeding to end a marriage; requires grounds in most states.

E

easement the right to use the land of another for a particular and restricted purpose.

endorsement/indorsement transferring a negotiable instrument to a third party by signing it in such a manner as to transfer the rights to another.

equity a court's power to act when no law governs the situation; a court order to stop an individual or entity from doing an act or to require that an act be done.

escrow a process by which legal title to property is transferred.

estate planning the process of creating a plan during one's lifetime regarding how the person's property will be distributed upon her death.

eviction a legal action in which a landlord removes a tenant from the property.

executor an individual appointed in the will by the decedent to administer the estate.

executory contract a contract whose terms have not yet been carried out and that may depend on a future event.

F

fair market value the price a seller could obtain for property if he sold it.

Fictitious Business Name Statement a certificate required to be filed in the county in which a business operates if the business functions under a name other than the owner's.

fiduciary relationship a relationship founded on trust and dependence in which an individual dominates or influences the other, generally by managing her money or property.

formal will a formally typed and witnessed will.

franchise a business arrangement whereby the owner obtains the right to market a company's goods or services in a particular territory.

fungible describes a unit of goods that is identical to every other unit of that type of goods.

G

goods tangible and movable merchandise.

grounds for divorce reasons for which the state allows a couple to obtain a divorce.

guardian ad litem a guardian for a minor for a particular lawsuit.

H

holographic will a will totally in the handwriting of the maker.

I

injunction a court order requiring an individual to perform an act or to refrain from performing an act.

intellectual property a broad category of law that includes patent law, trademarks, trade secrets, and the law of copyrights.

inter vivos trust a trust established during one's lifetime that takes effect while she is alive.

J

joint tenancy ownership of property by two or more persons each of whom has an undivided ownership interest in the property, with a right of survivorship.

joint will a will made by a married couple leaving property to each other and, if one dies before the other, leaving property to the same individuals.

jurisdiction the power of a court to hear a case.

L

lease a contract for the use of land or buildings.

license permission to enter another's land to perform a particular act; no property possession is granted.

M

marriage the legal union of a man and a woman as husband and wife in most states and of a couple of either sex in other states.

merger the taking over of a corporation by another corporation.

minor an individual who has not reached the age of majority.

mortgage a loan on real property in which the buyer acquires title to the property.

motion to strike a motion to the court to strike legally objectionable language from a pleading.

N

nonprofit corporation a corporation operated for charitable, religious, scientific, educational, or literary purposes, and not for profit.

nuisance invasion of one's interest in the use and enjoyment of property.

nuncupative will an oral will; valid in a few states.

O

offer a proposal to enter into a contract.

offeree the person or entity who accepts an offer to enter into a contract.

offeror the person or entity who makes an offer to enter into a contract.

option a separate contract under which one party pays money for the right to buy something from or sell something to the other party at a set price within a specified time period.

P

palimony support paid to one party after a relationship ends based on an implied contract between the couple while they lived together.

partnership an organization composed of two or more individuals who have jointly agreed to operate a business for profit.

patent infringement the unauthorized manufacture, use, sale, or distribution of a patented invention.

patent a right given by the federal government to an individual, for a specified number of years, to make, use, and sell his invention.

personal property all property that is not real property; movable property.

plea bargaining pleading guilty to a lesser offense with less jail time than the original offense.

points and authorities cases and statutes used as an argument in a memorandum to the court.

pour-over will a will made at the time a trust is established to account for assets of the maker that have not yet been transferred to the trust.

pre-incorporation agreement an agreement setting forth the preliminary arrangements of the parties who are forming the corporation.

preliminary hearing a hearing in court to determine whether there is enough evidence to hold the defendant over for trial.

pretermitted-heir statute a statute requiring that a child not mentioned in the will may take the share she would have received had there been no will.

primary sources statutes, constitutions, and cases in the same jurisdiction as the instant case.

probate a court procedure for proving the validity of a will and distributing estate assets.

procedural law the rules for enforcing one's rights in court; the procedures that must be followed.

professional corporation a special corporation owned by professionals, such as doctors, lawyers, psychologists, or optometrists.

prosecution the process of preparing the application for a patent and following through to its being granted.

punitive damages a monetary award to punish the defendant for her actions; also called *exemplary damages;* used when the wrong was as a result of gross negligence or intentional, willful, or wanton conduct of the defendant; used most often in civil actions.

punitive damages punishment damages assessed against the defendant if willfulness or bad faith is proven; damages will be three times the compensatory damages.

R

real property land or items affixed thereto or growing thereon.

request for admission the request of a party to admit points not in dispute.

restitution restoring the plaintiff to the position she would have held had the defendant performed according to the contract.

S

sales forms preprinted forms used by businesses for their sales transactions.

secondary sources sources for legal research that are not primary authority, such as legal encyclopedias, digests, treatises, and textbooks.

secrecy order an order made by the government to protect inventions that relate to national security.

self-proving will a certain clause in a will makes the will self-proving; this clause eliminates the need for the witnesses to sign a proof-of-subscribing-witness form to attest to the authenticity of the decedent's signature.

separate property property acquired before marriage or after separation, or during marriage by gift or inheritance.

Shepardize to update a case by using Shepard's citations to determine whether it is still good law.

sole proprietorship an unincorporated business usually owned by one individual.

specific bequest a gift of a specific item made in a will.

specific performance requirement to perform on a contract to the precise agreed-upon terms.

statute of limitations a law that sets a maximum amount of time after something happens within which it can be taken to court.

statutes laws passed by the legislature.

statutory law laws established by the state legislature or United States Congress.

subchapter S corporation a corporation with no more than 25 shareholders whose tax status enables it to be taxed similarly to a partnership. The corporation does not pay corporate income tax, but the shareholders declare income and losses on their personal tax returns.

subpoena a formal court document issued by the court to order a person's appearance.

substantial performance the condition in which one party has performed most of the obligations required under the contract; may be used as a defense in a breach-of-contract action.

substantive law the law that describes one's rights and duties; also known as *black letter law*.

summary judgment a judgment based on a motion that there are no disputed facts to be decided at trial and there is no defense that can be claimed.

T

tenancy in common ownership of property by two or more individuals, with each owning a proportion of the property.

testamentary trust a trust made in a will that takes effect after the maker dies.

testator one who makes a will.

transmutation melding of separate property with community property to a point at which it cannot be traced.

trust a fiduciary relationship in which property is held by one party (the trustee) with legal title for the benefit of another with an equitable title (the beneficiary).

trustee an independent party appointed by the court in a bankruptcy proceeding for the purpose of liquidating the assets and distributing funds to creditors.

U

Uniform Commercial Code (UCC) a comprehensive set of laws governing sales contracts with merchants.

unilateral contract a contract formed by the promise of one party and an act by the other party.

United States Code the federal statutes, organized by title and subject.

V

venue an appropriate geographical location to hear the case.

void marriage a marriage that is not legal; includes marriage between close relatives.

voidable marriage a marriage that may be voided by one of the parties or may be made legal on the occurrence of certain events.

W

will a written document setting forth the manner in which a person's estate will be distributed upon her death.

workers' compensation laws state laws established to pay funds to workers injured on the job.

written interrogatories written questions asked by one party of another.

CPSIA information can be obtained
at www.ICGtesting.com
Printed in the USA
FFOW04n1136190515
13552FF

9 781418 018375